LIBERTY AND EQUALITY

LIBERTY AND EQUALITY

Edited by

Ellen Frankel Paul
Fred D Miller Jr
Jeffrey Paul

BASIL BLACKWELL
for the
Social Philosophy and Policy Center
Bowling Green State University

© Social Philosophy and Policy 1985

First Published 1985

Basil Blackwell Publisher Limited
108 Cowley Road, Oxford OX4 1JF, England

British Library Cataloguing in Publication Data
Social philosophy and policy.——Vol. 2, no. 1
(Sept. 1984) —
1. Social sciences——Philosophy
300'.1   H61

ISBN 0-631-13718-1

Library of Congress Cataloging in Publication Data
Liberty and equality
  1. Equality——Addresses, essays, lectures.
  2. Liberty——Addresses, essays, lectures.
  I. Paul, Ellen Frankel.   II. Miller, Fred Dycus, 1944–
  III. Paul, Jeffrey.   IV. Bowling Green State University.
  Social Philosophy & Policy Center.
  JC575.L63   1985   320'.01'1   85-1361
  ISBN 0-631-13718-1

Typeset by Katerprint Co. Ltd, Oxford
Printed in Great Britain by
Whitstable Litho, Kent

CONTENTS

Introduction		vi
R. M. HARE	Liberty and Equality: How Politics Masquerades as Philosophy	1
JAMES M. BUCHANAN and LOREN E. LOMASKY	The Matrix of Contractarian Justice	12
JAN NARVESON	Equality vs. Liberty: Advantage, Liberty	33
ALLEN BUCHANAN	What's So Special About Rights?	61
MICHAEL LEVIN	Negative Liberty	84
DAVID BRAYBROOKE	Preferences Opposed to the Market	101
MAURICE CRANSTON	Rousseau on Equality	115
WILLIAM KRISTOL	Liberty, Equality, Honor	125
WERNER J. DANNHAUSER	Some Thoughts on Liberty, Equality, and Tocqueville's *Democracy in America*	141
J. R. LUCAS	Towards a Theory of Taxation	161

INTRODUCTION

Liberty and equality, in the Western political tradition, have been considered as intrinsically good things. However, philosophers of politics have differed rather markedly about how to fit both values into one system and, indeed, about whether one should be preferred over the other or even to the virtual exclusion of the other. Classical liberals, for example, held that the preservation of liberty in the sense of absence of coercion ought to be the principal function of government, and that any concern for equality beyond equality before the law exceeded the proper scope of government. Modern liberals see things quite differently. For them, equality – construed as either equality of condition or equality of opportunity – is a good on a par with liberty, and the attainment of both goods is considered a proper preserve of government.

The contributors to this collection have widely different views on, first, the definitions of liberty and equality and, second, the proper balance between them. Some authors would, clearly, fall within the classical liberal mold, while others more nearly identify with the modern liberals' quest for reconciling individual liberty with a measure of equality of condition. Our authors represent a variety of disciplines – economics, political science, and philosophy – and their approaches differ, yet they all share a belief that the theme at hand is of great interest to those concerned with the good society.

Most of our authors approach this topic from an analytical perspective, with the hypothetical social contract appearing quite often as the favored tool of analysis. This device figures most prominently in the papers of James Buchanan and Loren Lomasky, J. R. Lucas, and David Braybrooke, but with remarkably different results. Buchanan and Lomasky, in a co-authored work, present what they believe to be the limitations of a Hobbesian social contract when contrasted with the considerable methodological advantages of the Rawlsian model. More importantly, the two authors argue that the outcome of a Rawlsian deliberation would not only (as Rawls, himself, contends) accord a superior place to liberty in the order of political values, but would endorse a far weaker version of the difference principle than that advanced by Rawls. Such an outcome would give unequivocal support, Buchanan and Lomasky argue, to a free market society.

Braybrooke, in contrast to Buchanan and Lomasky, finds it far from obvious that rational contracting agents would necessarily accept the market as the most desirable economic system. Though the market is often touted as the most efficient (and just) means of satisfying preferences, there is in fact a large class of preferences which it does not and cannot satisfy at all, namely, those which are opposed to some aspect of the market process itself or its outcome. Braybrooke uses the fable of the Grasshopper and the Ant to illustrate some of these preferences. He then, considers briefly the question of what kind of society, if any, might be palatable to both the (pro-market) Ant and the (anti-market) Grasshopper.

J. R. Lucas discerns in the hypothetical agreement a suitable device for critically analyzing the taxation policies of contemporary welfare states, especially where these are employed to bring about an equality of condition among their citizens. Lucas argues that an adequate theory of taxation must be based on a consideration of the justice of tax policies, i.e., on a theory of "contributive justice." His principle of contributive justice is that taxes (i.e., contributions to collective goals) must be "what I can see good reason to pay as a matter of enlightened self-interest and reasonable identification with my fellow members of the State, and in reasonable confidence of their paying too." Hence, tax policy must be based on an understanding of what individuals who are representative of different interest groups in society would see as a "good bargain," i.e., a good price for benefits received.

The economic problems that plague Western democracies are alleged by both Jan Narveson and Michael Levin to derive from their mistaken commitment to what political philosophers have called positive, as opposed to negative liberty. The latter formulation, which underpins the classical liberal attachment to personal and property rights, has been eroded, in their view, by an unjustified injection of so-called "positive liberty," and "right" to equality of condition. Both Narveson and Levin reject the contention of many egalitarians that equality of condition is a right.

If positive liberty cannot be adequately defended as a coherent, universalizable principle, how certain can we be that negative liberty will not fall victim, also, to philosophical scrutiny? Allen Buchanan argues that we need not worry should such an alleged natural right to negative liberty be placed in jeopardy by philosophical discussion, since there are other more substantial reasons for thinking that governments should erect permanent impediments to certain types of anti-social behaviour, reasons that derive from the nature of a public good and not from speculation about "natural rights."

Allen Buchanan's point nicely anticipates the view of R. M. Hare who contends that the competing libertarian and egalitarian visions of the good society derive not from philosophical argument but from competing intuitions about the common good. Hare believes that quarrels about rights are, therefore, grounded in a kind of anti-rationalism. Rationality, he suggests, would lead us to conclude that utilitarianism supplies a defensible political standard for western societies.

Several authors attack our problem from a historical perspective. Rousseau, long associated in the popular mind with egalitarianism, is given a novel reading by Maurice Cranston. Cranston argues that this alleged partisan of equality of condition has been miscast in this role both by his supporters and detractors. Cranston contends that Rousseau was primarily a proponent of equal negative liberty. This implies that Rousseau is less an ally of twentieth century socialist experimentation than has been previously thought.

William Kristol proposes a different type of foundational support for a liberal society (in the classical sense) in his paper, *Liberty, Equality, and Honor*. His view is that the liberal society will be more adequately defended if it is grounded in a conception of honor which can constrain egalitarian and other baser impulses, a conception the genesis of which he finds in the writings of Tocqueville. Such a conception Kristol argues, must emanate from a religious rather than a secular philosophical framework. Tocqueville reappears in Werner Dannhauser's paper. Dannhauser points out that although Tocqueville never refers to "capitalism," the conception of liberty to which he subscribes is one that will necessarily give rise to a market order. Dannhauser, teasingly, wonders why the United States has a Statue of Liberty but no Statue of Equality.

From grasshoppers to ants, to hemophiliacs isolated in Alaska, to Statues of Equality, our authors have provided lively examples to illustrate their positions. Readers should find something novel from among the wide diversity of viewpoints represented within this volume.

LIBERTY AND EQUALITY:
HOW POLITICS MASQUERADES
AS PHILOSOPHY

R. M. HARE

It is my intention in this paper to highlight the dangers which arise when people appeal to moral intuitions to settle questions in political, and in general in applied, philosophy. But first I want to ask why all or nearly all of us are in favour both of liberty and of equality – why all our intuitions are on their side.

In the case of liberty it is easy to understand why. Although philosophers have held diverse theories about the concept of liberty – theories which have been drawn together into two main groups in a famous lecture by Sir Isaiah Berlin – there cannot be much doubt that in the mind of the ordinary man to have liberty (to be free; I shall not distinguish between freedom and liberty) is to be under no constraint in doing what one wants to do. This, at any rate, is a main constituent of the concept of liberty as all of us understand it.

Since, therefore, it seems self-evidently true that we want to be able to do what we want, we are bound to want liberty and, in general, to be in favour of it. We want it for ourselves; if we universalize our prescriptions, this constrains us to be in favour of it for others as well. That explains why, if any politician can claim that he is fighting for liberty, he is likely to win a large following.

In the case of equality the matter is not so clear cut. There have been many societies in which equality was not valued. As the well known hymn has it:

> The rich man in his castle,
> The poor man at his gate,
> God made them, high or lowly,
> And ordered their estate.

This has been the view of *anciens régimes* throughout the ages, and Plato is echoing an extremely common sentiment when he complains of the Athenian democracy of his day that it "distributes a sort of equality to equals and unequals alike" (*Rep.* 558c). If, today, it is as easy to get political support by appealing to equality as to liberty, this is because such regimes have become outmoded. I have given reasons elsewhere why equality (at any rate moderate equality) is a good thing, and I shall return to these reasons later.

Thus it has come about that in the mouths of most of us both "liberty" and "equality" are hurrah-words. But any well read political philosopher knows that this is only the beginning of a tangle of problems. Just because they are hurrah-words, the prescription to pursue liberty and equality in our society seems self-evidently right, but it is entirely unclear what in particular it tells us to do. Let me give some examples, not only of conflicts *between* liberty and equality as political aims, but of conflicts between different aims, each of which could claim to be motivated by the desire for liberty; and the same for equality. Of conflicts between liberty and equality we have heard a great deal in recent years. It is notorious·that if you start with an equal distribution of wealth in society, and give people the liberty to dispose of their own wealth as they think fit, you will very soon end up with an extremely unequal distribution. Thus in the economic sphere at any rate it has come to be generally accepted that there is no fraternity between liberty and equality: so far from being happy brothers they are natural enemies.

But even within each camp there is conflict. My wife and I were recently taken by a kind German friend to see the Befreiungshalle, or Hall of the Liberation, built on a magnificent site above the Danube gorge near Regensburg. It is a splendid rotunda in the purest classical style (looking a bit like a gasholder designed by Phidias), and was put up by King Ludwig of Bavaria to commemorate the liberation of the Germans, and of Bavaria in particular, from Napoleon. To my English eyes it was strange that, among the many military leaders who figure as liberators, the Duke of Wellington is not included (though Blücher is). Although far from being a liberal (were any of them?), the Duke could claim in some sense to be a liberator. But what is more to the point is that the "tyranny" from which the Germans were thus liberated was that of a man whose political roots lay in the Revolution, and whose armies were inspired by thoughts of liberty. For them, King Ludwig was a tyrant.

There is another example nearer home. When the American ex-colonists expanded into the West, they had the liberty to do so because the French were no longer there; and the French were no longer there because they had been expelled by British arms (assisted of course by vigorous local efforts); it was the freedom not to be taxed in order to provide for their own protection that the Revolutionaries above all sought. The French, naturally, were delighted. So here again the winning of one sort of liberty had militated against the preservation of another. Today in many parts of the world peoples have obtained freedom from imperial rulers only to fall under the power of the most odious local tyrannies. Think of Cambodia.

Equality is just as divided against itself. The best general example is the conflict between equality of wealth and equality of power. The principal motive for setting up socialist regimes all over the world has been to promote equality of wealth. Egalitarian sentiments always bulk large in the propaganda of socialist parties. Yet the putting into practice of these ideas has almost always resulted in (indeed required) the concentration of enormous power into the hands of a small number of people, who have seldom followed liberal principles in the exercise of it. This, indeed, is in accord with Marxist theory. It has proved possible in a very few western-style democracies to combine moderate equality of wealth with a moderate spread of power among the governed. But this is a very difficult political art, and the conditions under which it can be practised occur relatively rarely, and are very delicate and easily disturbed by extremist measures either of the left or of the right.

Some philosophers, viewing these conflicts between liberty and equality and within them both, of which I have been able to give only the sketchiest of examples, will try to provide a remedy by seeking better definitions of the two concepts. If we could only find the right kind of concept of liberty or of equality, they seem to be thinking, we should be able to recommend self-consistent policies which would pursue the best sort of liberty and the best sort of equality simultaneously. Some philosophers even think that they can thus reconcile other desirable political ends as well, such as order. Hegel is an outstanding example. But I am inclined to think that the ambition to solve these problems by finding a single definition of either concept is naive, and does not go to the root of the matter. A single definition there might be of each concept; but it would not help, because it would be too lacking in content (as indeed definitions should be) to provide specific political guidance.

The truth is that the conflicts are inherent. This is because liberty for one person to do one thing may be inconsistent, in the world as it is, with liberty for another person to do something else that he wants; and equality between people in one respect may, as we have seen, militate against equality in other respects. These conflicts, like all moral conflicts, should make us re-examine, in more depth than I have done so far, the reasoning processes which have led us to our conflicting aims and opinions. And the first thing that may then happen is that we shall acquire a healthy distrust of moral intuition.

It is common political form in most western countries to think that liberty must be a good thing, and that equality must be a good thing. It is even held, contrary to all the evidence, that democracy must be a good thing in all circumstances. I am a very strong believer in democracy; but there is a danger in letting our belief in it rest on simple moral conviction. This may weaken our power to argue; and then, when we need to show *why* democracy is, in certain familiar circumstances, preferable to dictatorship, we shall find ourselves at a loss. Having been brought up from our earliest years to think that it is a good form of government, we are convinced that it is so, but cannot for the life of us think why. Only by using our reasoning powers shall we be able to show why the democratic process is, in many societies which can manage it, the most efficient and best way of governing ourselves; and when there are exceptions (when it turns out, for example, that a democratic constitution leads to governmental impotence, corruption and chaos) to show what peculiarities of the particular society (deep communal divisions, for example) led to the collapse of democracy. In all this reasoning we shall have to have regard, not initially to our moral convictions (they will come later when we have done the reasoning) but to facts about societies. It is a relevant fact, for example, that it was the western democracies that defeated the dictatorships of Germany, Italy and Japan in the second World War, and not vice versa; they showed themselves the more efficient form of government in this formidable test. But even there Russia was the exception.

So to argue in defence of democracy, morally or in any other way, demands thought about our principles and about the situations to which they are to be applied. Our conviction that democracy is a good form of government is only secure when it can be defended by sound reasoning on the basis of established historical facts. And the conviction will become, albeit more secure, less extreme in the process: we shall remain convinced that democracy is a good form of government, but ready to admit that it may not be the best form of government in all societies at all times.

This digression about democracy has illustrated why it is a mistake, and weakens our political and moral thought, to rely on intuition. I now want to apply this lesson to liberty and equality. We need to be able to show by clear thinking in the light of the facts, not merely that liberty and equality are on the whole good things, but why they are, and, more importantly, what sorts of liberty and equality are good things, and in what circumstances. And in doing this thinking, we have to have an eye to the actual conditions under which the liberty is going to be exercised and the equality enjoyed.

I want you to see how radical a departure this would be from the practice of many philosophers. Both liberty and equality are often referred to as "rights". "The right to be free" occurred in a wartime slogan that I remember; and people are constantly demanding equal treatment in some respect as a right (and in many cases I applaud them for doing this). What I am going now to say about liberty and equality is simply an application of what I have said elsewhere about rights. When philosophers talk about rights, either in general or in arguing about particular rights, they commonly assume that we *know*, really, what rights people have. Our intuitions inform us of this, if only we can get them clear. So we find Judith Jarvis Thomson (*PPA* 1 (1971)) naively supposing that if only we can think clearly about her case of the lady hooked up to a great violinist, our intuitions will tell us what we ought to say about it, and thus we shall be able to generalize from this particular case and say something secure about abortion (something of course which will support the feminist view). This is an outstanding example of how, as I put it in my title, politics masquerades as philosophy. We start off with intuitions, which we hope will be sufficiently widely shared for us to attract a following, and apply them to particular well chosen cases. The answers come out as we wish, and we then derive a general conclusion about some important political question. Never, in the whole thought-process, is it asked whether the intuitions are ones which we should have. It is assumed that people (women for example or, if you are on the other side, foetuses) have rights, and that we can intuit what they are, if only we pay close enough attention to our own navels. It is never asked what rights these parties *should be accorded*. But that is the fundamental moral question on the answer to which all our practice should be based.

The same thing happens when Robert Nozick talks about liberty. In his famous Wilt Chamberlain example, he *assumes* that the snap answers that we shall most of us give are the right ones. We know already, by intuition, that he ought to be free to exchange his services for whatever fee he can get from other willing parties. The fact that the general application of this finding, which Nozick proceeds to make, would lead to the grossest inequalities in distribution, not only of wealth, but also of power derived from wealth, and that this runs counter to *other* intuitions which most of us have, is conveniently played down by Nozick. He is, like all those who use this method, highly selective in the intuitions to which he appeals.

John Rawls reaches very different conclusions by appeal to *his* intuitions. One is inclined to suspect that both of these writers *start* from a certain political position, just as Professor Thomson starts from a feminist position. This is what determines what intuitions they are going to have, and so, naturally, the arguments based on these intuitions come out as they wish. In fairness to Rawls, he does have, unlike Nozick, a method of moral reasoning. I think it is a good one, and would lead to the right conclusions if it were consistently applied. The method relies on asking what people would say in the original position, ignorant of the role which they were to play in the society governed by the principles of justice they were choosing. The great merit of this method is that it asks initially not "What social arrangements are just?" but "What are the principles of justice by which we should determine the justice of social arrangements?". Applied to questions about rights, this procedure will lead us to ask first, not "What rights do such and such people have?" but "How (by what principles) should we determine what rights ought to be accorded to those people?". Applied to questions about liberty, it will lead us to ask first, not "What rights to what sorts of liberty do what people have?" but "How should we decide what things people should be free to do and what things they should not be free to do?". Applied to equality, it would lead us to ask first, not "What rights to equal treatment do people have in various circumstances?" but 'How should we determine what rights to what kind of equal treatment should be accorded to people under varying conditions?".

Rawls is absolutely right to treat as basic the questions which I say should be asked first. We have to have, first, a method of arguing (his method is that of the original position), and then use the method to establish general principles. Only after that can we apply the principles to particular questions about justice, rights, liberty and equality. The sad thing is that, although he has a method for settling these questions, Rawls vitiates his procedure by continual appeals to his own moral intuitions, which he hopes his readers will share. He is not content to rely on the method; it has to yield results consistent with his intuitions in reflective equilibrium, or he will tinker with the method. In particular, it has to yield results different from those yielded by utilitarianism; for one of Rawls' firmest intuitions is that utilitarianism is wrong. Others besides myself have shown that, if the method is played straight, it does yield utilitarian conclusions. Rawls himself admits that an ideal-observer theory will yield such conclusions. But it is only by ad hoc tinkering, and by depriving them of the factual information on which sound moral judgement has to be based, that Rawls manages to get his ideal rational contractors out of the position of ideal observers and into a position in which they will make a non-utilitarian contract. In order to ensure their impartiality, which is the only function of his veil of ignorance, he only needed to conceal from them their individual roles, not other more material facts. If he had restricted himself to this 'formal' veil of ignorance, his rational contractors would have been subject effectively to the same restrictions as the ideal observer, and would have reached the same utiliarian conclusions.

My point is that we have to have a method of moral thinking before we start thinking – at least, the method is logically prior; though there may be perfectly good inarticulate intuitive thinking without any prior explicit grasp of method, the method is implicit in any sound thinking that can give reasons for what is thought. Thus, we have to ask how we should determine what liberties and equalities people should have before we address the substantial question. I shall go on now, to discuss how I would myself answer the methodological question, and how I think the answer to it puts on a much more hopeful basis all our arguments on practical questions about liberty and equality.

Like Rawls, I think that the first things to look for are principles of justice, determining rights, which are acceptable to rational thought. Unlike Rawls, who is rather contemptuous of appeals to the logic of our concepts, I think that the way to find these principles is first to study our moral language and concepts (which are, so far, neutral between different substantial moral and political standpoints). These concepts and their logic will determine for us certain rules which we have to obey in our thinking, if we are to do it rationally. When we do it in accordance with these rules, we find that, in the light of the facts of the world in which we live, some principles of justice and other moral principles are acceptable and some not. That is how we get our principles of justice.

I have explained the method much more fully in my recent book. Here, I can only summarize: the conceptual points about the logic of moral thinking are that moral statements in their central use express prescriptions, and these have to be universalizable. The recognition of this leads to a method which is at the same time Kantian and utilitarian. If we know that in making a moral judgement we are prescribing universally for all similar cases, we shall not prescribe for others what we are not prepared to prescribe for ourselves were we identically placed. This will lead us to give equal weight to the equal preferences of all, since we shall give equal weight to theirs and to ours, and of course it will be positive. Thus we shall be, as utilitarians do, counting everybody as one and nobody as more than one, and shall be trying to maximize the satisfaction of everybody's preferences, treated impartially. And, as Kantians do, we shall be acting so that we can will the maxim of our action to be a universal law; we shall be treating humanity in ourselves and others as an end; and we shall be acting as if we were legislating members of a kingdom of ends.

If this method were applied directly to acts, it would enjoin us to judge them by their utility, in the sense of preference-satisfaction. However, even an act-utilitarian (which is what I am) must recognize that our ability to predict the consequences of our acts (what we shall be in effect doing if we perform them) is very limited. Even an act-utilitarian, therefore, will only demand of himself that he give himself the best chance that he can: the greatest expectation of utility. And the way to do this, the world and human nature being as they are, is to cultivate and religiously follow sound general principles whose acceptance-utility is highest. There is much more to be said about this, but that will have to suffice.

The posture of the wise Kantian utilitarian will therefore be just like that of an intuitionist brought up on sound lines, except that he can justify his upbringing and the intuitionist cannot. Some of the intuitions he will have will be about justice and rights. He will have come to have those intuitions (acknowledge those principles of justice and those rights) which have the highest acceptance-utility: that is, whose acceptance in society, and in particular by him, is most likely to do the best, all in all, to satisfy the preferences of those affected. This, then, is how we should determine what rights we should acknowledge: in particular, what liberties we should safeguard either by law or by moral sanctions; and how equally we should treat people and in what respects.

Since all that is much too summary and general, I am going to illustrate it by discussing briefly a particular class of cases which seems to me to be an extremely good example of the application of this method in the political field. This is the case of legislation about employment and trade unions.

If we look at the rhetoric used by both sides in this area, it is obvious that appeals to liberty and equality are frequently made. One of the main motives of labour leaders is the desire for equality. But the equality desired may be of different kinds. There is, first, the wish to lessen differences in power and wealth between capitalists, or managers, and workers. But more prominent recently has been a wish to secure equality with other groups of workers. This has revived in miniature an old conflict between different interpretations of "equality". One interpretation is used to support higher wages for workers at present at the bottom of the scale, in order to make their pay more equal to that of others. But on another interpretation the others are then being unequally, in the sense of unfairly, treated because the differential has been eroded; it is assumed, on this interpretation, that the old differential yielded *proportionate* equality (in very much the sense supported by Aristotle, equal pay for work of equal value), and it is therefore claimed that equality demands a return to the old proportionate differential. However, this very same argument is looked on askance if it is applied to the pay of judges, army officers or members of parliament. As is well known, the alternation or leapfrogging of these two arguments is a potent rhetorical weapon in the hands of union leaders. It is a kind of ratchet device whereby pay can be increased indefinitely, provided that the unions who appeal to these conflicting intuitions have enough industrial muscle.

In order to preserve their muscle, union leaders frequently invoke other intuitions about liberty. If they are successfully to prosecute the class war, workers have to have the liberty to combine against their employers and coerce them into giving better terms of employment. "Liberty to coerce" is of course somewhat of a paradox. The liberty is secured by obtaining for trade unions legal immunities, so that they cannot, like ordinary people, be sued in the courts if, for example, they induce their members to break contracts, or damage third parties not involved in a wage claim. The liberty is even demanded to use violence in the course of strikes, at least by way of barring "blacklegs" from a factory by a threat of trouble, in order to avoid which the police, if the government is benign, will, in effect, help to keep the picket line peaceful but secure. But if the police are absent, the blacklegs know what to expect.

On the other side, employers and Conservative politicians will marshal another lot of intuitions. They will complain that firms are not being treated equally if the laws of contract and tort are not applied to trade unions as they are to everybody else, including the firms in their dealings with one another. And they will complain that employers' liberty is being infringed if they are not allowed to make enforceable contracts (the best they can obtain by free bargaining) with their employees. And the bargaining, they will say, is not free if they are subject to the threat of strike action. Not all those on the two sides would use all these arguments. It is far from my intention to support any of them. I think they are all bad arguments, in so far as they rest on unreasoned intuitions whose sole basis is political. Yet I should not be at all surprised to find arguments having just the same form, and just as little sound basis, in the writings of our philosophical colleagues. They are what their epistemology encourages. I have at any rate shown how deeply intuitions about liberty and equality are embedded in such disputes.

How *should* we decide what rights of liberty and equality should be accorded by the law, and sanctioned by morality, to those engaged in industry? The first part of the answer is relatively easy. The formal properties of the moral concepts require us not to differentiate morally between identical cases: a moral prescription for one case will have to apply to any identically similar case, whoever is at the receiving end. This is what is called formal justice, which comprises both formal equality (identical cases are to be treated equally by the moral law) and formal liberty (each person is to be the judge of what he here and now prefers and therefore prescribes). I am referring to singular prescriptions as to what should happen *to him now*. He is not necessarily the best judge of what he will prefer if things happen to him which he does not now fully represent to himself (for not everybody is prudent); and he is not necessarily the best judge of what prescriptions, if universalized, will maximally satisfy the preferences of all, considered impartially (for not everybody is moral). Misconceptions on these points are the source of vulgar objections to what I have been saying, with which I shall not bore you.

As is generally recognized, formal justice does not take us very far. But I have already said how it leads directly to a utilitarian method of moral reasoning which can settle more substantial questions. If, in choosing what principles to cultivate in the field of labour relations, we realize that we are prescribing universally, and subject therefore to the requirement of formal justice, we shall have equal regard to the equal preferences of all those affected. These will include, besides the workers and employers in a particular industry, all who buy its products, and in some degree the whole of society. This, as I have said, will make us choose the principles with the highest general acceptance-utility, in the world of industry as it is. So should we or should we not have combination acts forbidding trade unions? We should not, because the existence of trade unions has, by and large, brought enormous benefits to employees without actually harming industry or the consumer in the long run. But ought trade unions to be given all the legal immunities that they have in Britain, for example? That is at present being argued; and the way to argue it rationally is to ask "What principles covering legislation about trade unions and in general about wage-fixing are likely, if accepted, to result in the greatest preference-satisfaction for all, treated impartially?" If we follow such principles, the laws that we make will do better for the general preference-satisfaction than the present law does, unless it is already optimal. I doubt whether the present state of the law in Britain *is* optimal. It certainly gives in most respects greater liberties to trade unions than those of most other countries.

Will a law made in accordance with such principles be just? It will be formally just, because we shall be treating like cases alike, whoever is affected, as universalizability leads us to do. It will also be formally just as regards the operation of the law itself, in that the law applies to everybody who falls under the conditions specified in it, and is impartially administered by the courts. But the first kind of formal justice (the moral, as contrasted with the legal) is the more fundamental.

Will such a law secure substantial justice? It will, because it will be approved by principles of justice (moral principles) which have the highest acceptance-utility, taking into account the preferences of all those affected, considered impartially. The substance is put in by the preferences them-selves (different preferences will justify different laws). If the Chinese *prefer* industry to be ordered differently, a formally just way of legislating about it in China will come out with different laws from those in a country whose inhabitants have different preferences. In either case, the laws will *be* just, because they allot utility impartially; and they will be *seen* to be just, if people have the moral intuitions about justice and rights, in this area, that they should have – i.e. the intuitions whose content is moral principles having the highest acceptance-utility.

In other words, our object should be to get both laws and moral principles adopted in society which do the best, all in all, for the members of society considered impartially. If I may speculate about the outcome, it might be that ideas became current very different from those which now motivate a supposed class war. People would begin to ask themselves whether more good is done to all by cooperation than by conflict. Trade unions would have an important place; but their actions would be governed by principles directed to the good of all members of society, whether in the role of workers, as nearly everybody is, or of consumers, as everybody is, or, as many employees are now in Britain through the operation of pension funds, of capitalists. All this could be effected if people really understood how to think about these matters.

Philosophy, University of Florida

Further References

The method of moral argument here used, and its basis, are more fully set out in my recent book *Moral Thinking: its Levels, Method and Point* (Oxford, 1981), whose bibliography refers to relevant papers of mine on "Justice and Equality" and "What is Wrong with Slavery", as well as to my review of Rawls and my criticism of Judith Jarvis Thomson on abortion. Berlin's lecture referred to on p. 1 is "Two Concepts of Liberty" (Oxford UP, 1981). The references to Nozick are to his *Anarchy, State and Utopia* (Basic Books 1974).

THE MATRIX OF CONTRACTARIAN JUSTICE*

JAMES M. BUCHANAN
and
LOREN E. LOMASKY

I

There are no first principles etched in stone from which all moral philosophers must take their bearings. We must deliberately *choose* our point of departure in any attempt to respond to the question: "Must any defensible theory of justice incorporate both a commitment to personal liberty and to economic equality?" Basic to our own approach is a suspicion of seers and visionaries who espy an external source of values independent from human choices. We presuppose, instead, that political philosophy commences with *individual* evaluation.[1] A near-corollary of this presupposition is that *each* individual's preferences ought to be taken into account equally with those of others. That is, we suppose that there is no *privileged evaluator*, whose preferences are accorded decisive weight. *Conceptual unanimity* as a criterion for institutional evaluation follows naturally from the other two presuppositions. If there is neither an external standard of value nor a corps of resident value experts, only unanimity can ultimately be satisfactory as a test of social desirability. Our perspective then is *subjectivist, individualist,* and *unanimitarian.*

These presuppositions inform our *contractarian* analysis. There are, however, two separate contractarian traditions that we shall find useful to distinguish, the "Hobbesian" and the "Rawlsian." In the first, persons find themselves in the anarchistic war of each against all. They contract away their natural liberties in exchange for the order that civil society – through its sovereign – affords. In this contracting process, individuals are assumed to possess full self-knowledge; they know who they are, what conceptions of the good they hold, and what their endowments are. The contractual solutions that emerge will necessarily reflect this knowledge.

* We are indebted to Geoffrey Brennan for helpful comments on an earlier draft.
[1] External values may be rejected as an appropriate foundation for political philosophy either because such values are held not to exist or because, even if existent, they cannot be invoked for epistemological or moral reasons. We need not make a commitment to either of these positions, although, of course, the difference between them may be significant in other contexts.

The Rawlsian contractual process is distinguishable from the Hobbesian primarily through the introduction of the veil of ignorance. Individuals in the original position lack knowledge of their own features in post-contractual stages, including their conceptions of the good. They are unable to identify their roles in patterns of interaction that emerge under the set of institutions selected.

In Section II, we examine a highly simplified model of Hobbesian contract. Our purpose is not to derive substantive normative results.[2] Here we limit analysis to the demonstration that the equilibrium outcome may be one in which both parties are better off than in the pre-contractual state but in which they enjoy unequal quantities of economic goods and liberties. If either of these inequalities seems to violate our pre-analytical sense of justice, this clash will, in itself, offer reasons to examine an alternative contractarian setting.

In Section III, we start from the Rawlsian original position. We shall assume a general familiarity with the analysis in *A Theory of Justice*,[3] and we shall ignore issues involved with the conceptual status of "choice" behind the veil. Our interest, here, lies in the results that may be derived from the idealized Rawlsian setting, not with the epistemological coherence of that setting itself. More specifically, we want to answer the question: What must be built into Rawlsian choice to generate principles of justice that are similar to those derived by Rawls himself? We shall focus primary attention on the principle of maximal equal liberty, rather than on the difference principle of distribution. Moreover, we will show that individuals in the choice process must concern themselves with *relative liberties* as well as with *absolute liberties*. Section IV specifically examines the demonstration of the equal liberty condition, and Section V offers our observations on the assignment of value to relative liberty as opposed to relative economic position. It will be concluded that the case for equality of basic liberties is much stronger than any case for equality in economic goods.

We emphasize that our purpose is *not* that of offering yet another commentary on Rawls or, for that matter, on Hobbes. Our intention is, instead, to explore the place that liberty and economic equality occupy in contractarian theories of justice. Substantive questions concerning contractual agreement motivate our analysis rather than any intention to reinterpret distinguished philosophers. And, as the analysis will demonstrate, our results will differ substantially from those presented by these two seminal

---

[2] Both of us have discussed such derivations elsewhere. See, James M. Buchanan, *The Limits of Liberty* (Chicago: University of Chicago Press, 1975), and Loren Lomasky, "Personal Projects as the Foundations for Basic Rights" *Social Philosophy and Policy*, Spring 1984, 1(2).

[3] John Rawls, *A Theory of Justice* (Cambridge: Harvard University Press, 1971).

contractarians. Those who demur from our interpretation of texts may change our labels to "quasi-Hobbes" and "quasi-Rawls" at their own choosing.

II. HOBBESIAN CONTRACT

In Hobbesian anarchy, individuals are entirely free from socially contrived constraints on their ability to pursue that which they want to pursue. In this sense, the state of nature affords maximal natural liberty. But, of course, anarchic equal liberty offers hardly an idyllic existence. The solitary predator is an object of predation by others, and the fear of sudden, violent death is never far away. A large share of an individual's resources will be invested in attempts to avoid this worst of fates, but without assurance of success. Hobbesian anarchy almost cries out for amelioration. A leap into order can be accomplished if persons trade off natural liberty for security. The result is the achievement of a contractual equilibrium, one in which all parties to the contract are immeasurably better off than they were in anarchy.

The process is illustrated in the highly simplified two-person model in Figure 1. The position at I depicts the setting in Hobbesian anarchy, where both persons "enjoy" *maximum* and *equal* natural liberty. There are no formal constraints on behavior. Each person is at liberty to do as he chooses; but the *power* of each person to accomplish his own desires is restricted by the liberty of the other. From the initial position at I, there are mutual advantages to be secured by a trade of liberties. Individual A may agree to give up some (or indeed possibly all) of his natural liberties in exchange for B's giving up some of his own. The area of the shaded lozenge in the construction of Figure 1 represents the potentialities for mutual gain.

Assume that agreement is reached on position C. Since C is, by construction, on the contract locus, it is in the set of non-dominated positions. No further agreement is possible.[4] Note, however, that C is not on the diagonal, positions along which would reflect equal liberty for both persons. The contractually-attained position could, of course, have been shown at E. But there would seem to be no basis for a presumption that the agreed upon equilibrium will lie on the diagonal. The two persons, A and B, know their natural endowments and also their own preferences. As they interact one with another, each will acquire information concerning the

---

[4] The problem of enforcement of any contractual agreement is, of course, one of intense importance in both the Hobbesian and the Rawlsian models of contract. We do not examine enforcement in this paper, although we recognize that this problem must occupy a crucial place in any comprehensive theory of justice.

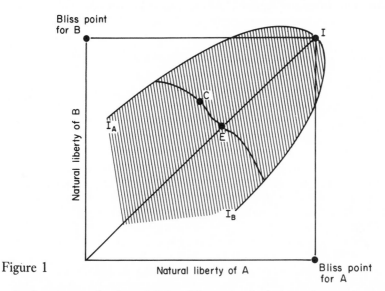

Figure 1

other's assets and vulnerabilities. If persons find themselves to be natural unequals in predatory ability and/or demand for deference, the equilibrium emergent from contract will tend to reflect such inequalities. Only if A and B are natural equals in these relevant respects will it be likely that the final equilibrium will lie along the diagonal.

There is no presumption of such natural equality and, hence, no inference that contractual agreement will feature equal liberty. Persons tend to differ in strength, guile, fortitude, ruthlessness, and bargaining skills. It would be exceptional if they should agree on arrangements embodying equal liberty. But this fact poses a problem for the normative status of Hobbesian contract: rational agreement may produce results that sharply diverge from pre-analytical intuitions to the effect that political justice must, at the very least, incorporate equality of basic liberties.

We suspect that Hobbes himself had some such intuitions, and that is why he attempted to impose conditions on the contractors that would insure attainment of a position on the diagonal.[5] Hobbes depicts persons in the state of nature as being equally vulnerable to the terrors of anarchy,

[5] With the notable exception of the Sovereign, who enjoys immeasurably greater liberty and power than anyone else. It is as if Hobbes believed that, by placing only one unequal in a position of power over a whole set of equals, he could dispel criticism that his outcome lacks formal justice. Critics historically have not been mollified.

downplaying the prospect that some are more vulnerable than others. But perhaps Hobbes also recognized that such a presumption was unconvincing, and for that reason he posited a further condition intended to guarantee equal liberties in contractual agreement:

> If nature therefore have made men equal, that equality is to be acknowledged; or if nature have made men unequal; yet because men that think themselves equal, will not enter into conditions of peace, but upon equal terms, such equality must be admitted. And therefore for the ninth law of nature I put this, that every man acknowledge another for his equal by nature. The breach of this precept is pride.[6]

By assertion, this statement constrains the feasible set of outcomes to the diagonal in Figure 1, or its n-person counterpart. Persons are vain, and they will not assent to any arrangement that limits one person's liberties more than those of others. With reference to the construction in Figure 1, C would be unacceptable to A because, in C, A is required to give up more of his natural liberty than B.[7]

The argument is not compelling. We are required not only to believe that each person displays vanity, but that this behavioral characteristic is lexically prior to all other motivations such that persons are unwilling to trade off even the slightest departure from equal liberty for other gains. This characterization is psychologically implausible, and especially so in the stark setting of the state of nature, where the indulgence of vanity would seem a dangerous luxury. Bargains need not be equal along any stipulated dimension for it to be the case that all parties are thereby made better off. Hobbes recognizes this in his argument for the emergence of a compact that allows one person, the Sovereign, to tower over all others. Were personal vanity so critically important, this most glaring of inequalities could scarcely be tolerated.

Our purpose in this section is not primarily to criticize a Hobbesian politics. It is, instead, to indicate just how difficult it is to ground a requirement of equal liberty within Hobbesian contract theory. Because persons may prove to be natural unequals along the relevant dimensions, it is reasonable to conjecture that civil society will not eradicate, and may indeed reinforce, such inequality. If this result is unsatisfactory for any conception of justice, the conditions of contract must be established so that individuals are either unable or unwilling to transform their natural advantages into a civil regime that embodies unequal basic liberties.

---

[6] Thomas Hobbes, *Leviathan*, ed. Michael Oakeshott (New York: Collier Macmillan, 1962), p. 120.

[7] The whole construction of preferences, indicated by the set of indifference curves in Figure 1, could not be as depicted under the Hobbesian constraint. Under the latter, no positions would dominate I, for A and B, except those on the 45 degree line.

III. RAWLSIAN CONTRACT

How did John Rawls reformulate contractarian procedures so as to generate his two principles of justice: that of *maximum equal liberty*, and lexicographically appended to it, the *difference principle* of distribution? What is necessary to produce these results?

The Meaning of Liberty. The first point to be made here is that the meaning of liberty is quite different as between the Hobbesian and the Rawlsian constructions. From the discussion above, it is clear that, if Rawls should have defined liberty analogously to Hobbes, the principle of "most extensive equal liberty" could only be satisfied in anarchy. It seems evident that Rawls' whole discussion applies to a comparison of institutional alternatives (or to a comparison of principles of justice that institutional alternatives represent) all of which fall within the limits of *civil order*. In contrast to Hobbes, Rawls does not compare order with anarchy; his task is a comparison of alternative social orders.

To be meaningful and useful in this comparison, the Hobbesian notion of "natural liberty" must be supplemented by what we can call "civil liberty." Rawls' own discussion as to the precise meaning he gives to "liberty" is not entirely clear, and we do not propose an exegetical effort, here. For our own analysis of the Rawlsian contract, however, it is necessary that we introduce a working definition of 'liberty,' even if we do not seek to defend this definition more generally. We shall define 'liberty' as the absence of constraints on the individual's choice among options. We want to restrict our definition to what has sometimes been called "negative" liberty; we do not want to confuse discussion by introducing the power of the individual to accomplish his desires with liberty itself.[8]

Even within this restricted definition of liberty, however, the dimension described as "liberty in civil order" is different from that dimension described as "liberty in anarchy." In civil order, the person who has

---

[8] Proponents of a conception of positive liberty maintain that person P has the liberty to do x if and only if no one or no social institution constrains P from doing x, *and* if it is the case that P has the ability to do x (i.e., does not lack the means necessary for doing x). On this conception, if someone lacks the means to take a round-the-world cruise, then that person is not at liberty to take the cruise even though no individual or institution is constraining such travel. We believe this to represent a serious conceptual confusion. Not all morally valuable commodities are liberties and, in particular, *power* or *ability* should not be conflated with liberty. Perhaps more to the point, it seems impossible to read Rawls as putting forth a positive conception of liberty. He distinguishes basic liberties (afforded by the first principle of justice) from the other primary goods to be allocated via the difference principle. Since the latter are instrumental to persons' abilities to pursue successfully their chosen conceptions of the good, Rawls is clearly not identifying liberty with the ability to secure desired outcomes.

liberty in person or property enjoys that liberty correlatively with a set of duties on the part of other persons to respect such liberty, duties which are enforceable by the agency of the collectivity. To use Amartya Sen's example, a person has the liberty to sleep on his back or his belly, and accompanying this liberty is the duty of other persons not to constrain the sleeping habits of the person in question.[9]

We can measure, at least ordinally, the predicted levels of liberty that will be available to persons under differing institutional regimes. (That is not to deny that there will be some genuinely hard cases.) Without attempting too much precision here, we can surely say that a regime that constrains a person in his sleeping habits, other things equal, offers such person a lower level of liberty than a regime that includes no such constraints.

The Rawlsian Vector. Persons who find themselves, place themselves, or are placed, behind the veil of ignorance have no knowledge of their future preferences. They know, however, that once they emerge from behind the veil under the set of arrangements chosen, they will have conceptions of the good that they will want to realize. Moreover, they know that what they choose to incorporate within their agreement will affect their subsequent abilities to act upon their various conceptions. We suggest that persons behind the veil be understood as assigning positive values to each of three components of what we shall label the "Rawlsian vector," namely, *absolute liberty*, *relative liberty*, and *economic goods*. From this central postulate, it is possible to derive the choice of institutions that embody Rawls' two principles of justice (although, as our analysis will show, the difference principle is less robust than Rawls seems to believe). This derivation may be accomplished without resort to utility-function logic, and, hence, without making the whole construction vulnerable to essentially irrelevant criticism concerning relative degrees of risk averseness. The construction remains, however, open to criticisms that challenge directly the three components of the vector, and particularly those that question the independent status of relative liberty in the absence of like status for relative economic position.

There is no numeraire or common denominator such as "utility" that allows the three components to be collapsed into a single measure. Over all ranges of possible levels of quantity, each of the "goods" is assumed to be valued in the predicted sense, but a contractor does not know how much absolute liberty he is willing to trade off for more relative liberty, or how much of either he would be willing to give up for more economic goods.

---

[9] The two dimensions are not, of course, independent one from another. An increase in civil liberty of one person necessarily involves a reduction in the natural liberty of others since the duty to refrain from interfering constitutes a limit in natural liberty. That is why natural liberty and civil liberty are both to be regarded as components of liberty *sans phrase*.

That does not preclude the possible recognition by the individual behind the veil of ignorance that, once the institutional structure is in place, and once roles are identified, persons who then know what they want may evaluate the three components relative to each other. But, behind the veil, the individual remains as uncertain about these future trade-offs within the post-constitutional decision calculus as he does about what his own role will be.

In this model of choice, therefore, the alternatives (which are represented as predicted patterns of achievement levels of the three separate components for each party) can be arrayed only by three scalars, identified for each person, one scalar for the absolute level of liberty, one for the level of liberty relative to that of others, and one for the level of economic goods. An alternative can be judged to be preferred to or better than another only if it carries a higher predicted measure for *all* three components and for *all* persons. Note that the scalars are not utility indicators; they are measures of objectively determinate predicted levels or quantities of the components specified.

The three components of the Rawlsian vector may be defined more carefully. *Absolute liberty* ordinally measures the size of the set of activities that the individual is permitted to exercise in the knowledge that other persons, privately or collectively, will not introduce constraints or interferences. Note, in this connection, that the absolute liberty of the individual is restricted even if he participates fully in the reaching of the collective decisions that impose the constraints.[10] For our purposes, we may assume that, for collectively imposed constraints, the individual "votes" on how his own and others' behavior may be limited. Because he is one among many, however, the single person exerts negligible influence on any collective outcome.[11]

Relative liberty is a ratio between absolute liberties. This scalar measures the absolute liberty possessed by an individual relative to that enjoyed by other persons in the community. If all persons have equal absolute liberty, relative liberty is standardized over all persons with a value of unity. If absolute liberty differs among separate persons, the scalar measure for relative liberty exceeds unity for those with the higher absolute liberty and falls below unity for those with lower absolute liberty.

Economic goods are measured in bundles of "commodities" predicted to be

---

[10] Cf. Robert Nozick's "Tale of the Slave", notably stage nine. *Anarchy, State, and Utopia* (New York: Basic Books, 1974), pp. 290–292.

[11] In this respect, the two-person models used to illustrate the analysis later may be misleading if not properly interpreted. In the strict two-person model, a single individual's vote is not without direct consequences for the collective outcome. Hence, it is necessary to keep in mind that the two-person example is designed to be illustrative of the more inclusive many-person setting.

available to the individual, bundles of "commodities" that are deemed generally desirable and positively valued for the maintenance of acceptable life standards (food, clothing, shelter, etc.).

The Matrix of Liberty. We shall now introduce a drastically simplified illustration of a two-person interaction, represented in the four-by-four matrix of Figure 2. The row and column dimensions are scalars for the absolute liberties of the two persons, A and B. And, since relative liberty is defined as a ratio between absolute liberties, only positions along the diagonal of the matrix reflect *equal liberty*.

Each cell of the matrix summarizes a separate institutional arrangement that may be chosen behind the veil of ignorance. Each cell contains the predicted "payoffs" for each of the two persons, the terms in the left bracket indicating payoffs for A, those in the right bracket the payoffs for B. Each bracket contains the predicted payoff, under the particular institutional alternatives depicted, for each of the three separate components of the Rawlsian vector. The top number in each bracket (Roman) depicts the predicted level of absolute liberty attainable under each of the institutional alternatives considered. The middle number in each bracket measures

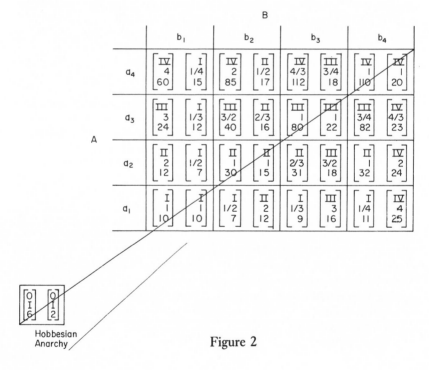

Figure 2

predicted levels of relative liberty. The bottom number measures predicted levels of economic goods, reduced to a single ordinal dimension.

As we suggested earlier, the dimension for absolute liberty that is relevant for Rawlsian choice is not the same as that relevant for the Hobbesian choice examined in Section II. In the latter, recall that natural liberty is maximal only in anarchy, where there is a total absence of formal constraints. In the Rawlsian context, however, absolute liberty, now defined as "liberty in civil society," is essentially nonexistent in genuine Hobbesian anarchy. Any institutional arrangements worthy of consideration behind the veil will dominate Hobbesian anarchy in terms of predicted levels of liberty, as now redefined. In Figure 2, therefore, the position of Hobbesian anarchy is placed outside of the central matrix to be analyzed.

The central matrix contains sixteen possible institutional arrangements; the four-by-four limit being, of course, arbitrary. Before examining the choice calculus of an individual, it is necessary to describe the illustrative construction more fully, at least in its stylized sense.

a_1 or b_1 – The behavior of the individual, A or B, is almost exclusively controlled by decisions reached by the collectivity, acting as a unit. The individual's sphere of activities over which he may exercise private choice is minimal. He is allowed no private property holdings.

a_2 or b_2 – The behavior of the individual, A or B, is extensively if not exclusively, controlled by decisions of the collectivity, acting as a unit. The individual's sphere of activities over which he exercises private choice is severely restricted. The individual possesses private property but over a tightly limited domain.

a_3 or b_3 – The behavior of the individual, A or B, is subjected to a relatively large number of collectively-imposed decisions, but his private property holdings are not directly restricted, and the individual is able to exercise private choice over a widely defined range of activities.

a_4 or b_4 – The behavior of the individual, A or B, is not directly subjected to collectively-imposed decisions except to the extent that is determined by recognition of and respect for the personal and property rights of other persons. The range and scope for the exercise of individual or private choice is maximal.

As we define absolute liberty in the Rawlsian setting, the scalar for A for this component increased from a_1 through a_4 (and from b_1 through b_4 for B). Relative liberty is defined as the ratio of absolute liberties, and is readily computed once absolute liberties are specified. Predicted values for the third component of the Rawlsian vector (economic goods), will depend on the predicted working properties of the institutions that are considered to be the effective alternatives, and particularly those properties relating to the production and the generation of economic goods along with predicted distributional patterns.

The Rawlsian Choice. Consider, now, the choice calculus of the individual behind the veil of ignorance as he examines the alternatives depicted in Figure 2. Recall our earlier statement to the effect that, without some knowledge of the post-veil trade-offs among the three valued components one alternative can be deemed preferable to another only if the dominance relationship is established for both ⌐persons and for all three valued components of the vector. An examination of the matrix reveals that there is no one cell that dominates all other cells in these respects, that simultaneously maximizes each of the three components for both A and B.

One step toward resolution of the choice may be taken, however, once it is recognized that, in the total absence of any agreement on some set of institutional arrangements, Hobbesian anarchy will necessarily emerge. In a real sense, this Hobbesian position becomes a benchmark from which all considerations of alternatives commence. If this benchmark is acknowledged, the dominance relationships can now come back into play. The alternatives to be considered must dominate the Hobbesian benchmark; the predicted values for the three components, for both persons, must exceed those predicted to be descriptive of Hobbesian anarchy.

Examination of Figure 2, as constructed, reveals that there are many positions described in the central matrix that dominate the Hobbesian benchmark for both parties in predicted levels of both absolute liberty and economic goods. Note, however, that only positions *along the diagonal* warrant serious consideration in terms of the third vector component, *relative liberty*. All such positions are characterized by *equal liberty*, and, hence, in this valued vector component, are equivalent to Hobbesian anarchy. In all off-diagonal positions, one of the two parties must predictably enjoy less relative liberty than the other, and, hence, less than he expects to enjoy in the Hobbesian setting.

If this initial step is taken, the relevant Rawlsian comparison reduces to that between the four cells: a_1b_1[12], a_2b_2, a_3b_3, and a_4b_4. Note, however, that

---

[12] Libertarian critics, in particular, may suggest that individuals will predictably enjoy lower levels of absolute liberty, even as defined in the Rawlsian sense, in the collectivist, highly regimented order described in a_1b_1 than they might expect to enjoy in genuine Hobbesian anarchy. There are two ways that we might counter such critics. We could point out that the illustrative descriptions in Figure 2 are designed to serve our expository purposes and are not meant to be actual settings, even as summarized. We might then redefine a_1b_1 to be that social order that dominates Hobbesian anarchy, in the sense discussed, but which embodies lower levels of absolute liberty than any other alternative that is considered to be within the Rawlsian choice set.

More straightforwardly, but less rigorously, we might simply postulate that the threshold values of the economic goods component in Hobbesian anarchy are so low that there is a presumptive, non-dominance argument for ruling this position out of account.

once the set is reduced to these four alternatives, the dominance relationship can again be brought into play. Both a_1b_1 and a_2b_2 are dominated by a_3b_3 and a_4b_4. Both persons are expected to secure higher levels of all of the three valued components in either of the latter two positions than in either of the former two positions.

The effective Rawlsian choice then reduces to a simple pairwise comparison: a_3b_3 and a_4b_4. These are the elements in the non-dominated set. Let us examine these two alternatives more fully. As stylized in the illustrative construction of Figure 2, note that both parties expect to enjoy higher levels of absolute liberty in a_4b_4 than in a_3b_3, while, of course, they expect to secure equal liberty in both positions. Also, as constructed, the predicted aggregate of economic goods in a_4b_4 exceeds that of a_3b_3. Given the Rawlsian vector, as defined, however, the aggregate level of economic goods nowhere enters the relevant calculus. The dominance relationship fails to distinguish between a_3b_3 and a_4b_4 because, for one of the persons, B in the illustration, the predicted level of economic goods is higher in the former than in the latter.

Without some further restriction, there is no purely contractarian basis for selecting an alternative from the reduced set of two. That is to say, if we interpret the veil of ignorance to imply the impossibility of predicting trade-offs among the three valued components of the vector, and, further, to include these three components and only these, as criteria for evaluation, there is no means of discriminating between the two alternatives that are left in the set.

This result carries through for Rawls himself *if we limit consideration to a barebones statement of his two principles of justice*. Indeed, our construction in this Section may be interpreted as little more than a presentation of the two principles in a somewhat more precise form than that which Rawls gives us. The initial statement of his two principles are familiar:

> First, each person is to have an equal right to the most extensive basic liberty compatible with a similar liberty for others.
> Second, social and economic inequalities are to be arranged so that they are both (a) reasonably expected to be to everyone's advantage, and (b) attached to positions and offices open to all. (*A Theory of Justice*, p. 60.)

If this were all there were to it, there would be no trade-off among the components inherent in the principles, and hence no choice between a_3b_3 and a_4b_4 (Figure 2) would be possible. But Rawls goes beyond these initial statements, and he does indeed introduce a suggested trade-off when he adds that the first of the two principles is lexically prior to the second.

These principles are to be arranged in a serial order with the first principle prior to the second. This ordering means that a departure from the institutions of equal liberty required by the first principle cannot be justified by, or compensated for, by greater social and economic advantages. (*A Theory of Justice*, p. 61.)

With this lexical ordering of his two principles, Rawlsian choice must involve the selection of a_4b_4 over a_3b_3. Note that, in a_4b_4, both persons are predicted to enjoy higher levels of absolute liberty than in a_3b_3. Only in the former, therefore, do both parties enjoy the "most extensive basic liberty," or "greatest equal liberty." (p. 124) The fact that, on cursory examination, a_3b_3 seems to meet the requirement of the difference principle becomes totally irrelevant for the choice. Only if absolute liberty is wholly eliminated from the calculus or if the lexical priority of the two principles is reversed, would a selection of a_3b_3 be indicated. If, however, absolute liberty is to count and if we are to take the words "most extensive" and "greatest" seriously, the alternative described in cell a_4b_4 in our illustration becomes the "Rawlsian solution" that necessarily emerges from choice behind the veil of ignorance, despite the apparent failure of Rawls himself to emphasize this result.[13] But if absolute liberty is to be valued, and the first principle is to be lexically prior to the second, how can the difference principle for distribution of economic goods, which has commanded so much attention from the Rawlsian critics, be applicable at all?

Simplified constructions simplify, and ours in Figure 2 is no exception in this respect. In order to clarify our exposition of the analysis, we have packed many variables in the three component vector payoffs depicted. Each set of institutional arrangements, very broadly defined, may contain within itself countless variations in institutional detail, variations that will make a difference for the payoff in predicted levels of distribution of economic

---

[13] It may be charged that we have connived to tinker with the Rawlsian choice situation so as to conjure up a set of institutional arrangements for a political-legal order that seems to describe something like a Nozickean minimal state. We should argue that a careful carrying out of the Rawlsian contractual exercise does produce a political order that, in a formal sense, is far closer to the minimal state than most commentators on Rawls have seemed to recognize. The discussion in Section V advances this finding. However, this result is a consequence of taking seriously the conditions Rawls stipulates as characterizing his contractors. Why, then, does Rawls himself not recognize the quasi-libertarian structure of the institutions he recommends as just? Perhaps, the absence of clarity here arises because Rawls does not clearly define the precise nature and scope of liberty. Consequently, the implications for social arrangements of the first principle of justice remain murky.

The extent to which the formally defined "Rawlsian solution," in a_4b_4, resembles in practical application, the Nozickean minimal state, *as this state is normally perceived*, will depend on the range and scope of "interpersonal" externalities, broadly defined, as these are predicted behind the veil of ignorance.

goods in particular. Consider the a_4b_4 cell as an example. We may assume that this set of arrangements, broadly defined, may embody differing details (e.g., differing assignments of property rights) that will alter the economic goods payoffs to A and to B. That which is specified by the explicit payoffs in Figure 2 can be reinterpreted as that one of this subset which maximizes the economics goods predicted to be available to the least advantaged of the two persons. That is to say, the difference principle is applied at a level of institutional detail *prior* to the construction of the payoff vectors reflected in the presentation of Figure 2. This relegation of the difference principle to within-institutional categories seems fully consonant with Rawls' own assignment of lexical priority to the principle of maximal equal liberty.

We shall not summarize Rawls' own arguments in support of assigning lexical priority to liberty.[14] We note only that in these arguments Rawls relies much more than in other parts of his analysis on empirical conjectures about the shape of utility functions and upon the context of application. He suggests that the marginal value of extensions of liberty relative to economic goods increases rapidly as a society's stock of wealth increases. Not surprisingly, Rawls' more radical critics tend to find this aspect of his argument unsatisfactory. We on the other hand, find it largely satisfactory as a rationale for the priority of liberty in societies where wealth levels approach those of Western democracies. But, in our view, Rawls does not need to limit his argument so much as he does. The weight of history and economic theory is sufficient to establish the dictum that a regime of personal liberty is necessary for the amassing of large quantities of economic goods, and for the tolerable distribution of such goods among the people. Maximum liberty is *desirable* on grounds of justice for rich countries; it is *necessary* for poor countries on grounds both of justice and of economic efficiency.

To summarize: we have supposed that persons in the original position are rationally committed to having a care for absolute liberty, relative liberty, and the quantity of economic goods. By means of a further stipulation, that liberty in civil society is more inclusive than Hobbesian natural liberty, we suggested that the Hobbesian Benchmark is properly excludable from the relevant choice set while remaining as a basis from which consideration of alternatives commences. Finally, by relying on Rawls' own considerations concerning the grounds for ascribing priority to liberty, we hit on a_4b_4 as the uniquely appropriate solution to Rawlsian contract. It should be reemphasized that this is our interpretation of the Rawlsian game, and it may not coincide with Rawls' interpretation.

---

[14] See, *A Theory of Justice*, especially pp. 243–251 and 541–548.

IV. WHY EQUAL LIBERTY?

We have demonstrated how something akin to the Rawlsian solution might be reached through the contractual process that Rawls defined. The discussion suggests the critical importance of the three separate components of the Rawlsian vector, but at the same time it suggests that the whole construction is vulnerable to criticism of the postulate that these components – and only these – are relevant.

We see little reason to question the postulate that individuals predict that positive value will be placed on both absolute liberty and economic goods. But why should relative liberty take on such importance? Is this merely another case where selection of premises is made with an eye on desired results? If we bring to the contractual process the presupposition that relative liberty is valued, then equal liberty will ultimately be derived as a condition for agreement to be reached. Is the Rawlsian contract superior to the Hobbesian in this respect? Does the shift behind the veil allow a derivation of equal liberty that does not emerge without the veil?

To get at these questions, it is useful to consider the possible clash between absolute liberty and relative liberty. Suppose that, behind the veil, it is predicted that a feasible set of arrangements exists that will offer all parties higher levels of absolute liberty, but, by definition, these higher levels come at a cost of imposing differentials among the parties. The problem may be illustrated in Figure 3, where point E depicts the setting of maximum equal liberty and where point F depicts a predictably attainable solution. By definition, no point on the diagonal northeast of E is feasible. Which set of institutions would be selected behind the veil of ignorance?

This question challenges the preliminary stipulation made above that only positions along the diagonal would be included in the relevant choice set. This stipulation might seem indicated if all departures from the position on the diagonal that feature maximum equal liberty would necessarily involve lower levels of absolute liberty for at least some parties. As the construction in Figure 3 suggests, however, this need not be so. Critics may, of course, claim on *empirical* grounds that no social arrangements exist that yield all parties higher levels of absolute liberty than those attained under the equal liberty constraint. But on the formal level of analysis, there seems no basis for ruling out such prospects.[15]

---

[15] One basis for arguing that such prospects may not emerge would be a presupposition that there are no "natural" differences among individuals. But this presupposition would be unsupportable on any formal grounds. If such natural differences are allowed as possibilities, even behind the veil of ignorance there may be predictions that institutional regimes that "treat individuals differently" with respect to allowable spheres of liberty may generate greater liberties for all parties.

Suppose, as an example, that there are "naturally" two types of persons, one of whom behaves morally toward others, the other of whom remains amoral. Behind the veil, of

How is the possibility of trade-offs of relative liberty for absolute liberty best conceived within a Rawlsian perspective? An analogy to the difference principle for economic goods suggests itself.

Such a principle maintains that equality should be the rule unless inequality improves the position of the least advantaged. Each party is to secure equal basic liberty except where all persons can benefit from some inequality in liberty, and that, among the feasible alternatives meeting the first requirement, one is to be chosen that makes the least advantaged (in terms of basic liberties) best off. Again referring to Figure 3, if both F and G are feasible alternatives to E, then the difference principle for liberty would state that F is to be preferred since B, the person who differentially enjoys lower basic liberty, is better off in F than in G.

If such a difference principle for liberty is adopted, there would be no need to build relative liberty as a separate component into the Rawlsian vector. In that case, however, we would have no initial assurance that the contractual process would generate a regime characterized by equal basic liberties. This result would seem to be almost as embarrassing in the

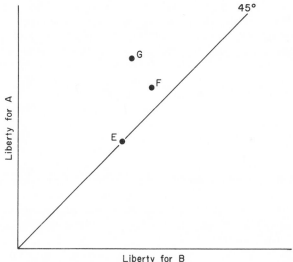

Figure 3

course, the chooser does not know which of these types he or she may be. Maximum equal liberty may be attained only in a regime that imposes relatively severe constraints on individuals' freedom of action. It may prove possible, however, that *everyone's* freedom of action may be extended by a regime that allows differential treatment for the moral and the amoral persons, once these two types are fully identified in the institutional operational sequence.

Rawlsian contract as in the Hobbesian. Can we buttress the former in ways unavailable to the Hobbesian?

Several prospects are open. First, it can be argued that an off-diagonal result is less objectionable if it emerges from Rawlsian than from Hobbesian contract. In both arrangements, the more favored parties enjoy an *ex post* advantage in relative liberty. However, in the Rawlsian setting, contractors do not know their own identities, and each regards himself, *ex ante*, as equally likely to be favored to enjoy greater relative liberty. The Rawlsian contract is like a fair lottery in that it can be judged to be equitable *ex ante* despite the existence *ex post* of differential treatment.

Second, it can be argued that the Rawlsian vector need not assign independent status to relative liberty; the contractual process will, nonetheless, produce results as if such status has been assigned. In a two person setting, suppose that A and B know that, once they emerge from behind the veil, each will value absolute liberty. Suppose, however, that they do not know whether or not they will place a value on relative liberty. A prudent course for the contractor to take would be to select arrangements that are predicted to distribute liberties equally rather than unequally, to select, say, position E rather than position F in Figure 3. If, post-constitutionally, individuals discover that they are indifferent to relative liberty, or regard it as much less crucial than absolute liberty, they can then agree *in period* so as to bring about the differential liberty allocation (assuming that the payoffs for both persons in economic goods are also satisfactory to both). In this case, the contractors lose nothing by the initial constitutional choice of the arrangement that promises equal liberties.

The reverse is not the case. Suppose that the contractors agree, constitutionally, to the arrangement that promises the highest level of absolute liberty to the person least advantaged in liberty (position F in Figure 3). Subsequently, beyond the veil, however, suppose that they find that each cares much for relative liberty. No agreement could then be made to bring about an institutional shift from F to the regime characterized by equal liberties, E. B would be eager to make such a shift, but A would veto it because it would lower both his level of absolute liberty and his level of relative liberty. There is an asymmetry in the prospects for post-constitutional change that suggests that persons behind the veil who have no reason to know whether they will or will not assign positive value to relative liberty should act *as if* relative liberty will be valued.

A third argument is indirectly related to the second; although, it does not depend in any way on uncertainty about post-constitutional evaluation of relative liberty. Even if the contractors predict with certainty that, post-constitutionally, A and B would agree to make a shift to the set of arrangements that promise higher levels of absolute liberty to both at the expense of some differentials in relative liberty, they may prefer, on grounds of *autonomy*, to select the equal liberty arrangements at the basic constitutional stage. Individuals will assign value to the retention of in-period autonomous choice to the extent that such retention does not involve major opportunity cost. They may predict that, post-constitutionally, they will enjoy enhanced self-esteem by having retained the option to remain under the equal liberty set of arrangements, even if they are sure, in advance and behind the veil, that agreement will be reached on abandoning the equal liberty precept.[16]

The lines of reasoning above at least partially meet the charge that Rawlsian contract is vulnerable in assigning overriding importance to relative liberty. We acknowledge, however, that this component of the Rawlsian vector is more problematic than the other two components. What this means is that the intuition that justice requires the assignment of equal basic liberties is also problematic.

We have been surprised to find how little has been said by Rawls, by Hobbes, and by others in justification of the equal liberty proviso. The issue here demands a closer examination. For example, libertarian philosophers profess unlimited support for a regime of liberty, a regime in which absolute liberties are maximal and in which these liberties are equal among persons. But what if these two requirements diverge? What if maximal liberty requires that liberties be differentially distributed? Is this "libertarian dilemma" to be resolved by giving priority to the rule of law (equal liberty) or to absolute liberty? So far as we know, the issue has not been addressed, let alone satisfactorily resolved.

V. EQUAL LIBERTY, ECONOMIC EQUALITY
AND THE DIFFERENCE PRINCIPLE

Persons are presumed to value both absolute liberty and their absolute level of economic goods. The concern for liberty was extended so as to

---

[16] A critic might demur, claiming that autonomy is simply a function of *who decides*, not whether decision is made in-period rather than at a constitutional level. However, the manner in which a decision is made may have a bearing on the autonomy of the one who decides. The conditions of constitutional choice are significantly different from those of in-period choice. The former is made anonymously and with no knowledge of particularities. One brings about an outcome that will be an outcome for oneself in one way or another, but what that way is remains unknown. The latter choice is made in full knowledge of who one is and what one wants. It is determinate; one is not merely accepting some outcome or other, in which one's own role is unknown, but *this outcome*. We maintain that this amounts to a significant difference in degree of autonomy exercised. One who knows what he is bringing about for himself and who acts intentionally to produce that result acts autonomously in a way no Rawlsian contractor can.

include relative liberty within the Rawlsian vector. Does not parity require a similar introduction of relative economic status? With this question, the egalitarian voices his chief complaint against our version of the Rawlsian construction.

We are under no illusion that we can settle, once and for all, the dispute between the libertarian and the egalitarian. We acknowledge that our interpretation of the Rawlsian contract does assign greater importance to relative liberty than to relative economic status. The critic might charge, however, that much of the argument set forth in defense of the equal assignment of basic liberties could be transformed into like arguments for equal assignments of economic goods. We are, therefore, under some obligation to show how the analogy between relative liberty and relative economic position breaks down. There is at least one crucial point at which the egalitarian's plea for parity is at risk.

As the examples make clear, and as ordinary common sense indicates, a choice of institutions that assign maximum equal liberties to all persons will insure results that involve at least some, and perhaps significant, inequalities in the distribution of economic goods. It is clear, however, that implementation of the equal maximum liberty principle does not, in itself, consign any particular person to any particular rung on the economic ladder. Some persons will be more talented than others, some will be lucky, and these persons will prosper relative to their fellows. But, behind the veil, no one trades off a known quantity of economic goods for a stock of liberty.

Suppose now, that an overriding concern for relative economic position should dominate institutional-constitutional choice. With reference to Figure 2, observe that such a concern would be fully realized only in cell a_1b_1. Strict equality with respect to both liberty and economic goods prevails, but absolute liberty is thereby minimized. To select a_1b_1 because of an overriding concern for relative economic status is *to abdicate for oneself and for everyone else any appreciable claim to absolute liberty*. On the other hand, to choose institutions that incorporate maximum equal liberty implies that *some* persons will have lower quantities of economic goods than others. But to opt for equality in economic goods means that *everyone's* liberty is minimized. Because persons are predicted to value absolute liberty, they have reason to deny to relative economic status a dimension within the basic Rawlsian vector.

The critic may, of course, suggest that this result is an artifact of the construction. He may suggest that the assignment of the lowest level of absolute liberty to the cell in which economic goods are equalized is arbitrary, that liberty and equality really thrive together.

We totally reject this criticism. Although almost every other particular feature of Figure 2 is arbitrary, this one is not. To guarantee a continuing order of strict economic equality requires continuous interference by collective institutions.[17] Persons will not be allowed to engage in activities that lead to differences in access to economic goods. "Liberty upsets patterns," says Nozick,[18] and, somewhat more directly to our point, patterns upset liberty. A choice of institutions that is dominated by a concern for relative economic status *will* land persons in cell a_1b_1. Liberties *will* be foregone by everyone, and the stock of economic goods will predictably be low.

For this reason and others that could be adduced, we reject the contention that there is an essential equivalence between a presumption in favor of relative liberty and one in favor of relative economic position. It is simply far costlier behind the veil to impose a regime of economic equality than to impose a regime of maximum equal liberty.

As has already been suggested, the difference principle does not occupy a central place in our analysis, despite the attention that it has received in the whole Rawlsian discussion. As was indicated, this principle is applicable only at a level of institutional choice that is far less general than the choice we have analyzed here. Such relegation of the difference principle to the level of institutional detail stems, expectedly, from the lexical priority of the maximum equal liberty principle, a priority which we take directly from Rawls. If institutional choice is constrained in the first instance by a proviso that equal liberty is to be maximized, scope remains for redistributional arrangements only *within the institutional choice emergent from the satisfaction of the proviso*.

Our analysis of the contractual process that generates the maximal equal liberty principle yields by-product implications for the basic economic organization of society. Maximal equal liberty would seem to require that all persons be free to enter and to exit from private contracts, to make voluntary exchanges without collective constraint, and to enter any occupational category. A society that even comes close to meeting the requirement for maximal equal liberty would, necessarily, have to be organized along the lines of a competitive economy in a constitutionally restricted democracy. Any socialist implementation of the principle of collective, centralized ownership-direction of production would violate the principle of justice. For that reason, we reject the following construal of the Rawlsian theory:

> It is necessary, then, to recognize that market institutions are common
> to both private-property and socialist regimes, and to distinguish

---

[17] This conclusion requires that these collective institutions operate ideally. In any realizable context, of course, collective ventures aimed at promoting economic equality introduce inequalities of their own, both in liberties and in access to economic goods.

[18] Nozick, *Anarchy, State, and Utopia*, p. 160.

between the allocative and the distributive function of prices. Since under socialism the means of production and natural resources are publicly owned, the distributive function is greatly restricted, whereas a private-property system uses prices in varying degrees for both purposes. *Which of these systems and the many intermediate forms most fully answers to the requirements of justice cannot, I think, be determined in advance. There is presumably no general answer to this question. . . .*

The author of the above lines is John Rawls.[19] The seminal proponent of the Rawlsian contract himself seems to have misapplied his own principles, a result that might have been avoided by the introduction of the Rawlsian vector in the matrix of contractarian justice.

Economics, Center for Study of Public Choice, George Mason University

Philosophy, University of Minnesota, Duluth

---

[19] Rawls, *A Theory of Justice*, pp. 273–274 (Italics supplied).

EQUALITY vs. LIBERTY: ADVANTAGE, LIBERTY

Jan Narveson

Introduction

The subject of this essay is political, and therefore social, philosophy; and therefore, ethics. We want to know whether the right thing for a society to do is to incorporate in its structure requirements that we bring about equality, or liberty, or both if they are compatible, and if incompatible then which if either, or what sort of mix if they can to some degree be mixed. But this fairly succinct statement of the issue before us requires considerable clarification, even as a statment of the issue. For it is widely, and in my view correctly, held that *some* sort of equality is utterly fundamental in these matters. We seek a principle, or principles, that apply to all, are the same for all. In that sense, certainly, equality is fundamental and inescapable. But this is a very thin sort of "equality."

It will almost equally widely be agreed that the principles in question should in some more interesting sense "treat" people equally, e.g., by allotting to all the same set of rights, and moreover, rights that are – again we have to say "in some sense" – nonarbitrary, so that whatever they are, persons of all races, sexes, and so on will have the same fundamental rights assigned to them. Taking this to be, again, essentially uncontroversial, though not without potentially worrisome points of unclarity, it needs, now, to be pointed out that this characterization does not settle the issue that this essay is concerned with. That issue is about *economic* matters in particular. The question is whether people should be required to bring about, or at least move in the direction of, economic equality, meaning by this equality of income and/or wealth, property, or possessions. There is, as I shall point out, a problem about identifying and then of measuring the variable thus to be equalized, though that problem won't be the major concern of this essay. Alternatively, should we require that people's economic *liberty* be respected? Economic liberty is generally identified with the free market, and again, I share this predilection. But again, there are questions of conceptual specification here. Some have even contended that the free market is *not* really "free," that it is itself somehow the enemy of liberty. We need a notion of liberty clear enough to enable us to discern whether there is any merit in such claims.

The procedure of this essay will be as follows. I begin by expressing some doubts about the coherence of the ideal of economic equality, and then proceed to examine, briefly, a very few of the principal defenses of that ideal. I then move on to the subject of liberty, and in particular economic liberty, beginning with the project of identifying the referent of that term, and of arguing for the coherence of the ideal. Finally, I proceed to the question of foundations: is there a good argument for one or the other, for economic equality or economic liberty? It will emerge that they are evidently incompatible as sets of social requirements, and thus that we must take our choice, or try to settle on some kind of mixture. The pure doctrine of liberty is often defended on grounds of natural rights or of self-evidence. As these terms are normally understood, I shall make no appeal to either of them. The argument will be contractarian, though not in Rawls' peculiar sense of that term, and as will be seen, the argument supports liberty, so far as I can see. There will be little space for discussing implications, but a very few will be noted in the course of the argument.

PART I: EQUALITY

Economic Equality: Some Queries

Since we are considering the claim that economic equality is a goal of justice, it is worth pausing to ask what that goal is supposed to be. There is certainly an obvious answer: two persons are equal if they have equal incomes or equal wealth measured in monetary units such as dollars. Since, one might say, the whole point of money is to enable us to compare the diverse things of which wealth is made up, this answer would seem as natural as the use of degrees of temperature on a thermometer for measuring heat.

The trouble with that suggestion for present purposes is that the value of a unit of currency in an exchange or market society is determined by the market mechanism. A unit of currency expresses a relation among batches of goods on a market, the equivalence class any of whose members would fetch that price on the market: for each such item, not enough people will pay more for it to make it possible for the seller to charge more profitably, whereas enough will pay that much for it to make that price profitable. What makes it all go around is free exchange. But now suppose we wish to equalize dollar-income: what now? In a market society, one expects a considerable range of incomes to develop as time goes by, and this has concomitant effects on the consumption patterns, hence the "demand curves," of the various agents – and this, in turn, affects what is produced and how much those things will bring on the market. If you begin with a market society at T_1 and impose a totally redistributive tax at T_2, then what will it mean to say that incomes following the redistribution, identical though they may be in point of numbers of "dollars," are now equal? Suppose that person A purchases with his post-redistributional income, i, bundle of goods j, whereas B purchases bundle k with hers: what *meaning* do we attach to the claim that k = j? Especially if, as is likely, the post-redistributive dollar would appear to its owner to be worth less than the pre-redistributive dollar was? Suppose that at T_1 income i would have bought j + m, or k + n, where n ≠ m? Are they now, A and B, more equal or less?

One way to solve such problems would be to pay people in kind instead of in money, giving each person as nearly as possible literally the *same* bundle of goods (as soon as there is *any* difference, the same problem quickly arises). But presumably this is not what the advocate of equality really wants. Thus, Bruce Landesman, a recent proponent of egalitarianism, writes:

> But they [anti-egalitarians] have attacked a 'straw man.' It is very implausible to think that an egalitarian has or must have uniformity as his fundamental aim. Why should he want or wish for uniformity? If he has a wish, it is that persons, all of them, do well, equally well, and it is a commonplace that equal well-being is at least logically compatible with the satisfaction of quite different preferences and the pursuit of different life-styles.[1]

But there *is* pressure toward uniformity. For in the absence of a free market, which would certainly make the desired equality impossible, it would be difficult to measure the share each was getting under the putatively egalitarian regime unless what each got was extremely similar in content.

To be sure, it is difficult to see why anyone should think that a condition of equality – in the sense in which each has pretty much the same assemblage of material (or any other, so far as possible) goods – was either required by justice or any kind of social desideratum. In fact, I shall insist that the same observation holds for any other sort of equality that might be thought to underpin the desirability of economic equality, but at the outset it must be evident that anyone driven to advocating the kind of parcel-by-parcel equality imagined above must be propelled by some other underlying vision: for example, (as in Landesman's case) equality of ultimate welfare or well-being; or, as recently advocated by Ronald Dworkin, equality of resources. And even then, surely the candidates do not have the ring of self-evidence. If someone thinks we ought all to have equal ultimate well-being as a matter of justice, it must surely be because that person thinks that we are all equally deserving, or equally entitled, or some such thing, to well-being; and similarly with resources. We can profit from having a closer look at such arguments; I shall consider each in turn, briefly.

---

[1] Bruce Landesman, "Egalitarianism," *Canadian Journal of Philosophy*, March 1983, 13 (1), p. 31.

Equal Welfare?

ᶜIf it is thought that all should have equal welfare, the first question is: just who is "all"? Probably all *humans*, one supposes from most advocates' writings. There is an immediate problem for one trying to be serious about this. Consider the human with the lowest welfare that is not, so far as anybody knows at present, capable of being significantly improved by any efforts of other people, no matter how strenuous, well-intended, and extensive. Does the advocate of equal welfare wish to assert, then, that it is the solemn duty of the rest of us to make ourselves as miserable as that unfortunate, in the interests of justice?

Advocates of equality usually talk as though we could all be quite happy, really: they want to fix things up by equalizing *up*, not *down*. But no one who has spent much time in a mental hospital, to say nothing of any other sort of hospital, can seriously suppose that we have it within our power to improve things for the most wretched of us to the level enjoyed by ordinary people, let alone persons of unusually blessed constitution, character, and personality. In some few of those cases, conceivably, the poor individual in question was made that way by some other human, and in such cases we could, perhaps, argue that the perpetrator of whatever deeds brought about that unhappy individual's condition should be brought down to match him, as a matter of retributive justice. And some few theorists do talk as though this were actually typical – e.g., that the miserable of the earth were all made that way by greedy capitalists. It is not easy to comprehend persons who can take such a view seriously, and I do not suppose that anything said in this essay would do much to persuade them of the utter unreality of their views (though I shall try, just a bit, in the next-but-one paragraph). But the rest of us can easily enough imagine cases in which any such assessment simply has nothing going for it. Congenital diseases and malformations that were quite beyond the ability of any current persons to predict might cause the misery I have in mind here, and what we want to know of aspiring equalitarians is: *then what?* Is it now to be inferred that we have the sacred duty, as a matter of justice, of each making himself as miserable as those worst cases?

Suppose, instead, that we *can* do something. Suppose, namely, that we can improve the lot of that worst-off individual just slightly by enormous and protracted effort of ours, with the foreseeable side effect that we would all be made about as miserable as he or she will still be after all these efforts? Does the advocate of equality want to say that this makes all the difference: that even if we are to be let off the hook concerning cases where we can do nothing, we are to be put back on it if we can do anything at all? If not, why not?

The question, Whose welfare is to be equalized?, is by no means as yet at an end. For it is hard to see why we should draw a line around humankind in particular for this purpose. What about the lower animals? And how much lower? Is it an injustice, one which we all ought to be doing whatever we can to rectify, that cuttlefish, newts, and perhaps even amoeba are incapable of the levels of welfare so unfairly enjoyed by you and I? If it isn't, why isn't it? And if it is, do we have an idea, here, that deserves to be taken seriously by any rational being?

The advocate of equality is likely, upon reflection, to declare that what he has in mind is only the welfare of normal people, people not afflicted with debilitating diseases or uncontrollably melancholy tempers, and definitely only people. We are still owed an explanation – aren't we? – for this seemingly arbitrary restriction, of course, but for the sake of argument we proceed. And we have to note immediately that the connection between equal welfare and equal economic circumstances is surely not straight-forward. If the point of equalizing Smith's and Jones' incomes and/or properties is to bring about a condition of equal well-being between them, then notoriously we can hardly be assured of success even in typical cases, and can be pretty definitely assured of failure in innumerable others. One will be of sunny temperament and robust constitution, and will take little interest in most of what she would have, given economic equality (whatever that may be), while another will not enjoy himself even tolerably with appreciably less than what a typical millionaire can now command. Or is it supposed that the new equalitarian regime will take care of such matters, supplying Smith and Jones not only with equal amenities and necessities, but also with equal dispositions and identical tastes to match? And if it is so supposed, is it not already evident that the project has gone very, very far off the rails? (Or should we say, very, very far *down* the rails, toward a condition that every serious person must surely find totally abhorrent?)

Arguing for Equal Welfare I: Desert

The big question about equality is Why? Of course, that is the question we must address to any substantive conception of justice, and we must, in the end, come up with a good idea of what justice is or should be before we could decisively answer that question in any case. For the present, I want only to ask this at the level of "intuition," though I hope reasonably sensitive and well-informed intuition, and not intuition in a sense incompatible with theory. So let us ask what sort of answers might be forthcoming at this level. The sort of terms in which we would expect them to be couched are, one supposes, such as Desert or Merit, and Fairness or perhaps Equity in the sense of equal consideration or "equal treatment." Let us begin with the former.

But equal desert or merit is what we would need in order to arrive at equal welfare – and, of course, equal desert for welfare, equal merit as pertinent to distributions of (sources of) welfare in particular. But considerations of desert have in general been pointed to as justifications of inequality, rather than equality. On any ordinary standard of desert, people will vary in their deserts. And besides, it is by no means clear that 'desert' is the only relevant variable, even if one could somehow establish equality of desert; if anything, it is quite clear that it is not the only relevant variable, at least in any ordinary understanding of desert. Both points deserve some elaboration here.

(1) To begin with, desert is in general what we might call "project-specific." One might deserve more from basketball fans for activities that would get you nowhere, or worse, in a symphony orchestra. The egalitarian who appeals to desert must evidently think that there is a general, project-indifferent notion of desert in which we are all equal and which is specifically relevant to economic distribution. But there is no such notion. Not even moral worth will do; the notion that we should pay people for being virtuous is wrong-headed from the start, and in any case people are not, by any stretch of the imagination, equal in moral worth, anyway.

Not only is desert project-specific, but it is also reward-specific. One could deserve praise without deserving an increase in pay; one could deserve the trophy without deserving a citation in Who's Who in Academia. The equalitarian requires not only a project-indifferent notion of desert, but he also requires, interestingly enough, a reward-specific response to this project-indifferent notion. For economic rewards are, at least ordinarily, considered to be specific. Moreover, what is, at least on the face of it, relevant to economic rewards – the "desert-base," the project to which economic rewards are peculiarly appropriate – is productivity, of whatever it is that the enterprise in question produces. And again, productivity, notoriously, varies enormously from one person to another.

It might, as a desperate measure, be hypothesized that although people do indeed vary greatly in any particular project-specific, desert-relevant variable, yet when we take all together, people come out equal. But this is desperate: there are persons who exceed at least some other persons in just about any respect one can think of, and at least tie them in the rest. Or at least, this is so if we take any sort of commonly recognized variables as our bases. Of course, if Jones is better-looking than Smith, it follows that Smith is worse-looking than Jones, and so if Jones deserves more of whatever good looks deserve, then Smith deserves more of whatever bad looks deserve. Let him (or her!) who will make what he (or she) can out of that one ... ! Meanwhile, we note also that in order to make any such scheme work at all, we also need some kind of workable cardinalization over different desert bases, since again we can expect many cases where A is far better than B at x, y, and z, and B exceeds A but only just slightly in respect of u, v, and w. And to top it all off, we again need to argue that somehow the aggregated sum of these diverse variables is specifically relevant to *economic* reward. I take it that we need pursue this particular hare no further.

It has become fashionable in the recent past to proclaim a deeper theory about this matter. True, we say that Joanne is more deserving than Kenneth because, say, she can program a computer much more quickly and simply than he; *but*, it will be pointed out, this is only because she is better trained/more highly motivated/whatever than he, and this she got from her superior environment which she did *not* deserve; or ultimately, perhaps, because her native ability is greater than his and she did nothing to deserve *that*. We shall take up such maneuvers in the next section, since the argument really is now an argument from fairness rather than desert.

(2) But in any case, desert cannot reasonably be held to be the only relevant variable, as Nozick has so elegantly reminded us.[2] Most of us skew the distribution of our resources very strongly in favor of persons we merely happen to love, not because they *deserve* more of our love than others but simply because they happen to be, e.g., our own children; and the same goes for friendship and other such human relations. Again, the trophy goes to the winner of the race, and not necessarily to the one who deserved to win, by virtue of far greater effort, sacrifice, or whatnot. And finally (another Nozick-inspired observation), it may be true that Vladimir Ashkenazy, if he needed my particular liver and no one else's would do, deserves it more than I, but it does not follow that I am required, in justice, to give it to him. More will be said regarding this deep and important matter later on; and of course we must acknowledge that some will simply want to reject all such claims. The main form of this rejection will be discussed next.

Arguing for Equal Welfare II: Fairness

Notions of fairness enter our lives at many points, most especially when we undertake activities as members of groups accepting certain common rules and pursuing more or less common purposes. It is then appropriate to appeal to the rules, and/or the purposes, to establish that someone has done one down (to use Lucas' adept phrase)[3] by violating the letter or the spirit of the relevant rules or purposes. This is what we might call "ordinary fairness"; but ordinary fairness will not lead one far toward equality. The weakest player on the team might have tripped up the strongest on the opposite team; this is unfair, but rectification will only widen the gap between the teams' respective scores. There can be no general expectation that narrowing of that or any other gaps, including economic ones, must follow from us all being fairer than we currently are.

But lately there has been an appeal to fairness at a deeper level. The

---

[2] Robert Nozick, *Anarchy, State and Utopia* (New York: Basic Books, 1974), Ch. 6.
[3] J. R. Lucas, *On Justice* (Oxford: Oxford University Press, 1980), p. 5.

apostle of this appeal in its current form is, no doubt, John Rawls. The principle he invokes by way of leading up to a theory of justice which at least appears to be massively redistributivist in its implications, is to be found in his discussion of what he calls the "system of natural liberty," in which there is "equal liberty and a free market economy," but no attempt made to "preserve an equality, or similarity, of social conditions," as a result of which "the initial distribution of assets for any period of time is strongly influenced by natural and social contingencies." His comment on this is that "Intuitively, the most obvious injustice of the system of natural liberty is that it permits distributive shares to be improperly influenced by these factors so arbitrary from a moral point of view."[4] But is it intuitive that all such influences must be "improper?"

We can concede that one's native endowment, and many aspects of one's environment, both natural and social, are things which an individual cannot be said to have "deserved." In that respect, at least, they are indeed morally arbitrary. But it hardly follows that everything about this is morally arbitrary: perhaps your parents really had the right to move to North Battleford, Saskatchewan even though the foreseeable consequence is that you too would wind up there at the age of nine, forever unable to attend Phillips Andover Academy. And in particular, as has been often noted by others,[5] it does not follow from the fact that *I* did not deserve distribution D that therefore someone else *does*. What if *none* of us deserves it? And there is a further point to note. Some of these undeserved conditions are so central to one's being that the whole idea of "my" deserving *or* not deserving them can make no sense at all. Some at least of my native endowment is essential to my being me at all: those bits of genetic matter that constitute my native intelligence, for instance. If "I" had been "given" quite a different parcel of such bits, then it would not be the case that *I* had gotten a different one; rather, the individual constituted by that different lot would be a different person, not me at all. To insist that things must go only to those who deserve them, is to deny that one has the right to be whomever one is. And if we deny *that* right, what could possibly be left that is recognizable, let alone worth having?

It, of course, also needs to be observed that nobody deserves to be a human being. We could, for all that desert has to say about it, have been squirrels, or – what? Microbes, perhaps? Moral arbitrariness, obviously, does not stop at the boundaries of *homo sapiens*, once we allow talk about the

---

[4] John Rawls, *A Theory of Justice* (Cambridge, Mass.: Harvard University Press, 1971), p. 72.
[5] By Nozick, for instance (*op. cit.*, pp. 216–224 especially); and by Fred D. Miller, Jr. "The Natural Right to Private Property"' Tibor Machan, ed., *The Libertarian Reader* (Totowa, N.J.: Rowman and Littlefield, 1982), pp. 278–280 especially.

arbitrariness of native endowments. For similar reasons, it does not stop, evidently, at the boundaries of intelligibility, either.

The subject of this essay is the design of social "institutions." The point of the various moral premises being scrutinized here is to direct people's actions. A premise to the effect that it was unjust of someone to do something is a premise that supports, or may be used to support, a call for action, namely to make amends. A premise to the effect that some state of affairs is unjust, however, needs to be explained in this crucial regard: *who* is to do *what* because of this? The equalitarian calls upon all of us to redistribute, if we have more than others, or to clamor for a share in a redistribution from such people, if we have less. Now, how does a premise about the undeservedness of one's natural assets or the assets one has from one's parents and one's social environment bear upon our actions? If the premise is:

P1 – People do not deserve their initial assets,

then on the face of it, the indicated conclusion would seem to be:

C1 – We should take away all initial assets from all persons,

together, one assumes, with everything they have since got by virtue of those assets. But equalitarians don't seem to want to take that line. Their reasoning, instead, seems to be this:

P2 – No person deserves native assets *any more than any other*,

therefore,

C2 – All assets should, as nearly as possible, be distributed equally.

If the native assets themselves cannot, as they obviously often cannot, be redistributed, then at least the results in terms of differential rewards to individuals differently endowed can, and the clear intent of equilitarians is to do that. But why, we should ask, does C2 follow from P2? For P2, after all, follows from P1, and what appears to follow from P1, as we noted, is C1, not C2. In order to get C2, we need to add to P2 the premise that at least some persons *do* deserve their native assets. Assuming that this would, then, give them a claim on what they can get by utilizing those assets, then subjoining P2 will indeed yield C2. But the trouble is that the only reason for affirming P2 was precisely the impossibility of making any sense of the claim that *anyone* deserves his or her native assets *at all*. If we were to go back on this – which we hardly can, but we can fudge it a little bit – and say, instead, that at least some people *do* deserve what they get by virtue of the exercise of their native assets, then the argument would proceed as follows:

P3 – Some people deserve what they acquire by the exercise of their native assets.

(P2, as before:) No person deserves native assets any more than any other.

Therefore:

(C2, as before:) All acquisitions should be distributed equally.

But this is absurd. For either P3 is understood to be compatible with P1 or it isn't. If it *is*, then it requires that we reject the inferability of any conclusion such as C2 *or* C1 from it: the desert or non-desert of native assets simply doesn't figure on behalf of normative conclusions any more, and instead the weight is shifted to what people do with them. But they do *different* things with them, and come to deserve different rewards, payments, and, in general, distributive shares as a result. And, thus, we can no longer infer anything like C2 from what we now have. And if, on the other hand, P3 is understood to be incompatible with P1, then we no longer have any argument if we retain P1, since we would then be drawing our conclusion from inconsistent premises, and obviously no conclusion has any more support than any other from such sets of premises.

The argument is, therefore, hopeless. The grand premise that we all are utterly undeserving of our native endowments and assets is quite true, but entirely useless in attempting to support equalitarian conclusions. Accordingly, it provides no support for rectification, and thus for redistribution so far as it stems from *this* source.

How much did Rawls' intuition about the arbitrariness of natural and (certain kinds of) social initial assets affect the theoretical construction in *A Theory of Justice*? As is well known, he proposed to derive the basic principles of justice from the choice of persons behind a "veil of ignorance," which operates to bar each chooser from any knowledge of his own subsequent identity: we are to choose without being influenced by that knowledge. But there are two ways to interpret this requirement. *One* way is to assume not only that these persons don't know anything about their own identity on the other side of the veil, but also that whomever they are, they will not only be quite capable of coherently choosing some principles while behind it, but also of being bound by them even after they know who they will become. In that case, the well-known arguments, give or take a few details, go through: we will, doing the best we can for ourselves but realizing that we could turn out to be just anybody at all, arguably rig things so as to favor the least favored, meaning that we choose equality except if it should turn out that somehow we can do even better. But a *different* way to interpret the veil is this: we are allowed to make what we can of the information that the people on the other side of the veil will, rationally and inevitably, act in the light of the actual, and varying, values that they will then have, and will *not* be capable of incorporating into their actual, practical bases of action any principles that make sense only if one might be somebody or anybody else. If people on the original position side of the veil know *that*, then they will choose, being constrained by these facts about people, very differently. They will choose the principles that they would choose on the other side, given full information about their fellow men and the constraints of their situation.[6]

The first of these two ways may well railroad the chooser toward strongly redistributive, equalitarian principles. But not the second! And which way is right? I shall be arguing further about this below, but to anticipate, I suggest that the second way is. If its assumptions about rational choice are right, it must be, for otherwise the output from the original position will be of purely academic interest: it will be used only by those persons whose interests happen to call for principles that coincide, at least in practice, with the original position ones. And if a case for redistribution or equalitarianism is to be made, it will have to be made on the kind of grounds that would be available to any well-informed individual placed in the sort of circumstances that call for principles of justice.

Utilitarianism

Rawls, and consequently Rawlsians and most critics of Rawls, have assumed that those in the original position à la Rawls would opt for principles other than that of the Principle of Utility. I have argued previously that this is an error, both in the sense that they should, indeed, choose that principle and, also, that one must infer from Rawls' systematic exposition that they actually have chosen it, and that given his assumptions it supports the famous Two Principles. Let us, however, view the matter independently and ask (a) what utilitarianism will imply about economic equality, and (b) what appeal utilitarianism has as a fundamental theory in this area.

Utilitarianism may be characterized sufficiently, here, as the view that utility counts and nothing else counts. All and only utility counts: acts large and small, from the nodding of one's head to a passing stranger to the establishment and operation of governments are to be appraised, ultimately, from the point of view of their promotion of aggregate utility, the sum of the utilities, positive and negative, of all affectable individuals.

What are the implications of this mighty postulate for economic justice? The equality asserted in utilitarianism, it should be noted at the outset, is

---

[6] This point was first made, to my knowledge, by David Gauthier in "Justice and Natural Endowment: A Critique of Rawls' Ideological Framework," *Social Theory and Practice*, Winter 1974, 3(1). A similar point is made in John Marshall, "The Failure of Contract as Justification," *Social Theory and Practice*, Fall 1975, 3(4).

only an equality of the like amount of utility of any two individuals. On the face of it, as commentators have been quick to point out, this means that if what we were distributing were utilities, then it would not matter how any *given* lot of it should be assigned to any given lot of individuals: 50 for A and none for B is as good as 25 for each; worse still, 150 for A and −75 for B is likewise just as good, just as recommendable a distribution. People have thought this highly unintuitive, to put the matter fairly mildly. But they speak over-hastily. We do not in fact know how unintuitive this is, or indeed whether it is so at all, until we know what relationship there is between the distribution of the various things we actually can distribute – money, for instance – and utility.[7] A standard assumption in the field is that the marginal utility of economic goods diminishes as the parcel for a given individual increases. It is an old idea – only the words used by recent writers (myself included) are new; so here is an elegant statement of it from David Hume:

> It must also be confessed, that, wherever we depart from this equality, we rob the poor of more satisfaction than we add to the rich, and that the slight gratification of a frivolous vanity, in one individual, frequently costs more than bread to many families, and even provinces.

It seems plausible, at first sight. But the standard defense of permitting inequality, adopted by Hume, Adam Smith, and for that matter Rawls, has been that if you deprive people of the incentive they have from the prospect of being able to better their own situations, then:

> ... you reduce society to the most extreme indigence; and instead of preventing want and beggary in a few, render it unavoidable to the whole community.[8]

Such defenses – certainly also plausible, so far as they go – bring up a theoretical conundrum of rather serious proportions. For about these industrious and enterprising persons who, in the process of promoting their own well-being, also promote the public good, we must ask: should they feel guilty about not sharing the portion of their product which they keep unequally for themselves? If justice requires, after all, that incomes be equalized, then why am I not always being unjust whenever I raise the lot of myself and my family, say, above the average level of the surrounding community?[9]

Nor, of course, is this all. What about the rest of mankind, outside one's

---

[7] See J. Narveson, *Morality and Utility* (Baltimore: Johns Hopkins Press, 1967), Ch. VII, where this point is pressed.

[8] David Hume, *Inquiry Concerning the Principles of Morals* (1751), Ch. III, sec. ii.

[9] For a development of this argument in relation to Rawls, cf. J. Narveson, "A Puzzle About Economic Justice in Rawls' Theory." *Social Theory and Practice*, Fall 1976, 4(1).

community? Socialist countries, we note, seem to have no compunctions about attempting to improve the lots of their own citizens relative to those in, say, Bangladesh. And liberals generally don't seem excessively bothered by the fact that the measures they propose, often including severe restrictions on foreign trade, even if they achieved their avowed purposes, would tend to maintain or increase a gap between the average domestic welfare and that in the poorer countries these measures discriminate against. Why aren't all these things really wrong? For the point is that they can't be said to be really "necessary," *unless* we think that self-interest is not only unavoidable, but also unavoidable in such a way as to be compatible with utilitarianism. But then we can, perhaps, go farther and ask whether it might not conduce still more to the general utility if people not only *did* what they wanted to do – in particular, skewing the distributions of their products quite strongly in favor of themselves and people they like – but also did so with a clean conscience? In short, perhaps the general utility will be maximized if we reject, as our theory of justice, the equalitarian pretension outright. Perhaps the losses of those who lose whatever is lost by no longer being an automatic recipient of the involuntary charity of their fellows, would be less than what virtually the whole of humankind would gain by not having to suppose that almost everything they do in life is morally unjust.[10]

But the upshot of all this is that utilitarianism may be completely useless for settling the question before us. For if theorists on polar-opposite sides of this issue can both mount plausible arguments, armed with the very same fundamental principle, then it would appear that all of our attention might as well be turned to the "supplementary factual premises" so obviously essential for applying it to anything in particular. Moreover, it is not clear that we should regard estimates of the utility of any particular state of affairs as counting among those "factual premises!"

Besides, there remains the other question: why accept utilitarianism, anyway? The question, here, must be at an abstract level, as the above arguments, I hope, sufficiently suggest. Now at this abstract level, we are being asked to regard all and sundry persons, whatever else one might think of them, as *equally deserving*, at least *prima-facie*, along with one's loved ones, friends, associates, workers toward valued causes, and oneself. And surely that is not the way we want to regard all and sundry others. It is not clear that we *can* so regard them, for that matter. But consider what sort of cases we seem to be contemplating if we do. I read in a newspaper quite some time

[10] Two quite different arguments within the context of utilitarianism are pressed in earlier publications of mine. See Narveson, "Aesthetics, Charity, Utility and Distributive Justice," *The Monist*, October, 1972, 56(4); and also "Rights and Utilitarianism," *Canadian Journal of Philosophy* Supplementary Volume V, Summer 1979 (Cooper, Nielsen, and Patton, eds., *New Essays on John Stuart Mill and Utilitarianism*), esp. pp. 157–160.

ago of someone in a village in China who, having learned his political lessons well, and upon finding the village being swept away by a flood, had to choose between saving Comrade X, the local Communist Party chairman, and saving his own wife and family – and elected to save Comrade X! Now, many of us would have our doutbs about whether more good is brought to the universe by Comrade X than by this man's wife, but that isn't why most people find this case rather astonishing. What we probably think is that any system that would require such conduct as a moral duty is outrageous on the face of it. Similarly, we have our doubts about a system that implies – if it does – that whenever we buy a $100 dollhouse for our children, we do grave moral wrong, since we could, instead, have sent $99 to distant lands, thus saving the lives of several people. Evidently, as I was at pains to argue in the preceding pages, we don't know that utilitarianism *does* imply that. It's just that it looks on the face of it as though it should and at least could, and the question is whether we want to buy a system which on the face of it implies such things. It will seem to many people that these are the wrong implications on the face of it, even though they might agree that in some suitably exotic circumstances which we might be able to cook up, we might have to accept some such implications nevertheless. And the utilitarian will insist that those on-the-face-of-it appearances are *only* that and can comfortably be disregarded in the here and now. Not all utilitarians will take this comfortable line, however.[11] But enough said for the moment.

Dworkin

In some recent writings[12] Ronald Dworkin has put forward a rather different conception of equality from any of the above, including the sort of outright income/wealth equality whose coherence I expressed doubts about at the outset of this essay. Instead, Dworkin proposes what he calls *equality of resources*. This involves distinguishing what counts as the (at least logically) external goods that the individual can be thought of as utilizing to forward his good life as he sees it, and what is inseparable from the person in question. And then, reminiscent of (but very different from) Rawls' original position, one must try to envisage each person as participating in a sort of primordial auction in which, equipped with the same purchasing power, all the existent resources are sold to the highest bidder, who bids with a view to supplying himself for his entire life. The idea is to divide what there is in such a way that no one would trade his lot, post-auction, for that of any other. This ingeniously retains the meaningful market notion of equality as

---

[11] Peter Singer, "Failure, Affluence, and Morality," *Philosophy and Public Affairs* Spring 1972, 1(3).

[12] Ronald Dworkin, "What is Equality?," *Philosophy and Public Affairs*, Summer 1981 (Part I: Equality of Welfare), and Fall 1981 (Part II: Equality of Resources), 10(3,4)

equality-in-exchange, while properly scuttling any thought of item-by-item equality. Of course, it also means that outright income equality is not necessarily, or even probably, the indicated outcome for fundamental social policy. But Dworkin supposes – plausibly, one imagines – that the scheme would support fairly heavily redistributive taxation, and taxation *for the sake of* redistribution too, and not just to ensure, say, a minimum level of welfare for all.

Having discussed Dworkin's views at length recently,[13] I will not recapitulate here, except to cite the fundamental question that seemed to me to arise in reflection on this intriguing scheme, and that is: why would one be moved to accept its basic idea? That idea was to follow from a still more abstract one, that "From the standpoint of politics, the interests of the members of the community matter, and matter equally."[14] That, too, sounds plausible, but then we have the question why the "standpoint of politics" should *matter*, even if it could be made out – which I doubt – that the Equality of Resources idea is what is maximally supported by that abstract principle, rather than something else. Surely the standpoint of politics has to be *shown* to matter to us, for it is far from obvious that political institutions are *necessary*, strictly speaking, and even if they are, there would still be the question of how *much* they matter. Suppose we agreed that from the standpoint of politics, everyone should have equal resources, but from the standpoint of our own personal selves, they should not. Then we would seem to have to decide how much politics counts vs. how much our own lives, as we see and live them, count. And then it may seem quite rational to decide that the latter count practically 100%, the former scarcely at all. And then we would have the question, which standpoint is basic? If we can face the question just framed, how would rival answers be assessed? And the trouble is, it looks very much as though they would have to be assessed from one's personal standpoint (which might, of course, include a lot having to do with others who mattered to one) – which really means that the personal standpoint is fundamental, and thus that politics only matters as a component of one's life. In that case, however, what a Dworkinian must really show is that from the standpoint of any individual person, everyone matters and matters equally, and/or that everyone should, as a matter of justice, have equal resources. And I think it implausible, even bordering on the incredible, that such a result would be forthcoming. (So, as I noted in the aforementioned treatment, does Dworkin.)[15]

****

[13] J. Narveson, "On Dworkinian Equality"; R. Dworkin, "In Defense of Equality"; J. Narveson, "Reply to Dworkin," in this journal, Autumn 1983, 1(1), pp. 1–44.
[14] Dworkin, "In Defense of Equality," p. 24.
[15] Dworkin, "What is Equality?," Part II, pp. 31–2.

Here I rest with the negative part of this essay. Certainly I have not exhausted the supply of conceptions of or arguments for equality, though I hope to have addressed several of the main ones. But even if I really had, as I don't even suppose I have, demolished all such arguments, the case for liberty, if it even makes any sense as a basic social principle, needs yet to be made. For after all, there have been regimes in plenty that gave not a fig for either liberty or equality, especially as basic principles. And perhaps they were right, for all we know as yet.[16]

II. LIBERTY

Liberty-Maximization? A Puzzle

If the equalitarian wants to enforce an equal distribution of income and wealth, what does the "libertarian" want? Presumably, to enforce an equal distribution of liberty. And there is a sense, which will be refined below, in which this is exactly right. Yet, just as the equalitarian also wishes his equal distribution to be at the highest possible equal level, so one would suppose that the libertarian would want liberty to be equally distributed at the highest possible equal level. "Maximize equal welfare/income/wealth," says one; "Maximize equal liberty," says the other.

But some reflection on this leads to a puzzle. On the one hand, we would be inclined to suppose that liberty in economic matters is compatible with (at least) considerable inequality. Start persons with equal shares, even, and ere long their free use of those resources will lead to some having much more than others. Yet some would wish to argue that the free market is not free: that a society enjoying maximum equal liberty could not be one in which people had varying levels of income. Why so? Because money is, after all, "purchasing power": the more of it you have, the more you are thereby enabled to do, hence free to do. Moreover, the goods end up being yours, which means that others may not use or enjoy them without your permission. When they are yours, you have the power to exclude others. Yet to exclude others is to restrict or limit their liberty; and the more of this power you have, the less liberty they have.[17] And so, to maximize equal liberty one must also maximize *equal* incomes! This is hardly the result that defenders of a free market would expect, and it seems odd to characterize a free market as "unfree." What is wrong?

---

[16] Roger Scruton, *The Meaning of Conservatism* (Markham, Ont.: Penguin Books, 1980) provides an example of a serious thinker who evidently thinks thus.

[17] See G. A. Cohen, "Capitalism, Freedom and the Proletariat," A. Ryan, ed., *The Idea of Freedom* (Oxford, U.K.: Oxford University Press, 1979) for one who argues thus.

Liberty: What it is

Evidently we require a closer look at the notion of liberty. But an immediate restriction may, happily, be put on the scope of the inquiry, for what is at issue, here, is *social* liberty, rather than, say, the liberty of the will in general. Liberty in general, I believe, is absence of impediment to one's actions, and it is beyond question that many such impediments are not put there – certainly not intentionally or even knowingly, at any rate – by one's fellows. Some of them, for that matter, are surely put there by oneself, and sometimes put there quite rationally. And many others are not "put" there by anyone: they're just part of the nature of things. But our specific question in this investigation concerns the class of impediments posed by the actions of one's fellow persons, and in particular those posed knowingly (intentionally or otherwise) by them, and those whose impedimentary character, even if not known or intended, is establishable and preventable by methods of social control.

When is one person's action, in the relevant sense, an "impediment" to another's? We must distinguish, at least, between two sorts:

(1) B's doing y makes it *impossible* for A to do x;
(2) B's doing y would render it (much) more costly for A to do x;

which in turn has two significantly different variants:

(2a) If B does y, then A prefers not doing x to doing x
(2b) A would prefer doing x given that B does not do y to doing x given that B does y (even though A will still do x rather than x̄)[18]

Impediments of type (1) are, as we might say, out-and-out. In the interests of liberty, we would want, and we would be able, to identify a set of acts of type (1) that are to be prohibited. But if we move to (2), and especially to (2b), things are more complicated, since B can rightly claim that he does not actually prevent A from doing x in such cases. Cases of type (2) include what we commonly term "coercions": I coerce you into doing x̄ if I threaten to do something to you if you do x that would render x, under the circumstances, a highly undesirable course of action. But what if it makes x only a little bit less desirable? Especially if, as in (2b), it still leaves A willing, as well as able, to do it? Has B interfered with A's liberty in the latter case? Can the objection to B's doing y in such a case be that it violates a right to liberty that A has? Or must we go to a theory that identifies some other rights A has, then show that this case violates one of those?

In the case where A doesn't have the right to do x in the first place, the

---

[18] (Reading "x̄" as "an act other than x")

interferences posed by B are, at least so far as A's x-ing goes, not wrong. Conversely, there might be some independent reason why B's y-ing is wrong, aside from its bearing on A's doing x. But otherwise, it seems to me that if A's doing x is something A independently has the right to do, then B should not be able to increase the cost of A's doing it either, unless there is an independent argument for his having the right to do the particular thing y whose impedimental character is in question here.

Consider, in particular, the case of coercion. If I attempt to induce A not to do x by threatening to do z if he does, where z is, for instance, killing A, then z would be independently wrong, since it would prevent A from doing anything whatever thereafter. This sort of coercion can be ruled wrong too, but not simply by virtue of being an impediment to A's x-ing. Suppose, instead, I attempt to induce A not to do x by threatening to foreclose on his mortgage, and suppose that I have, independently, the right to do that. It is not clear, then, that we can object to my doing it – indeed, it is pretty clear that we cannot, just as such. But we can still object to my doing it *qua* interference with A. If I have no other reason to foreclose, and if A has the right to do x, then my making this threat seems objectionable in that respect, and objectionable on the score of being an interference with A's liberty. The snag, however, is that we are considering the view that when actions are wrong, they are so because they violate liberty in *general*. And this raises very thorny problems. For giving A the right to do x ipso facto deprives B of the right to do y, where y interferes with x. Yet, that evidently interferes with B's liberty to do y. A right is a justifiable ground of interference. How do we establish that it is B, rather than A, who must get out of the way in the above case? If y interferes with x, doesn't x amount to an interference with y?

Answer: No, or at least we needn't give up so fast. Some interferences are simply that: the description of B's action y may be essentially that it was an interference with A's doing x and not an independent course of action that merely happened to collide with A's. That, at least, would put it squarely in the category of what we wish to rule out by proclaiming a general principle of liberty. And on the other hand, we can admit that there are many cases where the solution will be to negotiate. If the situation is that x interferes with y and y interferes with x, both can be declared in the wrong simply to proceed; negotiation could be required. The question is whether we can generate enough information from the root idea of a general right of liberty to enable us to see how such procedures are what are called for. So let us not give up yet!

And What it is Not

I interfere with your liberty when I make it impossible for you to do what you are endeavoring to do. But let us consider the case in which, though you *want* to do x, you lack some of what you would need to do it, say z. And suppose that I in fact have z. Some might wish to say that if I do not supply you with z, then I would be "interfering" with your liberty to do x. Should we go along with this? Certainly not! Or so I shall argue.

Why not? It is not a consequence of anyone else's *action* that you can't do x. It is, rather, a consequence of their inaction, in a sense. But "consequence" is misleading, here, anyway. Suppose that you are drowning 50 yards offshore, and that I could save you. Is your drowning a consequence of my not saving you? But suppose I was a thousand miles away and could do nothing about your drowning. Yet you still drown! How is it a "consequence" of something about me that you are in state S if you would be in it even if I didn't exist or was nowhere near?[19]

I could increase your ability to do various things by helping you, let us suppose. Is it the case, then, that I *increase* your *liberty*? Perhaps; though why shouldn't we just say that I increase your range of options, or your powers? However, we needn't stick at this. What we need to ask, rather, is what increasing liberty in the sense so defined has to do with a general principle that everyone has a right to liberty. And the answer is that it is not part of that right that others must increase our liberty when they have the chance to do so. We must distinguish, as has become happily customary in recent years, between "positive" and "negative" liberty, and likewise between "positive" and "negative" rights to liberty (or to anything else). The definitions go roughly thus:

A has the "negative" liberty to do x = nothing prevents A's doing x
A has the "positive" liberty to do x = A has whatever is needed in order for A to do x, as A wishes

And the parallel constructions for negative and positive rights go as follows:

A has the "negative" right to do x = No one may prevent A from doing x
A has the "positive" right to do x = Others must provide A with whatever A might need in order to do x, if A lacks it

Negative *social* liberty obtains when no other *person's* actions prevent one from doing as one wishes. Positive social liberty obtains when other persons are ready to assist one in doing as one wishes. To give persons a positive right to do as they wish is to impose a social requirement that others assist them. But to impose that requirement is to forbid them to refrain from offering that assistance, and hence to restrict their liberty. Positive rights conflict with negative ones. And so the notion of "maximizing" liberty is

---

[19] A similar argument is strongly pressed by Eric Mack in "Bad Samaritanism and the Causation of Harm," *Philosophy and Public Affairs* Spring 1980, 9(3).

ambiguous, or at least misleading. Maximization suggests promotion, not in the sense of removing obstacles but of increasing the power or ability to do things. It invites thinking in terms of positive rights. Yet positive rights cut into liberty. To be at liberty is, surely, for it to be up to you whether you do x or not, and if whenever I could help someone else do something I may be legitimately coerced into doing so, then how is this liberty? If, on the other hand, I am unable to do something because, through nobody else's fault, I have only one leg, or insufficient knowledge, then there is, nevertheless, no violation of my liberty by any other person, so far as it goes.

Maximization of positive liberty is a snare and a delusion. When do you have maximum positive liberty? When you are God, evidently: for only He lacks no powers at all. And if we were out to see to it that everyone has equal powers at a maximum level, how do we decide when two persons are equal? If Smith is proficient at ping pong, and Jones at playing the cello, are they equal? How would this be decided? More importantly for present purposes, how does this goal differ from that of maximizing equal welfare? And if it does not, then why not call a spade a spade?

To be concerned with liberty, to hold that what society should do is to respect liberty, and that it should be concerned to invoke coercion only in the interests of liberty, is to advance a distinctive project. It is to hold that people may do as they wish, even if some of the things they might have been forced to do would have done much more good for other people than the acts they chose to do. What the proponent of this idea needs to talk about under the heading of "maximization" is, actually, better construed as *minimization*: namely, minimization of interferences with liberty. People are to be constrained from doing what interferes with others' liberty; apart from that, they may do as they please – though, of course, many might greatly prefer that they do some things rather than others. Perhaps even *all* (others) might thus prefer: still, that is not sufficient reason for forcing them to do it. Here, if the idea is coherent, is a distinctive notion. The questions are: is it coherent? And even if it is, do we have good reason for embracing this idea?

Maximum Liberty as a Goal of Justice

First, let us address ourselves to the question of coherence. We want to try to fix the idea of "maximizing" liberty, which I have suggested should really be thought of as the idea of minimizing interferences with liberty. If we accept the characterization of justice as concerned with basic rights, then the social system we envisage with this as our leading idea is that in which society is concerned to give everyone the right of maximum liberty, the right to do whatever one wants to do, and thus the duty to refrain from interfering with the liberty of others.

To appreciate the looming problem of coherence in this scheme, we must ask how a society in which that was the sole basic right differed from a society in which everyone "could" do as he or she pleased with no restrictions at all. In an unguarded moment, one might entertain the idea of everyone's having the right to do *whatever* he or she wished, with literally no restrictions. But then we would have to ask what the term "right"is doing in this characterization. For to recognize a right is to accept a restriction on one's behavior. If I agree that you have the right to smoke in place X, then I agree not to attempt to stop you by any coercive means (though I may reserve the right to try to persuade you not to do so, or to request, politely, that you refrain). But on the view we are considering, I would in fact have the right to do anything I felt like in the way of stopping you, since I have the right to do anything whatever – and so do you! Obviously, this is to drain the notion of a right of all meaning, unless possibly one rather ghostly resonance. Perhaps the Hobbesian state of nature, in which we are told that "every man has a right to every thing; even to one another's body"[20] gives every man one right – the right not to be criticized:

> The Desires, and other Passions of man, are in themselves no Sin. No more are the Actions, that proceed from those Passions, till they know a Law that forbids them: which till Lawes be made they cannot know.[21]

Even this is dubious, since if we have the right to do absolutely everything, why not also the right to criticize? The most Hobbes can insist on is that any such criticism will be unreasonable in such a condition. And perhaps there he has a point.

Meanwhile, the point here is that such a condition is very different from one in which everyone has a genuine right, in the full ordinary meaning of the term, to do whatever he or she pleases, meaning by this whichever of those actions are consistent with the recognition of the same right on the part of everyone else. To envisage this is to envisage, not a state in which, in Hobbes' words, "the notions of Right and Wrong have no place," but rather one in which some actions are Wrong and all others are, at least in the weak sense of being permissible, Right.

One obvious thought is to try to quantify over the "extent" of interferences: some impediments to one's action are greater, more serious, than others. So we might be tempted to try to draw up an ordered list of interferences, ranked by their "seriousness" as impositions. But this would lead to inordinate difficulties, especially in view of the fact that one would surely expect people to rank different interferences very differently. Indeed,

---

[20] Thomas Hobbes, *Leviathan* (1651), Ch. XIV, 4th paragraph.
[21] Hobbes, *op. cit.*, Ch. XIII, 10th paragraph.

perhaps there will be some people who attach greatest importance to precisely some of the actions which we would also want to say are most obviously and outrightly interferences with others. And, thus, they would rank interferences with these actions as most serious. And there will arise the question whether this isn't just going to end up as a form of negative utilitarianism (Minimize Disutility).

Fortunately, there is a better way to handle the sort of problems to which such measures (e.g., as rank ordering) are proposed remedies: viz., by negotiation. Once we have a proper starting point, then when acts impinge on each other, the indicated solution is for the parties to them to reach an agreement concerning the area under dispute, an agreement specifying who is to be permitted to do what. Agreements, indeed, will bear the lion's share of the burden if liberty is our guide, since they are prototypically voluntary: no one is (in general) required to make any agreements, but once made, the obligations stemming from them have been self-imposed. The basis for future complaints is agreed upon, hence accepted, in advance.

Agreements, it should be noted, will typically reflect the relative strengths of the bargaining positions of the parties antecedently. They are not made behind the Veil of Ignorance, and nothing about them inherently requires or promises equality of outcome in the respects considered and rejected in Part I. The parties may take it or leave it so far as any particular proposal is concerned, and those taken will, provided that no fraud is involved in the negotiation, presumably be the best offers available, so that when taken the parties will find themselves better off, in their own views of what constitutes being better off, than before; but there is no need to expect that the degrees to which each will be better off will be equal, supposing that could be objectively measured anyway. This, I suggest, is as it should be. Nor is it to deny that, very often, the basis for agreement will be a proposal to split something equally.

In order to make sense of minimizing interferences, we need a conception of separate or separable areas, spheres, or "territories" – "turfs," as one subculture has it – that define the limits within which each person may properly operate: Mill's "appropriate region of human liberty,"[22] only with a twist. For Mill hoped to find a region in which no human activity *could* interfere with another, and that is in principle hopeless, at least if we allow that human action is in the natural, causal network. But what we can try to identify is a region in which impingements by others are necessarily interferences, are to be reckoned interferences if anything is, and to give the individual associated with that region the right to control such impingements, at a minimum. The initial such region is surely the person's body.

[22] J. S. Mill, *An Essay on Liberty* (1859), Introduction.

Here, surely, is a region which others may not invade without the consent of the person whose body it is.

This, of course, is equivalent to maintaining that a person's body is that person's property: if the body in question is that of A, then A may do and may permit or forbid others to do with it as A wants. A is the authority over A's body: insofar as this is controllable, others may not visit effects upon it that A does not want to have visited upon it.

Is this to be reckoned (part of) a basic right to *liberty*? Ordinarily, we would say that some damages to the body impede liberty, but not others. Broken limbs, diseases that confine one to bed, maladies that render parts of the body inoperable, are clearly enough impediments to liberty, but what of bruises, scratches, or headaches? It must be admitted that to conceive the right of liberty in such a way as to make the latter impediments to liberty is to stretch things a little. But not, I think, very much. The right to do as one likes with a thing, X, is the right to control X – to decide which states X shall be in, insofar as this is possible. If we accept this construal, then anything done to one's body without consent is a violation of one's right to liberty. And I do wish to insist that liberty rights are property rights, in general. To have the right to do x is to have the right to *use* whatever is involved in doing x in whatever *way* is involved.

The connection with property continues when we move to things that are not integral parts of one's body. When we own a certain thing, T, what we have are rights to do what we wish with T, within the limits of others' rights. That much is, I think, clear enough. But how does a right to liberty entail rights to ownership?

The general form of the answer to this question, I think, is as follows, or at any rate in the general direction indicated by what follows. To own X is to have the right to do whatever one wishes with X, within the limits imposed by others' rights. Therefore, there is an identifiable (though open-ended) set of (possible) acts the right to perform which is what ownership consists in. If none of those acts on the face of it conflicts with others' rights, then we have, by hypothesis, the right to perform any member of that set, as we wish, and, of course, if we *can*. To claim ownership is to claim the right to perform those acts. To rebut such a claim is to show that the claimant either simply isn't in a position to perform them, in which case others doing them instead cannot conflict with anything the claimant does; or to show that there are others' rights with which these *would* conflict. If somebody else already owns the thing, then the claim is invalid. But if no one does, and if there are no rival simultaneous claimants, then to be embarked upon the set of actions in question is to have a sufficient claim to be allowed to continue them. The rules of "finders, keepers" and "first come, first served" are the indicated ones, if liberty, and thus noninterference, is our maxim.

In John Locke's version, the initiating actions in question are those of producing, making – "mixing one's labour with," as he puts it. But it seems to me that this is more than we need. One must be using, and intending further use, but that the use must be productive is a problematic extra restriction. If people may do as they please, then the protected activities need not be in any special way productive. (Of course, we may take the view that all voluntary activity is intended to be "productive" at least in the thin sense of satisfying one's preferences at the moment. But Locke had more than that in mind.[23])

The strong connection between liberty and (private) property becomes clear, also, when one compares a property system to one in which decisions about who may do what and with what are always, in principle at least, in the power of a public authority or committee or deliberative body, ultimately subject to putatively democratic control. The hallmark of liberty, surely, is that one may do things "without asking the leave of any man" (Locke's phrase). Being at the beck and call of the majority of one's fellows is hardly that. And if nobody owns anything, then everything will be so subject, for we can't do anything at all unless we do it *with* something!

It will be objected, no doubt, that persons with no incomes in a society lacking social welfare systems will be at the mercy of their fellows, namely for the very rudiments of life – food, clothing, etc. Now, in a society *with* such institutions, one is also at the mercy of one's fellows, corporately rather than individually. Whether that is better or worse than being at the mercy of individuals or voluntary associations whose purpose it is to cater to such persons is surely not *a priori* decidable, even from the point of view of the indigent. But that it is worse from the point of view of all of those whose involuntary support contributes to the public institution seems beyond peradventure; that such institutions could thrive in the name of *freedom*, at any rate, seems a perversion of the notion.

The conceptual problems of initial acquisition, while appreciable, do not seem to be overwhelming, given the device of negotiation. And, of course, very little in the modern world is available for initial acquisition, and certainly only a tiny portion of the world's real wealth. Overwhelmingly, goods and services are produced by human activity. And if we aim at liberty as the guide of institutional design, then the indicated format is the free market society, in which what is produced and who gets it depends upon voluntary decisions of the persons who make and receive these goods. If I may do as I please with x, and you with y, then we may also arrange a trade of x and y if we like. And we may make such trades with anyone with whom we wish to do business.

[23] John Locke, *Second Treatise on Civil Government* (1690), Ch. V.

Freedom of association is also a straightforward entailment from the general conception; and associate we do, in innumerable ways and, sometimes, at great depth. This puts in perspective the claim that liberalism presupposes "atomic individualism":

> For atomic individualists, the ultimate constituents of social reality, the atoms, are individual men and women, essentially independent of one another and of society, bearing only extrinsic relations to one another. Like atoms in an enclosed space, individuals in society do come into contact with one another. But this contact is in no way constitutive of the individual's nature. Society no more constitutes individuals than space constitutes atoms . . . Society is no more a part of social reality than physical space, in the traditional atomist view, is part of matter.[24]

It is difficult to know what to make of this, since it is difficult to be sure just what the liberal is supposed to be denying in this passage. All of us are born into and grow up in particular families and particular societies, with heritages that unquestionably shape us forever after. And we are deeply attached to, and involved in, the societies we live in – often. But if it were a universal truth that individuals are "constituted by" their societies, "intrinsically" and "essentially", then why do people sometimes reject their societies and go elsewhere, or attempt to reform, even in revolutionary ways, the ones they do live in? Should not such efforts at detachment be *impossible* on the view in question? But indeed, non-individualists don't really want to deny those possibilities. They want, instead, to insist that when people do that, they are radically wrongheaded. But how do we get *that* thesis out of the facts about people and their societies? If the claim is that there is always sufficient reason to continue all the attachments of one's society without question, that is an interesting one: but what argues for it? Once the question has been raised, the nonindividualism apparently asserted is already refuted in its most salient form. And what is left?

Since the sort of principle under consideration here permits indefinitely many associations, with whatever strength and extent of obligations people may see fit to take on (or not see fit to renounce, once an "age of reason" is reached at which the question can arise whether to do so), it is hard to see how anything further can be gained by embracing the nonindividualist thesis than the blessings of fascism, such as they are. Perhaps this makes an apt point to move to our final question: why liberty?

---

[24] Andrew Levine, *Liberal Democracy: A Critique of its Theory* (New York: Columbia University Press, 1981), p. 45.

The Argument for Liberty

Defenders of liberty tend to assume that the rights they proclaim are self-evident, requiring and affording no further argument. There is some excuse for this procedure – equalitarians, after all, do no better – but still, it is hardly satisfactory. The aim of political argument, I should think, is to provide good reasons for anyone to accept the system being proposed, that is, the system which would be determined by the principle being proposed.

Now, the acceptance of a system, in the sense of a preference for it, on the part of isolated persons is hardly of any interest. One cannot get very far in public matters by acting on principles that no one else respects. And even if they respect your right to believe those principles, that is hardly going to do much for you if what you are concerned about is acting on them. Ideally, our argument should show that no rational person can do better than to accept the proposal being put forward; or that he has reason to complain about any alternative.

It is also no use insisting that rational and free beings necessarily respect the like status of other beings. Free and rational beings, I think, are simply beings with preferences that are modulated by, or capable of being modulated by, information about the world around them and by considerations of internal consistency. It hardly follows from this characterization that the beings in question will respect, in the form of granting rights to their liberty, their fellow rational animals. What follows is only that their actions might well be altered on the basis of information about their fellows; but not that it will be altered in that particular manner.

What matters about one's fellow beings is that their actions might affect one's interests and pursuits. The effects can be of all kinds. Some of these fellow beings will be people one is extremely fond of; others will at least be useful, e.g., in removing one's inflamed appendix or one's garbage. And doubtless there are various things one might *like* to have guaranteed, i.e., that one's fellows would have no right to refuse to do them for you. Indeed, everyone might conceivably like this, though I doubt it. But we can't necessarily have everything we want. These "strong" rights to "positive" services are not free. If everyone has them, so too does everyone have the obligation to contribute to them if possible. And it is not so obvious that one would want so to contribute. *Prima facie* one will be willing to do so if (1) the expected benefit is at least equal to the expected cost, and (2) there are no alternative ways of achieving a sufficient level of assurance without resorting to coercion.

Now, what are the options here? One possibility is to agree to nothing. This option, the "State of Nature", is to be understood as the situation in which, as Hobbes has it, nothing is right or wrong, i.e., there simply are no rules at all. I wish to add here the understanding that this includes the rule, say, of keeping agreements: that too goes by the board in this alternative. No objection can be made to the use of force for *any* purpose, because there are literally no rules. Hobbes' classic prediction is that such a condition would afford a life that was "nasty, brutish, miserable and short", and it is difficult to see why he would not be right, unless one sneaks in the assumption that the argument is already over and that certain rules, such as that forbidding wanton killing, are *already* in force, by virtue of being inherent in the nature of man.

If the State of Nature is rationally to be rejected, then which of the various alternatives is possibly capable of universal assent? It is likely that some persons, such as the exceedingly unlucky – paraplegics, for instance – would like to have a system in which people had no choice but to render life as tolerable for them as possible. But it is difficult to see why others should accept this. There is, of course, the possibility that one will end up a paraplegic oneself. But in a system of liberty, one has two important options here. The first is to try to ensure oneself against such options, e.g., by literally buying insurance. And the second is to appeal to the benevolence of one's fellows. And if some would find these options between them preferable to the option of being maintained by coercing all the sundry into supplying one's needs, then I propose that the argument is complete. For if any proposal fails of unanimity, we must choose either some other or we are forced back to the State of Nature. Now those who opt for coercion must ask how they are going to get unanimity on *that*, given that some reject it? For the no-agreement option is the State of Nature, and surely not only paraplegics but everyone will do worse there than in the Liberty condition; and it is hard to see how we can get agreement beyond this.

Nor is it easy to see why we need it. It is odd that so many liberals talk as though the typical human being in the very liberal society he champions is already solitary, mean, nasty, brutish, and short-sighted. Why? In fact, I hardly know any person so uncharitable that he or she would not expend some effort voluntarily aiding the desperate, given ready opportunity to do so. And on the other hand, most persons are not only able-bodied but have sufficient talent so that, given also some incentive and enterprise, they would and could do reasonably well in a society in which enterprise was not substantially impeded, or substantial incentives offered for avoiding it.

Concluding Remarks

All manner of large issues are certainly stirred up in the preceding pages. Among the largest, for example, is the question of anarchism. The strong view on individual liberty and property doubtless implies, at least on the face of it, that governments should do much less than they currently do, and no doubt also makes it difficult to see how they could function at all within the set of constraints proposed. But it should be appreciated that these are proposed at an extremely general level, and that one should not proceed too cavalierly from theoretical cup to practical lip: slippage, as we know, is common in such transitions. Consider the Welfare State, for example. Suppose that it is overwhelmingly popular: say, that 90% of the adult population would vote for it even if they knew (as they doubtless do not at present) what they were getting in for. A determined majority of that size acting quite without recourse to government could, in principle, readily induce the remainder to go along with programs of that sort, e.g., by boycotting their services if they didn't. Such tactics could not be forbidden within the structure of rights proposed here, and they would have the effect of reenacting the State in practical terms if used; it is hard to deny that their effective use would make life (even?) less comfortable than it now is for dissenters whose monetary support, at least, is coerced by the political system as it now operates. Whether the State can be retrieved in anything like its present form within the constraints imposed by such principles as have been argued for is not easy to say, but we should not simply assume that it must be impossible.

Nevertheless, I do suppose that the principles advocated here have teeth. The alternative to liberty, it is claimed, is always the permissibility of coercion of someone or other in order to benefit someone else or \other, and we surely need to ask whether that, as it stands, is morally acceptable. If it is not, then we must ask how practice can be made to square much more nearly with this fundamental requirement. Many others have labored on these matters;[25] it behooves us to take them seriously, if the foregoing arguments are near the truth.

Philosophy, University of Waterloo

---

[25] Most of the contributors to Machan (note 5) are cases in point. I should also mention that the original version of this paper, running to rather more than twice the present length, contains more detailed discussion of many points, and also examines several more arguments for equality than those considered here. The author can supply copies of this longer version upon request (within reason).

WHAT'S SO SPECIAL ABOUT RIGHTS?

Allen Buchanan

Future historians of moral and political philosophy may well label our period the Age of Rights. In moral philosophy it is now widely assumed that the two most plausible types of normative theories are Utilitarianism and Kantian theories and that the contest between them must be decided in the end by seeing whether Utilitarianism can accommodate a prominent role for rights in morality. In political philosophy even the most bitter opponents in the perennial debate over conflicts between liberty and equality often share a common assumption: that the issue of liberty versus equality can only be resolved (or dissolved) by determining which is the correct theory of rights. Some contend that equal respect for persons requires enforcement of moral rights to goods and services required for the pursuit of one's own conception of the good, while others protest that an enforced system of 'positive' rights violates the right to liberty whose recognition is the essence of equal respect for persons. The dominant views in contemporary moral and political philosophy combine an almost unbounded enthusiasm for the concept of rights with seemingly incessant disagreement about what our rights are and which rights are most basic. Unfortunately, that which enjoys our greatest enthusiasm is often that about which we are least critical.

My aim in this essay is to take a step backward in order to examine the assumption that frames the most important debates in contemporary moral and political philosophy – the assumption that the concept of a right has certain unique features which make rights so especially valuable as to be virtually indispensable elements of any acceptable social order. In philosophy, whose main business is criticism, a step backward need not be a loss of ground.

There are, it seems, only two archetypal strategies for challenging the thesis that rights are uniquely valuable. The first is to argue that rights are valuable only under certain defective – and temporary – social conditions. According to this position, the conflicts that make rights valuable can and ought to be abolished. Thus even if rights are very valuable in a society fraught with conflict, they are not valuable in all forms of human society. Our efforts should not be directed toward developing and faithfully implementing more adequate theories of rights; instead, we should strive to establish a social order which is so harmonious as to make rights otiose.

Variants of this view provide different accounts of the source of the conflicts that make rights valuable and alternative recommendations for how to eliminate them. Marx, I have argued elsewhere,[1] believed that the sorts of interpersonal conflicts that make rights valuable are rooted in class-conflict and the egoism to which class-conflict gives rise, under conditions of scarcity. Marx also predicted that class-divided society would eventually be replaced by a system of democratic control over production that would eliminate class-division and so reduce egoism and scarcity, and hence interpersonal conflict, that reliance upon rights would become largely, if not totally, unnecessary.

Perhaps the greatest flaw in this type of view, including Marx's specific version of it, is that it rests on an unduly narrow understanding of the sources of interpersonal conflict that make reliance upon rights valuable. I have argued that the sorts of interpersonal conflicts which rights-principles are or can be invoked to cope with do not presuppose egoism or class conflict, but merely conflicting preferences and the need to coordinate social activity in an efficient way. I have also argued that Marx's prediction that communism would eliminate those sorts of conflicts that make rights valuable presupposes a theory of democratic social organization which Marx's social philosophy failed to provide.[2]

In the remainder of this essay, I shall explore a second, more promising strategy for challenging the thesis that rights are so uniquely valuable as to be indispensable. This second approach frankly acknowledges that at least some of the types of interpersonal conflict which rights are invoked to handle are not eliminable by changing the mode of production or by any other acceptable and feasible transformation of the social order. It then seeks to show that there are other kinds of moral principles, which do not employ the concept of a right, which can or do successfully perform the functions that are uniquely attributed to rights principles.

If it turns out there are valuable functions that cannot be achieved without the distinctive features of rights, we shall know what is so special about rights. In particular, we shall know whether the reconciliation of liberty and equality, if it is possible at all, will rely upon a theory of rights. Further, in attempting to see whether rights are replaceable and hence dispensable, we will get clearer about what rights are. Whether or not our current enthusiasm for rights will be enhanced or diminished, it will at least be rationally supported, rather than dogmatic, and we will have a better idea of what we have been, or should be, so enthusiastic about.

---

[1] A. Buchanan, *Marx and Justice: The Radical Critique of Liberalism* (Totowa, New Jersey; Rowman and Littlefield 1982), pp. 50–85.

[2] *ibid.*, pp. 162–179. See also, A. Buchanan, "Marx on Democracy and the Obsolescence of Rights," *South African Journal of Philosophy*, Marx Centenary Issue, forthcoming.

We can begin by listing, in summary fashion, the features that are said by various writers to make rights uniquely valuable. (1) Because valid claims of right 'trump' appeals to what would maximize social utility, rights provide the strongest protections for individuals and minorities. (2) A moral (or legal) system that included no provision for compensation to those whose interests have been invaded would be a very defective system; but compensation is appropriate only where a right has been infringed. (3) Rights enable us to distinguish between those moral principles that can justly be enforced and those that cannot. (4) The concept of a right expresses the idea that something is owed to the individual, that a certain performance or certain forms of non-interference are his due or that he is entitled to them. Consequently, in a moral (or legal) system that lacked the concept of a right, individuals could only make requests, or beg, or ask favors; they could not demand certain treatment, but would be at the mercy of the generosity or personal whims of others. (5) Respect for persons simply is, or includes, recognition of the individual's status as a holder of rights. In a system in which such recognition is lacking, respect for oneself and others as persons is impossible, and to fail to respect persons as such is a grave moral defect. (6) A unique feature of rights is that the right holder may either invoke or not invoke or waive his right. For several reasons, this special feature makes rights principles more valuable than principles that merely state obligations or other moral (or legal) requirements. Each of these six features must now be examined in detail.

1. Three of the most prominent contemporary rights theorists, John Rawls, Ronald Dworkin, and Robert Nozick, place great emphasis on the idea that valid claims of right, at least in the case of basic rights, take precedence over, or as Dworkin puts it, "trump" appeals to what would maximize social utility.[3] It is easy to see that having some sort of interest-protecting principles that take precedence over appeals to social utility maximization is extremely valuable. It is more difficult to see, however, why the attractiveness of the utility-trumping feature itself shows that *rights* are indispensable. For there is certainly nothing conceptually incoherent or even impractical about interest-protecting principles that have the utility-trumping feature but that include none of the other features said to be distinctive of rights. In particular, there seems to be no conceptual or pragmatic connection between the trumping feature and the idea that something is owed to the individual, or that the individual may or may not invoke his right or waive it. After all, to say that the requirement laid down by a principle possesses the trumping feature is to make an external relational statement, a

---

[3] R. Dworkin, *Taking Rights Seriously* (Cambridge, MA: Harvard University Press, 1977), pp. 184–205.

statement about the weighting or priority relation between that principle and other principles, in particular, the principle of utility. It is not to say anything at all about the distinctive content of the principle in question.

Consequently, even if the utility trumping feature were necessary for a principle to be a rights principle, it hardly seems sufficient. Thus, although it may be true that any system that lacked this feature would leave individuals or minority interests vulnerable, it does not follow that a system that lacked rights would be intolerable. To put the point differently, to adhere to utility-trumping, interest-protecting principles is to recognize that certain *interests* (e.g., in food or shelter or in freedom from bodily invasion) are to be protected even at the cost of losses in social utility. But this seems to fall short of recognizing that *individuals have rights.*

2. If a system that awards compensation for invasions of interests has significant advantages over one which does not, and if compensation presupposes infringement of a right, then rights are distinctively valuable, at least for this reason. Assuming for a moment that rights alone provide a basis for compensation, why is a system that includes compensation better than one that does not? The most obvious reply is that compensation is an intuitively attractive response to an infraction of an interest-protecting principle. After all, if the infraction made A worse off, then it seems fitting to try to restore A's interests to the condition they were in before they were set back by the infraction.

Whether or not we describe this restorative function as a matter of doing justice (or rectifying injustice), it is certainly not the only attraction of compensation. Just as obviously, the prospect that the victim will be awarded compensation can serve as a deterrent for those who would infringe the interest-protecting principle in question, if the perpetrator of the infraction is held responsible for supplying compensation. However, as the criminal law shows, deterrence can be achieved (when it can be achieved at all) just as well by punishing the perpetrator as by requiring him to compensate the victim.

A more subtle and less appreciated advantage of a system of compensation is that the prospect of compensation provides an incentive for reporting infringements and, hence, facilitates effective enforcement of the law. In many cases a rational victim will conclude that the cost to him of reporting an infringement (and of testifying, etc.) will exceed the benefits he would receive from doing so, unless he can expect compensation. This may well be the case if (a) the probability is low that one will be a victim of this sort of infraction again in the future, or if (b) the probability is low that punishment will achieve a significant deterrent effect.

Even if I know that the probability of my being a victim in the future would be significantly reduced if everyone, or a large number of others, took the trouble to report (and help prosecute) violations, I may conclude that the contribution that my reporting of this infraction would make would be negligible. I may reason that either enough others will report infractions (testify, etc.) to reduce the probability that I will be a victim again or they will not, regardless of what I do. Since reporting is a cost to me, it may be rational for me not to report. If enough others reason as I do, infractions will be under-reported and enforcement will be hampered.

However, when the prospect of compensation enters the picture, I have an incentive to report the infraction, even when conditions (a) and (b) are present. Thus, compensation is attractive in part because it promotes reporting of infractions and, hence, facilitates enforcement of interest-protecting principles.

It does not follow, however, that only compensation can do this job. A simple reward system would also provide the needed incentive. If C can expect a reward for reporting an infraction of a principle that occurs when B's interests are invaded by A, then all C need be concerned about is whether his expected gain from the reward surpasses the expected cost to him of reporting the infraction. So it seems that compensation is not an indispensable aid to reporting infractions and, hence, to enforcement of interest-protecting principles.

Nevertheless, one might argue that compensation offers certain *efficiencies* in reporting and enforcement which would be very difficult, if not impossible, to attain with a simple reward system. Just as the absence of rewards or compensation may, for the reasons noted above, result in under-reporting of infractions, so a reward system, as opposed to a compensation system, may lead to over-reporting (and hence over-enforcement). In a simple reward system, C's decision to report B's infraction against A is in no way constrained by an assessment of A's losses due to the infraction; it is only constrained by the cost to C of reporting the infraction. On the other hand, in a compensation system, B's incentive to report the infraction in order to reap compensation is constrained not only by the cost of reporting the infraction, but also by the cost of the infraction to B. If the amount of compensation B can expect is determined by the loss to him due to the infraction, then it will be rational for B to report only those infractions that cause losses that exceed the cost of reporting the infractions. A simple reward system, because it lacks this constraint, will tend toward over-reporting, other things being equal. A system which provides for compensation may achieve more efficient enforcement, and this may be one reason why rights are distinctively valuable – *if* compensation presupposes rights.

However, a more complex reward system might also minimize the problem of over-reporting. Suppose the amount of reward C receives for reporting A's infraction regarding B is determined by the cost of the infraction to B. As in the compensation system, one will have an incentive to report infractions only if the amount one expects to gain (through the reward) exceeds the cost of reporting and the amount one expects to gain will be determined by the cost of the infraction to the victim.

If there is a distinctive advantage to the compensation system, then, it is not that compensation alone provides an incentive for reporting infractions and an incentive against over-reporting, since a reward system may also do this. Instead, what distinguishes the compensation system is that the same arrangement that provides an incentive against over-reporting also insures that the "reward" for reporting the infraction serves to help restore the victim to the condition he enjoyed prior to the infraction.

Even if we conclude that this feature makes compensation distinctively valuable, this does nothing to establish the unique value of rights unless compensation presupposes rights. The thesis that compensation presupposes infringement of a right is ambiguous. It may be understood either as a claim about the meaning of "compensation" or as a claim about the necessary conditions for justified compensation.[4] On the first interpretation, the thesis can be dismissed rather easily. There is nothing incoherent or meaningless about the idea of a principle of compensation which requires A to be compensated whenever certain of his interests are invaded, but which does not imply that A has any rights against the invasions in question. All that is needed is the principle of compensation itself and some way of picking out which invasions of interests are to be compensated. The difficulty lies in determining which interests count for purposes of compensation. But precisely the same is true for a theory of rights – not just any interest will count as the basis for a right. It seems, then, that the burden of proof is on those who claim that no system could provide an adequate moral justification for compensation in the absence of infringement of rights.[5]

Finally, although those who have assumed that compensation requires infringement of a right have somehow failed to notice it, our own legal system, in the law of torts dealing with fault liability, provides instances in which a successful case for compensation does not depend upon establishing that a right was infringed. Rather, one need only show that a legitimate interest was invaded and that the one who invaded it was at fault, i.e., that his action was unjustified in that it failed to measure up to the standard of care exercised by the reasonable person.[6] Thus, although establishing that a right was infringed provides one basis for compensation, this does not tell us what

---

[4] J. Coleman, "Moral Theories of Torts: Their Scope and Limits: Part II," *Law and Philosophy* (1983), 2, p. 22.

[5] See for example, J. J. Thompson, "Rights and Compensation, 1980," 14 *Nous* pp. 3–15.

[6] T. Benditt, *Rights*; (Totowa, New Jersey: Rowman and Littlefield, 1982), pp. 53–64, and J. Coleman, "Moral Theories of Torts: Their Scope and Limits: Part II," pp. 19–20.

is distinctively valuable about rights, even in our own system at the present time.

Granted our earlier point that compensation promotes efficiency in reporting and, hence, in enforcing interest-protecting principles, it should come as no surprise that justification for a principle of compensation need not appeal to rights. A utilitarian system, or indeed any system that values efficiency, would find compensation attractive, even if such a system had no use for rights.

3. The thesis that rights play an indispensable role in distinguishing those moral principles that can justly be enforced from those that cannot is ambiguous, lending itself to four quite different interpretations. (1) A valid claim of right is sufficient justification for enforcement (if enforcement is not only sufficient but necessary to avoid violations of the right). (2) A valid claim of right constitutes a *prima facie* case for enforcement (if enforcement is not only sufficient but necessary to avoid violations of the right), and thus shifts the burden of proof to those who would deny that enforcement is justified. (3) A valid claim of right is necessary for justified enforcement (i.e., only rights principles can justly be enforced). (4) Enforcement of a principle is justified only if that principle is a rights principle or if it is a non-rights principle whose enforcement would violate no rights.

The first interpretation may be eliminated, for at least two reasons. First, when rights conflict, not all of them can be enforced. Second, even those celebrants of rights who emphasize the idea that rights trump appeals to what would maximize utility admit that in some (presumably rare) cases valid claims of right must give way in order to avoid enormous disutility.

The second interpretation certainly seems to capture at least part of the connection between rights and enforcement. Indeed, some theorists, including Mill, tend to define rights as something that society ought to guarantee for the individual. A presumption of enforceability seems natural enough, granted the trumping feature. If rights are such important items that protecting them requires foregoing gains in social utility, then it is not surprising that we believe they should be protected, by force if necessary, absent some substantial reason for not doing so.

The more interesting question is this: what kinds of considerations defeat the presumption that rights may be enforced in cases where enforcement is necessary to avoid violations of rights? One plausible place to begin is with the suggestion that the presumption is *not* defeated by the mere fact that non-enforcement would maximize social utility. My purpose here, however, is not to develop a theory of the justified enforcement of rights but rather to see whether the connection between rights and justified enforcement is so close that the need for justified enforcement makes rights uniquely valuable. The mere fact that the existence of a right constitutes a *prima facie* case for enforcement does not go very far toward showing that rights are indispensable. It would do so only if there were no serviceable non-rights-based arguments for enforcing moral principles.

The third interpretation, though more plausible than the first, is nonetheless insupportable, or at least not adequately supported by those who assume or assert it. There is indirect evidence that claim (3) is widely held. Almost without exception, those who argue that legal entitlements to goods or services are morally justified do so by arguing that there are moral rights to the goods and services in question. Their opponents, again almost without exception, attack the claim that legal entitlements to "welfare" are morally justified by arguing that there is no moral right to the goods and services in question. A plausible explanation of this behavior is that both sides assume that a legal right to X can only be adequately justified by showing that there is a moral right to X; in other words, that only (moral) rights principles are enforceable. A case in point is the debate over whether there is a sound moral justification for a legal right to a "decent minimum" of health care (or to resources for obtaining a "decent minimum" of health care).[7] The implicit assumption in this dispute seems to be that an enforced "decent minimum" policy, if it is morally justified, must rest upon a moral right to health care, either as a basic moral right or as a derivative moral right based on something more fundamental, such as a moral right to equal opportunity.

The assumption that only rights principles are enforceable, however, seems to be an unsupported dogma. There is at least one rather widely recognized type of argument for enforcement that provides a serious challenge to the assumption that only rights principles may be enforced: principles requiring contribution to certain important "public goods" in the technical sense. It is characteristic of public goods (such as energy conservation, pollution control, and national defense) that if the good is supplied it will be impossible or unfeasible to exclude non-contributors from partaking of it. Hence each individual has an incentive to withhold his contribution to the achievement of the good, even though the net result will be that the good is not achieved. Enforcement of a principle requiring everyone to contribute may be necessary to overcome the individual's incentive to refrain from contributing by imposing a penalty for his own failure to contribute.

In some instances, enforcement is needed not only to overcome the

---

[7] See, for example, D. Gauthier, "Unequal Need: A Problem of Equity in Access to Health Care"; N. Daniels, "Am I My Parents' Keeper", and N. Daniels, "Equity of Access to Health Care," all in *Securing Access to Health Care, Volume Two: Appendices, Sociocultural and Philosophical Studies Report of the President's Commission for the Study of Ethical Problems in Medicine and Biomedical and Behavioral Research*, Government Printing Office, Washington, D.C. 1983.

individual's incentive not to contribute to some good, but also to ensure that contributions are appropriately *coordinated*. To take one familiar example, enforcement of the "rule of the road" ("drive only on the right") is needed not only to ensure that all will contribute to the goal of safe driving but also to coordinate individuals' efforts so as to make attainment of that goal possible. Or, more accurately, in cases of this sort, a certain kind of coordinated collective behavior just is the public good in question. To argue that enforcement of principles of contribution is sometimes justified when necessary for the provision of important public goods, it is *not* necessary to assume that anyone has a moral (or legal) right to the good, whether it be safe-driving conditions, energy conservation, freedom from toxic wastes, or adequate national defense. If one believes, as I do, that there are at least some cases in which public goods arguments justify enforced contribution principles, in the absence of a right to the good in question, then one must reject the sweeping thesis that only rights principles can justly be enforced.[8]

To admit that some enforced principles requiring contributions to public goods are morally justifiable (in the absence of a right to the good) is not, however, to say that whenever a public good problem exists, enforcement is justified. First of all, since enforcement, even if not always an evil, is never a good thing, public goods problems generate enforceable principles only if the good cannot be attained by other, less undesirable means (e.g., moral exhortation, leading others to contribute by one's example, etc.). Second, and perhaps even more obviously, enforcement is not justified if the cost of enforcement is not surpassed by the benefit of attaining the good in question. Third, even when the preceding two conditions are satisfied, a further limitation may be needed to restrict the scope of public goods arguments for enforcement, simply because the class of things which can qualify as public goods is so extremely large that overuse of this type of argument for enforcement may result.

At this point, the attractiveness of the fourth interpretation of the thesis that rights are necessary for making a distinction between those principles that can rightly be enforced and those which cannot becomes apparent. On that interpretation, the connection between rights and enforcement is more subtle: if a principle can rightly be enforced, then either (a) it must itself be a rights principles or, (b) if it is not a rights principle, its enforcement must not violate any rights. Clause (b) places an important additional and very reasonable restriction on the scope of public goods arguments as justifications for enforcement.

---

[8] For an elaboration and defense of the view that problems of collective action provide sound, non-rights-based arguments for enforced principles requiring contributions see A. Buchanan, "The Right to a 'Decent Minimum' of Health Care," forthcoming in *Philosophy & Public Affairs*.

It is not difficult to see why the libertarian might mistakenly think it is virtually self-evident that coerced contributions are justified only if someone has a right to the good in question. For the libertarian may reason as follows. "Everyone has a basic moral right against coercion (i.e., a right to negative liberty). The only thing morally weighty enough to justify infringement of this right against coercion would be another basic moral right. Therefore, if enforced contribution (to collective goods) is ever morally justified, then its justification presupposes that individuals have a moral right to the good in question." My criticism of this libertarian view is straightforward. The claim that there is a general moral right against coercion (or to negative liberty) is non-question-begging only if the right in question is viewed as a presumptive moral claim, (i.e., a *prima facie* right) rather than as a justified moral claim (i.e., a right, all things considered). In other words, if the libertarian supports his premise that there is a general right against coercion (or to negative liberty) merely by an appeal to our moral intuitions, but views the right as a justified moral claim rather than as a *prima facie* right or moral presumption, he begs the question against the non-libertarian. For the non-libertarian can simply point out that his moral intuition is that a general moral right against coercion is simply too unlimited a right to be plausible. In other words, the non-libertarian can say that though he finds a strong presumption against interference to be intuitively plausible, he does not find intuitively plausible the much stronger claim that there is a moral right against coercion, if this claim entails that the only thing morally weighty enough to justify coercion is a basic moral right. Yet, if the libertarian admits that an appeal to our moral intuitions only supports a *prima facie* general moral right against coercion, then he cannot assume that the *only* consideration morally weighty enough to defeat this presumption would be a moral right (to receive some good).

Indeed, the non-libertarian can even admit that there is a right against coercion (not just a *prima facie* right) – but he can argue that when it comes to specifying the scope and content of this right, one morally relevant consideration is the need to overcome barriers to successful collective action. Once the proper content and scope of the right against coercion have been determined, it may *then* be correct to say, with respect to the *specified* right, that only another basic moral right could justify its infringement. What the libertarian overlooks is the possibility that in moving from the intuitively plausible assumption that there is a *prima facie* right to negative liberty or against coercion to a specification of the scope and limits of that moral right, non-rights-based considerations – including the need to use coercion to secure certain important collective goods – may be legitimate.

In sum, the libertarian's premise that there is a general moral right to negative liberty (i.e. against coercion) may be understood either as a claim about a *prima facie* right or as a claim about a right *tout court*, (i.e., a right all things considered). If the former, then the premise is intuitively plausible, but it does not follow that the only thing morally weighty enough to override the (merely *prima facie*) claim to negative liberty (against coercion) is a moral right. If the latter, then it may be true that only a moral right would be weighty enough to override the (justified) claim to negative liberty or against coercion, but the premise that there is a right to negative liberty or against coercion is not something which the libertarian can support simply by an appeal to intuition. It appears, then, that the libertarian cannot support his assumption that coerced contribution is justified only when there is a right to the good in question, by an intuitive appeal to a right to negative liberty or against coercion. Instead, he is stuck with the onerous task of providing a principled justification for a right (not a mere *prima facie* right) to negative liberty or against coercion that is so unlimited as to rule out *in principle* attempts to justify coercion for the provision of collective goods (public goods, coordinated beneficence). To my knowledge no libertarian theorist has successfully executed this task.

The purpose of our investigation of the connection between rights and enforcement was to determine whether rights are indispensable for distinguishing between those principles that can rightly be enforced and those which cannot. We have seen that rights can serve a valuable function in providing a *prima facie* justification for enforcement. We have also seen that although rights are not indispensable in the sense of providing the only basis for enforcement, they may play an important role in restricting the scope of non-rights-based justifications for enforcement.

One question remains: even if rights principles provide one plausible way of restricting the scope of non-rights-based justifications for enforcement, could the needed restriction be achieved equally well by non-rights principles? If, as I suggested earlier, the utility-trumping feature is at best necessary, but not sufficient, for a principle's being a rights principle, then the answer seems to be in the affirmative. A utility-trumping principle which merely protected certain interests from being subordinated to the pursuit of utility, without including any of the other features associated with rights, would provide a significant restriction on the scope of public goods arguments for justified enforcement.

4. Some writers, including Richard Wasserstrom, have held that at least part of what is distinctively valuable about rights principles is that they express the idea that something is *owed* to the individual, that something is the individual's *due*, or that he is *entitled* to something. Wasserstrom considers the case of a racist who fails to recognize that Negroes have rights and then emphasizes two consequences of this failure. First, the racist's way of conceptualizing Negroes denies to any Negro ". . . the standing to protest

against the way he is treated. If the white Southerner fails to do his duty, that is simply a matter between him and his conscience."[9] Second, failure to recognize that Negroes have rights ". . . requires of any Negro that he make out his case for the enjoyment of any goods. It reduces all of *his* claims to the level of request, privileges and favors."[10]

Wasserstrom's example is graphic. Nonetheless, the conclusions he draws from it do not fully capture what is distinctive about the notion that what is mine as a matter of right is *owed* to or *due me*, or that I am *entitled* to it. Consider Wasserstrom's first claim. Is it true that one can protest the way one is being treated only if one is owed (or entitled to) a different sort of treatment, where being owed (or being entitled to) is not reducible to someone else's being obligated to treat you in a certain way? Suppose that there is a legal system of interest-protecting principles, including prohibitions against murder, but that this system does not base the prohibitions in question on any notion of a right not to be murdered. If you threaten to kill me or if you kill my friend, surely I have a basis – namely, the existence of the publicly recognized prohibition – for protesting your behavior.

Further, if the prohibition is enforced, your failure to heed it will not simply be a matter between you and your conscience; instead, it may be a matter between you and the hangman. So contrary to Wasserstrom's first point, it is simply not true that rights provide the only basis for an individual's having standing to protest certain forms of behavior in such a way as to achieve enforcement or punishment. Under a system of interest-protecting principles, I can be effective in protesting your behavior as being prohibited and invoking enforcement of the laws you have violated, without having to establish that your behavior has failed to measure up to what you owe me or what you owe any other individual.

Wasserstrom's second point is equally unconvincing because it confuses two distinctions. The first distinction is between demanding something and requesting it; the second is between demanding something *as one's due* and demanding it as being required by some recognized system of laws or principles. If the notion of something's being one's due is unique to the concept of a right, then a system in which rights are not recognized is one in which one is not able to demand something as one's due. But it does not follow that in such a system you cannot make demands and, instead, are reduced to making mere requests. In the legal system described above, you need not merely request that you not be murdered; you can demand that the power of the law be brought to bear against the one who threatens you with

[9] R. Wasserstrom, "Rights, Human Rights, and Racial Discrimination, in *Rights*, edited by D. Lyons (Belmont, California: Wadsworth Publishing Company, 1979), p. 56.
[10] *ibid.*, p. 57.

murder and you can say to that individual that he is prohibited from killing you, not just that it would be awfully nice of him if he didn't.

Though this is only a conjecture, Wasserstrom may have gone astray, here, by uncritically assuming that only rights principles may be enforced. For if it were true that only rights principles may be enforced, and if it were also true that one can demand only what may be enforced, then it would follow that without rights one could make requests but not demands. We have seen, however, that at least the first premise of this argument is false.

If neither of the two features Wasserstrom emphasized does the job, how are we to capture the notion that a right is an entitlement or that what is a matter of right is due or owed to one; and what, if anything, is uniquely valuable about this peculiar notion? Part of what is crucial to the notion that I am owed or entitled to something, or that it is my due, is the idea that *I*, or my good, or my interests, constitute an independent *source* of moral (or legal) requirements.

Yet, the idea that the individual is an independent source of requirements is not by itself sufficient to distinguish rights, simply because it also applies to some moral requirements regarding others, in particular, duties of beneficence, where there are no correlative rights. If I ought to advance your interests or satisfy your needs, then your interests or needs are the *focus* of my duty – I have a duty regarding them. But if I ought to advance your interests or satisfy your needs only because doing so will advance my own or someone else's good, then your interests are not the *source* of my duty, even though they are the focus of it.

The moral principle of beneficence, as I understand it, implies particular duties to individuals in need under certain circumstances (Jones is in need and I can help him without excessive costs to myself, etc.). When those circumstances obtain, it is my duty to help this particular individual, Jones, because *he* is in need, not simply because doing so may serve interests other than Jones'.

In this sense, if I ought, as a matter of beneficence, to help you, then it is not just that I ought to do something regarding your interests; there is a sense in which your interests are the source, not merely the focus, of the requirement. I ought to help you because *you* are in need, independently of whether in doing so I would fulfill anyone else's needs or advance anyone else's interest or good. Nonetheless, it is still true that you have no right to my aid, that you are not entitled to it.

My suggestion is that we can best appreciate what the notion of "owedness" or entitlement adds to the idea that the individual (or his needs or interests or good) is an independent source of moral (or legal) requirements if we concentrate on two facts which have so far gone unremarked in my analysis. First, when one is not treated as one is entitled or is not accorded what one is owed, one is wronged; second, if one is owed or entitled to something, certain excuses for nonperformance are ruled out which might be acceptable in the case of non-rights-based requirements, such as duties of beneficence.

The judgment that you have violated my right and thereby wronged me has certain implications which the judgment that I have failed to give you something you ought to have, or failed to treat you as you ought to be treated, does not have, even in cases in which you (or your interests or good) are the source of the requirements in question. The judgment that you have wronged me implies a presumption that you ought to provide restitution, compensation, or at least apologies *to me.* This is not the case if you merely fail to fulfill a non-rights-based requirement, such as a duty of beneficence. If your duty toward me has a correlative right, then your failure to fulfill that requirement *changes your moral (or legal) relationship to me* in ways in which your failure to fulfill a non-rights-based requirement does not. Further, as we saw earlier, if rights provide a *prima facie* justification for enforcement, then the fact that you have wronged me (violated my right) may also *change your relationship to others* in the community at large by creating a presumption, though often a rather easily rebuttable one, that you may now be penalized, or that your liberty may now be limited, in ways that would have been impermissible had you not wronged me.

If I ought to give you food because you are hungry, but you are not entitled to the food, the fact that I *prefer* to give the food to another needy person may be an acceptable excuse for my not giving it to you, even if there is an enforceable, publicly recognized principle stating a requirement that I render aid to the needy. However, if you are entitled to the food as a matter of right, my preference, as such, is irrelevant to the moral (or legal) assessment of my not giving you the food.

We now at last can understand how the recognition that Negroes have rights changes things in Wasserstrom's example. As we saw earlier, it is not that the recognition of rights alone makes it possible for the Negro to protest the way he is being treated or to invoke the power of the law against his oppressor; nor does the lack of a recognition of rights necessarily reduce him to making requests, rather than making demands, if the laws in question impose strict requirements. But even though the Negro can invoke enforceable prohibitions against the racist, and is not limited to asking favors, there are some things he cannot do unless he has rights. He cannot correctly claim that the racist's failure to fulfill certain requirements *itself* changes the relationship between him and the racist so that the presumption is that the racist is required to offer restitution or compensation or at least apologies to him. Further, if the Negro is entitled to be treated in certain ways and is wronged if he is not, then certain kinds of excuses for noncompliance with the requirements in question will not be available to the racist. Finally, if the racist fails to accord the Negro what he is entitled to or owed, then this failure itself constitutes a *prima facie* case for enforcing the requirement, even in the absence of any previously existing enforcement arrangements.

5. Perhaps the most suggestive and influential formulation of the thesis that respect for persons is or entails recognition of their rights is that offered by Joel Feinberg. Feinberg states that (a) ". . . respect for persons . . . may simply be respect for their rights . . ." It is not clear how much weight Feinberg intends the term "person" to bear, here. If "person", here, means "moral agent" or if personhood at least entails moral agency, then (a) is incompatible with another thesis that Feinberg also endorses: (b) some animals who are not moral agents have rights (and we can and should show respect for their rights).[11] According to Feinberg, a being can have rights if (and only if) it is a source of claims, i.e., if (and only if) its interests can be represented. Hence, those beings, and only those beings, that have interests, that have a good of their own, can have rights.

The difficulty is this. If some nonpersons (i.e., animals who lack moral agency) have rights and if it is possible for us to respect those rights, then respecting rights (or recognizing a being as a right-holder) cannot *itself* entail, much less be equivalent to, showing respect for persons, as persons. If personhood simply is moral agency or if moral agency is distinctive of persons, then it is clear that respect for persons as such must involve recognition of their distinctive capacities *as moral* agents. But recognizing a being as having interests that are an independent source of claims does not itself involve recognition of any capacities of moral agency.

Since on Feinberg's own analysis, merely recognizing a being as a right-holder implies nothing at all about moral agency, respect for rights neither can be nor can entail respect for personhood. Feinberg's view is, of course, compatible with the claim that recognition of certain rights, namely, those which presuppose moral agency, such as a right of self-determination, shows respect for persons. But this latter claim is clearly a retreat from the more exciting proposal that respect for persons just is respect for their rights.

Although merely respecting a being's rights does not itself show respect for that being as a moral agent (and hence as a person), it is, nonetheless, true that when we show respect for a person as a moral agent this characteristically involves respecting his rights. We need an explanation of why this is so. The explanation rests upon an account of the difference between a being with interests and a person.

To say that moral agency is what distinguishes persons from other beings

---

[11] J. Feinberg, "The Nature and Value of Rights," in *Rights*, ed. D. Lyons; (Belmont, California; Wadsworth Publishing Company, 1979), p. 87.

who have interests is not terribly informative unless something is done to fill out the concept of moral agency. Here I can only offer a sketch. "Moral agency," as I understand the term, is short-hand for a set of capacities, including not just the capacity to assess the suitability of means to given ends, but also the capacity to evaluate ends. It includes the capacity to act for reasons, and the capacity to evaluate reasons for acting as well. A moral agent can ask himself whether a reason is a good or sufficient reason for acting.

A moral agent is more than a being who has interests. To put the point somewhat paradoxically, a moral agent, can *take an interest in his interests,* in the sense that he possesses the higher-order capacity to criticize, evaluate, and revise his interests. Moral agency, on this view, is that kind of practical rationality which enables a being with interests to distinguish himself from the interests that he happens to have at a particular time, or on the other hand, to identify with certain interests. To say that a being is a moral agent is to say that his behavior and even his attitudes and dispositions are subject to moral assessment because he is subject to moral requirements. Only a being who can stand in a critical relationship to his interests can be subject to moral requirements.

Although what distinguishes a moral agent from a mere being with interests is that he stands in a critical relationship to his interests, we show respect for a being as a moral agent by acknowledging principles that protect his interests. It is because capacities of moral agency are manifested only in the evaluation, revision, and pursuit of interests, that protection of interests can count as respect for persons as moral agents.

Now in our society, the protection of an individual's interests and, hence, the recognition of him as a being who stands in a critical relation to his interests, is achieved, at least in great part, by adherence to principles that specify his rights. It does not follow, however, that the needed protection of interests can be achieved only by rights principles. As I argued earlier, there seems to be no conceptual or pragmatic barrier to a system of enforceable, utility-trumping, interest-protecting principles which lack the other characteristics that are thought to be distinctive of rights.

We are still left with a puzzle. Why would a theorist like Feinberg, who views rights principles primarily as especially valuable devices for protecting individuals' interests and, consequently, draws the reasonable conclusion that rights are sometimes correctly ascribed to lower animals who lack moral agency, be tempted to assert the incompatible thesis that respect for persons just is respect for their rights?[12] And regardless of whether Feinberg's view is consistent, if we concentrate on the interest-protecting characteristics of

[12] J. Feinberg, "The Rights of Animals and Unborn Generations," in *Rights, Justice and the Bounds of Liberty* (Princeton, N.J.: Princeton University Press, 1980), pp. 165–167.

rights, especially the utility-trumping feature, why should anyone balk even for a moment at the propriety of ascribing rights to nonpersons, such as dogs?

The puzzle disappears if we distinguish between two questions: (a) can we coherently ascribe rights to beings who lack moral agency; and (b) are we morally justified in ascribing rights to beings who lack moral agency? If, like Dworkin, we concentrate on the idea that rights trump appeals to utility and are primarily devices for protecting an individual's interests, then we must answer the first question affirmatively, as Feinberg does.

An affirmative anwser to the first question, however, does not preclude a negative answer to the second. A distinctive feature of Kantian moral theories is that they maintain that only moral agents have rights. On such a view only the interests of moral agents are of such moral significance that they warrant the especially strong protections afforded by rights. Or, perhaps more accurately, it is only because certain interests are the interests of moral agents that they should be protected so stringently.

A crucial element of Kantian moral theory, then, is the thesis that only those beings who are *subject to* moral requirements, are also the proper *objects* of those especially stringent interest-protecting principles we call rights principles. Thus, a Kantian can admit that while it is conceptually coherent to ascribe rights to any being who has interests that can be protected, it is nonetheless true that respect for persons just is respect for rights. For if one believes, as the Kantian does, that rights can justifiably be ascribed only to moral agents and only in virtue of their moral agency, and if one identifies moral agency with personhood, then one will conclude that respecting an individual's rights just is respecting him as a person. Whether or not one will conclude that proper respect for persons can *only* be shown by respecting their rights will depend upon whether one thinks there are other ways of adequately acknowledging the distinctive moral importance of moral agents. I raise this question, but cannot hope to answer it here.

6. Surprisingly enough, the fact that the right-holder can invoke or not invoke or waive his right has received relatively scant attention in recent celebrations of the distinctive value of rights. However, at least two contemporary philosophers have stressed this feature: Joel Feinberg, in a "Postscript" to the paper discussed in Section 5,[13] and Theodore M. Benditt, in his book, *Rights*.[14]

Feinberg proposes to "supplement" his account of the distinctive role of rights and "to correct some of its emphases" by pointing out that because right-holders are not always obliged to exercise their rights, rights make supererogatory conduct possible. Now, it may be true that if, as a matter of

[13] ibid., pp. 156–158.
[14] T. Benditt, *Rights*, pp. 45–50.

right, you owe me something, but I refrain from exercising my rights even though it would be greatly to my advantage to do so, my conduct is supererogatory. However, it does not follow that supererogation is possible *only* through the decision to not exercise a right.

Suppose that we lived in a system of laws or moral rules which included the obligation, without correlative rights, of each person to contribute N hours of labor a week to the state or to the deity. If some generous individuals freely chose to contribute N + M hours a week, we might well describe their conduct as supererogatory. It seems, then, that even if some forms of supererogation presuppose the non-exercise of a right, others do not. And it is certainly not clear that a society which lacked only those forms of supererogation which presuppose rights would be seriously morally defective.

It might be replied on Feinberg's behalf that the act of supererogation in my hypothetical example does presuppose at least one right, the right to devote one's 'extra' labor-time to purposes other than that of serving the deity or the state. This, however, appears to be stretching a point toward triviality. It seems more accurate to say that in the society in question there is a list of obligations (without correlative rights), along with the understanding that it is permissible to do whatever one is not obligated not to do. Should one insist on saying that this amounts to a right to do whatever one is not obligated not to do, this will still fall short of showing that life without rights – i.e., without a set of substantive rights – would be sorely impoverished because supererogation would not be possible.

Benditt believes that rights are especially valuable because they alone make possible a very useful distinction between what one ought morally to do, all things considered, and what one is morally required to do. For example, it may be that what I ought morally to do, all things considered, is to forgive your debt to me. However, since I have a right to what you owe me, I may nonetheless insist that you repay me, even though, all things considered, I ought not. Benditt's point is, in a sense, the mirror-image of Feinberg's: for Benditt, rights are important because they provide a moral justification for less than morally optimal behavior, including selfish or stingy behavior.

Benditt thinks that a morality which includes rights, and thus provides a justification for departures from what is morally optimal, has several advantages. (a) Without the discretion which rights allow, morality would be over-demanding – it would fail to take into account the unavoidable weaknesses of human personality. (b) The freedom to depart from the morally optimal, which rights provide, can serve as a kind of "safety valve" for "self-assertion within a framework of requirements often seen and felt as oppressive and quasi-coercive." (c) A morality which recognized no justified departures from what is the morally best thing to do "would frustrate individual goals and life plans."[15]

What Benditt fails to see is that even though rights have all of these advantages, a non-rights system might attain them just as well. Instead of a rather extensive and, hence, demanding moral code, softened with loopholes provided by rights, there is the option of having a less extensive code consisting of a rather undemanding and narrow set of obligations, without any rights. Benditt wrongly assumes that the needed latitude for individual choice must be located *within* the moral code. An alternative is to constrict the moral code itself and make room for a great deal of discretion in matters not covered by morality.

I agree with both Feinberg and Benditt that part of what is distinctively valuable about rights is that they may be invoked or not invoked or waived. However, in my view the *unique* advantages of this feature of rights are different from any of those which they cite. The ability to invoke or not invoke or to waive one's right is uniquely valuable because it (a) makes possible certain efficiencies which are not available in a pure obligation system; (b) allows rights to function as *non-paternalistic* protections of the individual's interests, and, indeed, allows rights to function as *non-paternalistic protection against paternalism;* and (c) avoids a situation in which every instance of the nonperformance of an enforceable duty constitutes a *prima facie* case for complaints against the enforcement mechanism.

The first point, though rather obvious, has not to my knowledge been emphasized by philosophical rights theorists. If A can release B from an obligation by A waiving his right (or by A simply not insisting on B's performance by not invoking his (A's) right), A can sometimes gain more than if he insists on his right. In fact, in some cases both parties may be better off if the right holder is able to release the other party from an obligation.

It would be possible, of course, to have an arrangement whereby some third-party judge would be able to release B from his obligation, but the judge's decision would have to be made in either of two ways. Either the judge would release B from-his obligation if and only if A wished him released, in which case the added cost of having a judge would be sheer waste; or the judge's decision to release B would be independent of A's wishes. The obvious difficulty with the second option is that it would render the whole arrangement much less valuable for anyone in A's position because one would no longer be able to rely upon B's performing (if one wishes him to). Such an arrangement would be about as satisfactory as a system in which one can refuse to do what one has promised to do whenever

[15] *ibid.*, p. 47.

refusal would maximize social utility. In both systems obligations would not provide a reliable framework for expectations. The ability to invoke or not invoke or waive a right allows enough flexibility for efficiency, without sacrificing stability and predictability.

It is also important to emphasize what may be called the essentially anti-paternalistic character of rights. On this view, valid claims of right trump not only appeals to *social* utility-maximization, but also appeals to what would maximize *the right-holders's own utility*. To borrow Hume's example, I must return my profligate friend's money to him, even though doing so will result in his financial ruin, because he has a right to it. Thus, rights, even without the ability to waive them, provide protections against paternalistic interventions. Without the ability to waive, however, a system of enforceable rights may itself be paternalistic. For example, if I have a right to informed consent for medical treatment, but I am not permitted to waive that right in order to authorize my trusted physician to make certain decisions without consulting me, my autonomy to restrict my autonomy is limited by the very right that was designed to enhance it. A waivable right provides a non-paternalistic barrier against paternalistic interventions because it allows the right-holder to raise or lower the barrier at will. To the extent that respect for persons entails recognition of their autonomy, ascribing *waivable* rights to individuals does show respect for persons as such.

Finally, the third distinctive attraction of rights, so far as they may be invoked or not invoked or waived, can best be appreciated if we again consider a system lacking this feature. In some cases, nonenforcement of a generally useful law may be highly beneficial. Some flexibility is desirable. But in a system of enforceable obligations (without correlative rights) the failure of B to do what he is obligated to do *ipso facto* raises questions about the nonarbitrariness and effectiveness of the enforcement mechanism. In such a system, flexibility comes at a price: a burden of proof must be borne to show that this instance was a justifiable exception to a valid principle specifying an obligation. Otherwise, the legitimacy of the enforcement system is impugned.

In contrast, if A has freely and knowingly waived his right (or perhaps even merely refrained from exercising it when he had every opportunity to do so), B's nonperformance does not even trigger *prima facie* concern about the effectiveness or fairness of the enforcement mechanism. Flexibility is achieved without the cost of showing that this particular nonperformance was a justified exception to a valid principle of obligation.

Conclusion

The most fundamental disputes in contemporary moral and political philosophy are viewed as conflicts between competing theories of rights, the assumption being that rights are uniquely valuable and, hence, indispensable. Considerable confusion exists, however, as to what the distinctive features of rights are and why they are uniquely valuable.

The perennial issue of conflicts between liberty and equality now focuses primarily on the question of whether there is a sound moral justification for positive legal entitlements – legal rights to goods and services – or whether the enforcement of positive rights would unacceptably infringe individual liberty. Both sides of the dispute tend to proceed as if a sound moral justification for positive legal entitlements requires showing that there are moral rights to the goods and services in question. What this suggests is that they share a common assumption, namely, that only those moral principles which are rights principles can justly be enforced. This assumption, I have argued, is based on a misunderstanding of the connection between rights and justified enforcement. While a valid rights principle provides a *prima facie* case for enforcement, the existence of a right is neither necessary nor sufficient for justified enforcement. Rights principles, however, may play a valuable, though not necessarily indispensable, role in restricting the scope of justifications for enforcing requirements that do not themselves rest on moral rights, such as the requirement to contribute to the provision of certain public goods.

This last point has rather surprising implications for the current state of the liberty versus equality debate. It has seemed to many that those, such as Nozick, who claim that there are only negative moral rights enjoy a great strategic advantage over those, such as Rawls, who claim there are positive moral rights. Most simply, the point is that rights to goods and services seem harder to justify than mere rights against interference with liberty. If one assumes that the only sound moral basis for legal entitlements to goods and services is a moral right to them, then those who endorse positive legal entitlements are saddled with a much stronger burden of proof than their adversaries. However, the strategic situation is greatly altered once we acknowledge that there are sound non-rights-based justifications for positive legal entitlements. The burden of proof now shifts to the negative rights theorist to show that otherwise-compelling, non-rights-based arguments for positive legal entitlements are ruled out by negative moral rights. To bear this burden of proof, the negative rights theorist must provide a solid justification for a set of negative moral rights principles and then show that respect for these moral rights is in fact incompatible with enforcing the non-rights-based principles in question.

Some theorists have argued that it is misleading and unfruitful to ask whether equality and liberty are compatible; instead we should ask: What sorts of restrictions on liberty are required by equal respect for persons? Given the further assumption that respect for persons simply is, or at least entails, proper recognition of their rights, we are again brought back to the conclusion that everything depends upon the correct choice of a theory of rights.

Some of those, such as Dworkin, who emphasize this strong connection between respect for persons and recognition of rights focus almost exclusively upon the idea that certain interests ought to be protected even if this means losses in social utility. I have argued that this trumping feature, however, does not seem to be peculiar to rights. There is nothing incoherent or impractical about the notion of interest-protecting principles that override the principle of utility but which include none of the other features associated with rights. To say that one principle trumps another is simply to make an external relational statement about the priority relation between the former and the latter; it tells us nothing of the content of either principle. Moreover, if we concentrate exclusively on the idea that rights protect individuals' interests from appeals to utility, the concept of a person and hence of respect for persons as such, never comes into view. Respect for persons entails proper recognition of their capacities as moral agents, not merely acknowledgement that they are beings with interests.

There is at least one feature associated with the concept of a right which implies moral agency, not just the existence of interests – the idea that the right holder may invoke or not invoke or waive his right. This feature, which seems to be unique to rights, adds several important advantages to the notion that a right is simply an especially strong protector of interests. One is that the ability to release others from obligations by waiving one's rights makes possible certain efficiencies that are not attainable in a pure obligation system. Another is that the ability to waive rights allows interest-protecting principles, including those which protect our interest in self-determination, to function in a non-paternalistic way. Since respect for persons involves respect for their autonomy, recognition of waivable rights is one important way of showing respect for persons.

It has not been my purpose to deny that rights are valuable, nor even to show that rights are not *uniquely* valuable items in our current moral framework. Instead I have tried to examine critically the dogma that rights are so distinctively valuable as to be morally indispensable. I have argued that most of the features which are thought to be peculiar to rights are neither as clear individually, nor as closely related to one another, as is usually thought, and that many of the characteristic functions of rights principles could be fulfilled equally well by a combination of alternative moral principles.

Even if all this is true, however, rights may still be distinctively valuable to us. The best argument in favor of our according a central role to rights principles in morality may be one of simple efficiency. Granted that a number of quite conceptually distinguishable functions have come to be clustered under the concept of a right, it may be most economical to use this concept as we find it, rather than to devise alternatives to do these same jobs.[16]

Philosophy, University of Arizona

[16] I am grateful to Holly Smith for her comments on the issue of what is distinctively valuable about compensation and to Loren Lomasky for helping me to clarify my conclusions in this essay. I am also indebted to Deborah Mathieu for correcting several important errors in an earlier draft, especially in the discussion of the idea that what one has as a matter of right is owed to one.

NEGATIVE LIBERTY

Michael Levin

1. *Freedom*

Philosophers have articulated six notions of human freedom. Four are metaphysical. According to one, a man acts freely when *he is doing what he wants to*; according to the second, he acts freely when he is *not being compelled by outside forces*; according to the third, he acts freely when *the prior state of the universe was not a sufficient cause* of what he is doing; according to the fourth, he acts freely when *he*, not any preceding event, is the cause of what he is doing. The third and fourth theories may be called "indeterministic freedom" and "the agency theory," named only to be rejected. I reject indeterminism out of agreement with a long tradition which holds that (a) there is no reason to think that human actions are ever undetermined, and (b) an undetermined human action would not be "free" in any sense in which we desire our actions to be free and believe that they are in fact free. To appreciate (b), reflect that agents should control and be accountable for "free" actions. Now, we control an event by assembling or obstructing its sufficient conditions; therefore, an event without sufficient conditions, a random event which just happens, would lie beyond human control and, hence, the sphere of human freedom. Similarly, a man is no more responsible for what happens independently of his choices – and an event without sufficient conditions cannot have a choice as a sufficient condition – than he is responsible for the behavior of a roulette wheel.

The agency theory for its part claims that previous events never necessitate a human action, but instead of holding that free human actions have no sufficient causes, it holds that free actions are caused by selves. The window was caused to break by the collision of the hammer with the glass, whereas *I*, not any prior event in my nervous system, cause my fingers to wiggle. Agency theorists emphasize what they take to be the distinctive schema for human action sentences: [Personal name] – [transitive verb] – [noun phrase]; for example "I wiggle my finger." Against the agency theory generally there stands the obscurity of agent causation – since the fields of paradigmatic causal relations are sets of events, little sense attaches to a causal relation whose domain is a set of substances – and, more particularly, against its linguistic argument there stand exact natural-causation counterparts to the agentival language of human action. We often say, after all, that *the hammer* broke the window. To be sure, "The hammer broke the window" is equivalent to "Some event involving the hammer caused the window to break," but if agent language gives way to evential language here, the corresponding evential explication of human-agent language is surely in order. "An event involving me caused my finger to wiggle" is an adequate paraphrase of "I wiggled by finger."

The first two theories stand, with a little bolstering. Both must accommodate compulsive desires, post-hypnotic suggestions, and other manifestations of will that seem somehow "alien." I have elsewhere[1] argued at length that a man acts freely when he acts from desires he tacitly approves of himself having. In Lawrence Davis' more graceful formulation, a man is free when he acts from desires he doesn't mind having.[2] A parallel analysis of "internal compulsion" rescues freedom conceived as non-compulsion from counter examples based on psychopathology. Free will itself, then, becomes the capacity to act on one's chosen desires, or the capacity to act without external and internal compulsion – and, by implication, the capacity to modify one's desires.

The two surviving metaphysical conceptions of freedom have verbal counterparts in political philosophy. It is sometimes said that a man is *positively* free when he is doing what he wants to, and *negatively* free when no one is interfering with him. Negative freedom, that is, consists in the absence of constraint by the rational will of another. Picture a hemophiliac living in rural Alaska who cannot afford to visit a Park Avenue hematologist. On the positive conception of political liberty he is not free to see the specialist, since even though he wants to, he cannot do so. On the negative conception of political liberty, however, he *is* free to visit the specialist because no one is stopping him. Here is a parting of the conceptual ways whose ramifications extend all the way to public policy. People are said, after all, to have a *right to liberty* so strong that the state must protect it. What is more, everyone is said to have an *equal* right to liberty, or a right to equal liberty; liberty is a good the state must not apportion selectively. But the rights of individuals and the correlative duties of other individuals and the state vary considerably with how we understand the liberty to which each man is entitled. If our rightful liberty is negative liberty, the hemophiliac is not suffering any deprivation of his rights. On the positive theory, however, his right to liberty is being violated. His right to equal positive liberty is certainly being violated if someone else can afford to see a famous hematologist. The positive conception of political liberty, conjoined with the right to liberty, entails that he has a right to visit the doctor – and, therefore, a right to the means to get

---

[1] *Metaphysics and the Mind-Body Problem* (Oxford: Oxford University Press, 1979), Chapter VII.
[2] *Philosophy of Action* (New Jersey: Prentice-Hall, 1979).

to the doctor. The negative conception of political liberty, even when conjoined with the right to liberty, entails no such right. Positive and negative liberty yield fundamentally different arrays of rights.

2. *Metaphysical and Political Liberty*

The apparent parallel between our two concepts of political liberty and our two concepts of metaphysical liberty might suggest that each pair is an instance of some more fundamental distinction – positive and negative liberty *simpliciter*. This would be a mistake. The two metaphysical notions are extensionally equivalent, while, as we have just seen, the two concepts of political liberty are not. It is a matter of indifference whether metaphysical freedom, the freedom of the will, is described as doing what one wants or as the absence of hindrances. If I am running because I want to – and am thus free in the positive sense – nothing is stopping me and nothing is forcing me, so I am running freely in the negative sense. If I am not doing what I want to do, something must be hindering me or forcing me to do what I don't want to do. This equivalence obviously depends on not distinguishing, in the definition of negative metaphysical liberty, between interference by other people and unintended hindrances. This is as it should be. I am equally hindered from moving whether pinned under a boulder by a landslide or held down by a bully. There is a moral difference, of course, but not a metaphysical one.

This moral difference, however, is just what prevents rapprochement between the two concepts of political liberty. I have a cause for complaint against the bully that I do not have against the boulder; if the time spent getting out from under the boulder proves costly to me – if I was on my way to my stockbroker – no one owes me restitution, whereas the bully obviously does; and so on. The damage to my *rights* is quite distinct in the two cases, a distinction obliterated if we insist that there is no *moral* difference between an inability due to unintended circumstances and an inability due to the will of another rational agent. To be sure, many people do think that an indigent hemophiliac has a right to see a doctor. They rightly note that he will die whether he is prevented from seeing a doctor by a landslide or a roadblock or lack of funds. But even if such people are right, and the government's obligation to "protect his liberty" extends to subsidizing a trip to New York, those who are funding his trip – the taxpayers – are not obliged to fund it because they actively deprived him of means rightfully his. If the taxpayers owe the hemophiliac his trip, it is not as indemnification – which is the reason the bully owes me money for having wrestled me down. Perhaps, a mature and compassionate society ought not care about this difference, but the difference does exist. That the hemophiliac's "right to liberty" covers m/n dollars from each of n citizens toward his m air fare, just as my "right to liberty" includes damages from the bully, is a substantive moral thesis, and conflating positive and negative political liberty simply obscures the need to defend it. Indeed, so central is the positive/negative distinction for political philosophy and so trivial is the corresponding distinction for metaphysics that I will henceforth use "positive and negative liberty" to mean "positive and negative *political* liberty", and "metaphysical liberty" to refer to positive and negative metaphysical freedom indifferently.

3. *Further Clarifications*

I will soon argue that the proper conception of political liberty is the negative one, that the liberty we have a right to, or are entitled to, is liberty from interference by others. The state is obliged to protect each of us from interference by private parties and, of course, must be careful in its own right not to invade the liberty of private persons. The hemophiliac, in my view, has no right to see the Park Avenue doctor. However, before turning to this constructive task, I want to clarify some further distinctions and confusions.

The contrast between positive and negative liberty is often expressed by the slogan that the former is "freedom to" while the latter is "freedom from." This is a useful mnemonic, so long as the objects of the preposition do not get out of hand. It is all too easy to personify and diabolize any impediment, any condition one does not like, as interference to be freed from. Thus, Hitler promised a *Judenfrei* Germany and Communists promise a world "free from" the seductions of capitalism and its products. An American President once promised "freedom from want" as of a piece with freedom of speech.[3] Now whatever else want may be, or a particular man's want, it is not a rational agent. If freedom from want is subsumed under negative liberty, then all inability becomes something to be "free of" and negative liberty immediately warps into positive liberty. Indeed, the positive liberty thus fabricated is nothing less than full metaphysical liberty, and if the state is guarantor of one's entitlement to liberty, the state becomes the guarantor of whatever one wants.

The presence of metaphysical liberty entails the presence of negative liberty, but the presence of negative liberty does not entail metaphysical liberty. Thus, a man who voluntarily wiggles his finger is not being hindered by anything and, therefore, not being hindered by the will of another, but our hemophiliac is politically free to see a doctor without being able, metaphysically free, to do so. If negative liberty exhausts political liberty, there conceivably can be men – such as a victim of paralysis under police guard – whose political liberties are complete but who are utterly unable to do anything they want. This sounds odd, but it averts greater oddness at other

---

[3] Franklin D. Roosevelt, Message to Congress, Jan. 6, 1941.

junctures. Ernest van den Haag[4] for example, also observes that once "freedom is defined as a positive ability," the way is open for a welfare-maximizing state to push people around in the name of "maximizing freedom." I gave three examples of this tactic in the previous paragraph, and van den Haag cites more modern instances from Lawrence Tribe and Ronald Dworkin. But to forestall such abuses of the notion of positive liberty, van den Haag goes so far as to claim that there is no such thing. He bravely denies that being unable to afford an airplane ticket deprives one of the freedom to fly. I appreciate van den Haag's concern about the cries for government assistance that go up the instant an absence of freedom is discerned, but he forgets that there is a morally neutral sense of freedom – the metaphysical sense – that can be disengaged from the percept that people have "a right to freedom." There is a perfectly straight-forward sense in which a man stuck in the Alaskan wilderness is not free to see a doctor, and it does needless violence to language to deny this. He is unable to see a doctor, and, as English is ordinarily used, "A can do X" is interchangeable with "A is free to do X." One may admit that the man stuck in Alaska is not free to travel without conceding that society or the state owe him air fare. The man has no grounds for complaint because the liberty he lacks is not liberty he is entitled to. It was not taken from him; his unfreedom is nobody's fault, perhaps not even his own.

It should be emphasized that my disagreement with van den Haag is purely verbal: where he says "liberty" I say "negative liberty," and where he says "ability" I say "liberty." That trivial translation maps our views onto each other.

A final point: the terse definition of negative liberty as absence of constraint by the rational will of another overlooks unintended invasions of moral territory. My liberty to do with my lawn as I please is infringed if a discarded cigarette butt sets my lawn on fire, even if the careless smoker did not intend to harm my lawn. The operative factor, in such cases, however, is the failure of the smoker to exercise reasonable caution about the foreseeable consequences of his actions. The definition of negative liberty must, thus, expand to include freedom from the foreseeable consequences of the actions of rational wills. Preserved under this expansion is the essential reference made by negative liberty, negative rights, and all their conceptual cognates to rational agency. My negative liberty has not been infringed by a meteorite which happens to land on my lawn by natural chance.

4. *The Justification of Negative Liberty*

My argument for negative liberty, in a nutshell, is that negative liberty but

---

[4] "Liberty: Negative or Positive?," *Harvard Journal of Law and Public Policy*, 1978, 1, pp. 63–86.

not positive liberty can be shared equally by everybody. It is the *only* form of liberty that can be "distributed equally." Negative liberty ought to be embraced by all lovers of equality, since – beyond its other merits – it alone uniquely satisfies a strong Kantian requirement of universalizability.

Everyone agrees that the *basic* rights of a political community should apply equally to all. Any basic right must be one that all citizens can enjoy simultaneously. This is not a recondite demand – we all recognize for example that everyone is entitled to free speech. On the supposition that no one in the United States is being gagged at this moment, everyone is simultaneously enjoying free speech. Even so harsh a critic of equality and "equal opportunity" as Robert Nozick bases his system on the universal right of free transfer. Indeed, one might explicate the arbitrary exercise of power as the granting of different privileges and immunities to different groups without explaining what distinguishes one group from another. Governments usually oblige young men to serve in their armies, but quickly point out that young men make the best soldiers. Because it is always possible to contrive a distinguishing description for a group about to receive special state attention, the generality requirement is in practice only a regulative principle which cannot decide details of policy – but even so this requirement imposes an important constraint: if the satisfaction of a purported right for some members of a community *entails* that there are other members who *cannot* enjoy this right, the right cannot be basic. Such a "right" offends Kantian moral intuitions in much the way cheating and other forms of freeloading do. According to Kant, immorality means acting from a maxim that the agent cannot coherently will to be universal, either because the universalization of the maxim is itself an absurdity ("Let everyone use counterfeit money") or because there is an absurdity in *willing* it ("Let me commit suicide to escape my troubles, since I'll be much happier if I no longer exist.") The cheater's maxim is clearly of the former sort; in acting on the maxim "Break the rules in order to win," the cheater must also intend that everyone else abides by the rules. Cheating is advantageous only when it allows the cheater a *unique* freedom to maneuver; a wrestler gains nothing from using dirty holds if his opponent uses them also. The core of the cheater's moral offense is adopting a policy that logically requires him to be exceptional. He is counting on everyone else to count on everyone else to obey the rule he intends to break.

Now, your right not to be interfered with can obviously coexist with my right not to be interfered with. Both are respected if neither of us interferes with the other and no one else interferes with either. The enforcement of your right to noninterference by a rights-enforcing mechanism – that is, the state – does not entail the denial or abridgement of anyone else's right to noninterference. Any right, positive or negative, limits the freedom of others to frustrate the exercise of that right, and in particular your right not to be interfered with limits my freedom to interfere with you. However, this is consistent with the imposition of an entirely symmetrical curb on you – you are no longer free to interfere with me. As logicians would put it, our rights are identical up to variation in individual constants. A's having a right to noninterference in the pursuit of A's ends in no way compromises B's identical right to noninterference in the pursuit of B's ends. It is logically possible for all the negative rights of every member of a political community to be satisfied.

This is *not* true of positive rights. If you are guaranteed some concrete good – a shirt, say – no one else can have a right to that good. I cannot have the right of ownership in that same shirt. Only one person can wear that shirt whenever he wants to. (People do own shirts, but as entitlements *derived* from the particular exercise of the universal right to acquire property.) Any conception of rights that exceeds noninterference must play favorites. This is even clearer and more significant for systems of positive rights in society's product, the systems of greatest interest to social philosophers. If you have a right to a portion of the total product of society, I am excluded from having a right to that portion. Such systems not only play favorites, they lead to a Kantian absurdity when pressed toward full generalization. The tendency of such a system to self-destruct is hidden by our tendency to imagine people continuing to work when basic positive rights are invented, and so to imagine that there is always enough for those who claim their rights. But if the claim that people have a fundamental right to (say) subsistence is to mean anything at all, it must mean that you and everyone else can do nothing and yet rightfully demand enough food to stay alive. After all, you don't have to *do* anything, beyond refraining from aggression, to claim a right to free speech. That is what makes free speech a basic right. But there can be sufficient food for some only if others continue to produce, and do not simply throw down their hoes and get in line for their own share of society's product.

A system of subsistence rights, if acted on by everybody, would annihilate itself. The government could enforce the subsistence rights of some only by compelling others to work, and it would be a poor joke to tell farmers that while they, too, had a categorical right to subsistence, they did not have the right to *act* on that right. Communism plays the poorer joke of promising everyone a subsistence portion of the social product and, then, making everyone work to insure that a social product exists. A system of positive subsistence rights need not come to this in practice, since some people will work no matter what, out of habit or pride or ignorance of their entitlements, but that just makes my point all over again: a system of positive rights to the social product requires that some do not claim these rights. It presupposes a distinction between recipient grasshoppers and worker ants. Positive liberties cannot be shared equally; however "egalitarian" they may sound in verbal formulation, they are inconsistent with equality.

No system of assigning positive rights can avoid this result. If the state decides to augment the powers of poor Paul by giving him money instead of concrete goods, it must either take the money from Peter, or occasionally run the state printing presses exclusively for Paul – thereby inflating the currency and again decreasing Peter's purchasing power. Systems of rights to natural objects are equally partial. If I have a right to a grain of sand, you cannot have the same right – a right to that grain of sand. Even if everyone merely has a generalized right to some grain of sand or other, and conflicts are somehow avoided between those who covet the same grain of sand, these rights are simultaneously satisfiable only if there happens to be enough sand to go around. Let enough children be born and the system of general rights will again have to play favorites. It is easy to appreciate the contrast with free speech, for the right of all to speak freely does not require the caveat "as long as there are fewer than n people". Indeed, the situation created by rights to grains of sand is at bottom the same as that in which all claim a right to a portion of society's product. In that previous case, satisfiability of all takers depended on the contingency that enough people would continue to engage in productive work; in the present case, the satisfiability of all takers depends on the coincidence that nature has produced enough sand. Both systems can function only when there are not as many takers as there are entitled to be. No comparable condition limits negative rights, which would remain simultaneously satisfiable were all the galaxies teeming with rational agents.

Let me hark back to the "poor joke" of two paragraphs ago. A number of philosophers have suggested that positive rights can be sustained if conditioned by duties. A system in which each man is guaranteed subsistence *if* he contributes as much as he can to the common good, is said to be coherent and invulnerable to the Kantian objection. Even if this is granted, however, a fundamental difference remains between negative rights and positive rights so conceived. Only negative rights can be universal and unconditional, as good a criterion as any of fundamentality. Such rights as free speech are conspicuously unconditional: guarantees of noninterference with one's efforts at expression are not thought to apply only to citizens who fulfill some further condition. True, one intuitively distinguishes acceptable from unacceptable conditions that may attach to positive subsistence rights, such as "being unable to support oneself through no fault of one's own" as opposed to "having red hair." Whatever one makes of this intuition, it already presupposes that positive rights to the social product must be limited to some segment of the population, which is my central point. And reflect, finally, that a system of even conditional positive rights depends on total contributions to the social product at least equalling the demands of subsistence. Such a system in principle bestows rights to goods that *may not exist*, rights moreover not conditional on the existence of those goods, a situation on its face absurd.

As I have said, the inegalitarian and self-defeating character of basic positive rights goes unappreciated, in part, because of a failure to think through their ramifications. It is due as well, although perhaps to a lesser extent, to a confusion between the *extension* and *intension* of "social product." That foodstuffs must be produced is of course only a contingent fact. They might appear on dinner plates out of nowhere. Thus, it is by no means logically necessary that food must be produced, so it is by no means necessary that universal rights to food are non-Kantian. Yet, while it is a contingency that food is part of the social product, it is not a contingency that the social product, whatever it happens to include, must be the result of human effort, and so the impossibility of universal positive rights to *the social product* is not a contingency. It is not exactly a *logical* impossibility because a social product need not exist, just as men need not have labored to survive. On the other hand, if men had no need to labor, and "labored" only to amuse themselves, there would certainly be no pretended claims on the social product.

5. *Further Observations on this Argument*

I have not discussed the utility of a system of universal positive rights for the sufficient reason that the question is ill-formed – if they do not exist, for Kantian reasons, it is idle to ask if having them is a good or bad thing. It is also the part of conventional philosophical wisdom to distinguish the utility that would be generated by persons acting on a system of rules, from the utility generated by people believing that they ought to act on that system. (A society of Kantians might be happier than a society of doggedly hedonistic utilitarians, so that utilitarians should, in public, advocate Kantianism.) Nonetheless, it is instructive to contrast the *sociological* tendency of negative liberty to expand with the sociological tendency of positive liberty to contract. The less interference there is, the more is fostered an atmosphere of mutual tolerance. The more competition there is for protected access to goods, the more frantic becomes the scramble for privileges. This is why the welfare state has, in less than half a century of existence, proven unstable. As a practical analogue to the Kantian dialectic, its productive base has proven vulnerable to the upward elasticity of the supply of the truly needy. One of the most striking features of the welfare state is its tendency to treat its forces of order – deputized to protect the negative liberties of all – as a special interest in its own right, with its palm extended for its own positive share of the social product. People become accustomed to viewing every claim on the social product as a positive claim – and, since the ostensible constituency of the forces of order is quite small (military officers, arms contractors), this constituency is viewed as especially "greedy" and unworthy of attention. When the Carter Administration became alarmed at its budget deficit toward the end of its tenure, for example, Carter economized by curtailing Coast Guard Patrols.

It is frequently alleged in the popular media that liberty and equality are mutually entailing. Sometimes it is claimed that the welfare state has enhanced the liberty of all without in any way sacrificing the liberty of anyone, and sometimes that, while the liberties of some have, indeed, been curtailed (somebody, after all, has to foot the bill for social services), there has been a net expansion of human liberty. These declarations are due solely to inattention both to the social processes and the logic of the welfare state. These claims embody the notions that "liberty" is identical to "positive liberty," and that income transfer policies are gradually bringing the purchasing powers of the lowliest slum dweller up to that of the wealthiest Rockefeller. Even on these grounds, however, the net amount of liberty is decreasing for the simple reason that transfers of positive liberty are not frictionless. If liberty is functionally equivalent to purchasing power (as it is for liberals), liberty is lost as it flows from the rich to the poor because somebody has to pay the state supervisors of the pipes. These officials themselves contribute nothing to the social product, and their salaries are like thousands of tiny leaks in the pipes through which the money flows. And, as should be obvious, any transfer scheme not only makes those with more purchasing power give some of it to those with less, it also in the end makes the wealthier ones pay for this dubious privilege.

An honest liberal would probably say that, equality being an intrinsically good thing, a net decrease in (positive) liberty is worth its equalization. This, I must emphasize again, is an illusion. In practice, distributions of positive liberty do tend to stabilize at some lowered level of productivity, at least temporarily, since some people keep working and the general population remains satisfied with a partial system of positive legal rights. It is to my mind a completely open question whether the bubble of positive rights enforced by government will not expand until the productive base undergoes a reciprocal implosion.

6. *The State*

Nothing in my Kantian argument assumes that rights, positive or negative, are enforceable. I have used the state as enforcer merely as a heuristic device, to heighten the contrast between universally satisfiable negative rights and unsatisfiable positive rights. However, we do in fact suppose that basic rights, and certainly negative rights, are enforceable. If the state may enforce only basic rights, and the only basic rights are negative, the state may enforce only negative rights. But why are even negative rights enforceable at all? Some rights are clearly unenforceable – I have some right to candor when I ask your opinion of my new tie, but I can hardly sue you if you fib. How if at all did I acquire the further right to stop you by force if you try to gag me, or to deputize the state to stop you?

The general Kantian character of negative rights makes their enforcement by a central power morally *possible*: the state can do it without playing favorites. Everyone's negative rights can be simultaneously enforced because enforcing the negative rights of some spares the negative rights of others. It is moreover a *good thing* for there to be a central power with a known disposition to go after negative rights violators. A negative-rights-enforcing state gives men "public peace" to get on with their lives. In fact, the creation of such an authority is the only good reason that rational men would ever have for leaving the state of nature. Whether rights of noninterference are "natural" and merely safe-guarded by the state (Locke), or created by state decree (Hobbes), confidence that these rights will be respected would prompt rational egoists to transfer their individual powers of self-protection to a central power. The existence of this authority will reduce their gross expenditure of self-protective energy, since as long as A knows that there is a superior power ready to stop B from attacking him, A will be less prepared to launch a preemptive attack against B. Knowing this, B will be less apt to launch a pre-preemptive attack against A, and A can relax further. . . . The state protects negative liberty not by actual enforcement, but by this divisor effect on the mutual perception of threat. On the other hand, rational agents would *not* create a positive-rights-enforcing authority because such an authority could not effect a comparable net savings in the effort needed to secure positive goods. There is no divisor effect by which a central authority can satisfy people's hunger through promising to feed them.[5]

It seems unnecessary to go further in justifying state enforcement of negative liberty. One can hardly want more than a power able to protect negative rights by the unobtrusive expedient of declaring its intention to protect them. Notice that this justification of the state does not rest the central power's right of enforcement on prior individual rights of enforcement, as does Locke's. The state's right to defend individuals is created by the mutual agreement of all to surrender their war-making powers to the state. The agreement is binding because of the prior obligations of individuals to keep their word, but the agreement itself is prompted by pure considerations of utility. The state, thus, acquires no "emergent" right, but it is consistent with this argument that individuals have no prior right to repel invasions by force.

[5] See my: "A Hobbesian Minimal State," *Philosophy & Public Affairs*, Fall 1982, 11 (4).

7. *Objections to Negative Liberty as Exhaustive*

If a baby is abandoned on a public thoroughfare, the negative theory of rights gives him only the right to be left alone. It allows him no right to food or shelter. If indifferent passersby let him die, his rights remain intact. If the police rescue him, they are squandering the taxpayer's money. This hard doctrine does not appreciably soften when applied to destitute adults – a welcome switch away from babies, since determining the mutual obligations of *rational* beings is difficult enough. Imagine, then, that that vagabond who wanders in and out of philosophical examples, having just escaped the act-utilitarian sheriff about to frame and execute him in order to quell a riot, comes to town to meet a chilly reception. Unable to get work or credit from the grocer, he is reduced to sleeping in a ditch, near death from exposure and starvation It seems terrible for the state to refuse to put him on the dole, and conservatives will complain that letting him die will destroy the emotional bonds of community.

It *is* emotionally intolerable to say that the man should be allowed to die, but that does not address the question of whether anyone has the right to coerce others not responsible for his fate to save him. The best way to think through this dilemma is to strip away the layers of bureaucracy which soften the sharp outlines of coercion when the alternative to letting him die is described as "putting him on welfare." Instead of imagining taxes for welfare withheld on your paycheck, imagine someone coming along and making you give the vagabond your overcoat at gunpoint. That's not very tolerable either, and it would not be made much more tolerable by his assuring you that the townspeople had decided by majority vote that he is to force you to hand over your coat, so that everything has been done democratically.

Conservatives are right to emphasize that a society in which the man were left to die is unlikely to endure, and they are right to criticize libertarians for investing everything in a value as spiritually anemic as noninterference, for without a sense of a natural order of which they are a part, men fall into an abyss of meaninglessness. But conservatives are wrong to see coercive compassion as expressing social concern or providing meaning. The problem is not simply that forcing people to help each other does not generate emotional solidarity, but that the social bonds already have frayed beyond repair in a community which must be forced to help the suffering. No act of human will – certainly no act of government – can repair these bonds once they lose their hold. A spiritually exhausted community cannot be revived by design. Libertarians point out that a majority ready to support welfare legislation is already numerous enough to help the needy by their own efforts without need of government intervention. This prompts a quasi-Kantian question: how is welfare possible? Why would a majority ever enact welfare legislation when their own self-coordinated action will be more effective? Very probably, because these majorities no longer feel any communal obligations and are attempting to counterfeit a form of compassion which they fancy will relieve them of further effort. Instead of doing it themselves, they plan on "letting the government do it." Yeats defined rhetoric as "the will attempting to do the work of the imagination"; welfare is a kind of moral rhetoric, the will attempting to do the work of the conscience.

8. *Applications of Negative Liberty*

In this section I consider some issues of public policy which are best understood as conflicts between negative liberty and other values. These conflicts are especially instructive in clarifying negative liberty, since in most of them an invasion of negative liberty is disguised. This ought to displease proponents of invasive measures as much as negative libertarians, since the proponents presumably find some value more compelling than negative liberty and would like to see their favorite a clear victor in battle. That the conflict is seldom frankly admitted, that curtailments of negative liberty are so often and so aggressively advertised as *extensions* of negative liberty, suggests that even its opponents sense that it is overriding in nearly every instance.

To be sure, there have been numerous state actions which conspicuously create positive and, therefore, biassed legal rights. Minimum wage laws, for example, obstruct the freedom of employers to offer certain wages, as well as the less frequently noticed freedom of employees to accept those offers. The practical effect of truncating a range of mutually acceptable bargains, of course, is to decrease general utility. Since an employer would rather hire no one than hire someone at a rate higher than an employee's estimated marginal productivity, minimum wage laws guarantee no one a "decent" wage while guaranteeing unemployment to many. Equal pay laws war similarly with both freedom and utility. Forbidding employers to pay blacks or women less than white males for the same work may seem to enhance the "dignity" of the "protected" populations, but this policy curtails the freedom of employers to make certain offers and the freedom of "protected" parties to accept those offers. It is hard to see how being unable to close an acceptable deal enhances anyone's "dignity," especially when the alternative may be unemployment. A bigoted employer, after all, will simply hire a white if he cannot hire a black for less. Indeed, the difference between his white and black pay scales is as much the wasteful premium he is willing to pay for a white work force as it is a smear. Those distressed at his values can happily be sure that the market will penalize him further by inviting less prejudiced employers to undercut him.

Most violations of negative liberty, however, go unremarked because of public misinformation or sheer conceptual confusion. An example of the former is the common impression that the National Labor Relations Act in the United States gives workers "the right to unionize," a negative liberty, when what it does do is forbid employers from firing employees who organize. The right to join a union always existed but, in pure bargaining situations, actually joining a union has the downside risk that one's employer will exercise his freedom of association by issuing a pink slip. The NLRA, then, guarantees no one's freedom of association; it curtails the employer's freedom of association while creating a positive right in one's job.

The recently resurgent idea of "the right to a job" itself nicely illustrates how confusion can obscure an invasion of negative liberty. The principle of negative liberty is sometimes captured in the aphorism that an act is pemissible so long as it harms no one but the agent. (Even this familiar precept is too broad, since much harm is not wrongful harm. I harm but do not wrong Jones if I counsel his wife to leave him.) It is tempting, then, to represent the voluntary *withdrawal of benefits* as a *wrongful harm*, and thereupon deploy the aphorism as an excuse for forbidding the voluntary withdrawal of benefits. In particular, the courts and (very occasionally) elected officials have forbidden employers to fire employees for what are deemed arbitrary reasons, since "a job is too precious to be destroyed by a capricious supervisor."[6] This completely contravenes the traditional negative libertarian "at-will" doctrine that, consistent with contractual obligations, an employer may fire an employee for "good cause, no cause or even for cause morally wrong."[7] Obviously, an employer who fires an employee makes the employee worse off than the employee would have been had his employer retained him. The great mistake in the "employee rights" doctrine lies in taking this to entail that his employer has harmed him. Put more generally, the offending doctrine assumes that: If, as a result of A's doing X, B is worse off than B would have been had A done Y, A has harmed B. In fact, A has harmed B only if A was *obligated to do Y*, or some other action Z which would have made B as well off as action Y. If A was under no such obligation, A has simply done less for B than he might have, in doing X. I do not harm a starving man if I pass him by without giving him a bite of my sandwich. If everyday I give him some of my lunch and he expects me to continue without benefit of any signal from me that I will do so, I do not harm him the day I terminate my charity. His presuming my continued aid places no obligation

---

[6] David Ewing, "*Do It My Way or You're Fired*," (Wiley, 1983), p. 13. For more on this topic, see my "Do Employees 'Own' Their Jobs?," *Fortune*, Feb. 7, 1983, and "Rights to Public Employment," prepared for the Office of Personnel Management's "Conference on Risk-Taking and Earning Rewards in Federal Employment," June 1983.

[7] *Payne v. Westen and Atlantic Railroad Co.* (13 Lca, 507) *The American Reports*, Vol. XLIX, 1884, 673.

on me. I harm him only if I hit him on the head with a hammer, because that is something I should not do.

This point applies immediately to employment. Julius asks Michelangelo to paint his ceiling, and is so pleased with the job he asks Michelangelo to paint his wall and fix the roof. Such contracts as bind the two extend only to the end of each particular project. One day Julius "fires" Michelangelo, who has come to expect further commissions as a matter of course. Julius dislikes dealing with an ego nearly as large as his own; he no longer wants to be involved in Michelangelo's affairs. Arbitrary though Julius' action may be, he has not *harmed* Michelangelo. This grates against our moral sensibilities because Julius did make Michelangelo worse off than he could have made Michelangelo by associating with Michelangelo further, but Michelangelo has no *right* to associate with Julius. If Julius needs Michelangelo's permission to withdraw from his affairs just as he needs Michelangelo's permission to enter them, Julius is near to becoming Michelangelo's slave.

Other invasions of negative liberty are camouflaged by the ambiguity of rights that could be positive or negative. The "liberty of travel," for example, might mean the negative right to be free of interference in one's attempts to travel, or the positive right to a pot of gold at the end of one's journey to make the trip worthwhile. While the Constitution implies a "right to travel" in the former sense, the Supreme Court endorsed the second interpretation in 1969 when it found New York City's 30-day residency requirement for public assistance in violation of a Constitutional "right to travel." A parallel ambiguity sustains the construction put by the Departments of Transportation, Education, and Health and Human Services on the 1973 Rehabilitation Act, which bars federal aid to programs from which the handicapped are "excluded from participation." While this statute, under a normal interpretation of its language, is directed against institutions which forbid handicapped persons from participating in their activities, the federal bureaucracy ruled in effect that *refusing to assist* the handicapped amounts to excluding them. It promptly added stairs to its list of exclusionary devices – even stairs built before their were wheelchairs that could not negotiate them – thereby ruling that unintentional failure to help the handicapped, sheer obliviousness, is discriminatory. This is why unused concrete ramps now surround every facility in the country connected in any remote way to federal money.

Construing stairs as a device to "exclude" the handicapped illustrates the single most effective smokescreen for invasions of negative liberty: the tendency to reify and then personify the byproducts of private decisions as the work of an actively malevolent force. Once these byproducts are diabolized, forbidding the decisions which caused them is magically transformed into a way of freeing their victims from the evil force. This muddling has distorted the concept of discrimination, perhaps permanently.

The Civil Rights Act is almost universally justified for "freeing blacks from discrimination" and guaranteeing their "right to be free of discrimination."[8] But surely when A chooses not to associate with B – by not hiring him or renting him a room – because of B's color, A is no more depriving B of what is rightfully his than was Julius depriving Michelangelo in a previous example. A may hurt B's feelings, but Julius hurt Michelangelo's feelings, also. A has harmed B only if B had a prior right to bargain with A with reasonable prospect of success. It is not clear how B could have such a right, especially when A retains his right not to bargain with people of his own race. Indeed, if B has a right to force A to bargain with him, the word "bargaining" becomes inappropriate and, again, the word "slavery" takes its place. If B truly wishes to be "free of A's discrimination," his best bet is to avoid A altogether, which by hypothesis would be just fine with A. Laws which compel association in the teeth of dislike might be justified if racial prejudice were virulent enough to threaten the social fabric and thereby the system of liberty itself. It is noteworthy that this utilitarian justification of civil rights legislation is virtually never offered,[9] and that the Supreme Court upheld the Civil Rights Act on the slender reed of a Constitutional "right to dignity." It is an embarassment to this utilitarian argument that quotas, which followed the passage of the Civil Rights Act within nanoseconds, have introduced far more racial and sexual discrimination, all of it state mandated, than existed in the United States when the Civil Rights Act was passed in 1964.

Discrimination, to be sure, is not the utter fiction that "exclusion of the handicapped" is, but it does not invade the negative liberty of others and it is certainly not a force apart from particular human wills. Yet, once the initial conceptual gaffe of regarding discrimination as an intrusion into innocent lives is allowed to stand, it becomes easy to detach discrimination from the human will altogether and turn it into an independent force against which people must be shielded. This is the origin of such grotesqueries as "discriminatory effect," "unintended discriminatory consequence," and "institutional racism." These notions are literally baseless. "Institutional discrimination," for example, ubiquitously invoked to explain low black

---

[8] John Bunzel speaks of "the right to be free of discrimination" in "Rescuing Equality," in P. Kurtz, ed., *Sidney Hook* (Prometheus, 1983), p. 179. This is also the phrase used by Rep. Emmanuel Cellar in the Congressional debates on the Civil Rights Act in 1964; see *Legislative History of Titles VII and XI of the Civil Rights Act*, E.E.O.C., Washington, 1964, p. 328.

　　Even adamant critics of quotas, like Bunzel, prefer to base their opposition on the fictitious right to be free of discrimination or the even more fictitious right of the best-qualified for a job. In my view, no effective case will be mounted against quotas until they are recognized as violating liberty.

[9] Kent Greenawalt tries in *Discrimination and Reverse Discrimination*, Borzoi Books in Law and American Society (New York: Alfred A. Knopf, 1983), but his argument consists in asserting every few pages that civil rights legislation and quotas are good things.

participation in various activities, has no source in the social science literature. Robert Merton introduced the term in the late 1940's to describe the practice of an unprejudiced restaurant owner who bars blacks because his customers refuse to eat with them, but while the restaurant owner himself may not be bigoted, his discriminatory practice does involve discriminatory *intent*. Later writers adopted this usage as if Merton had identified a form of discrimination independent not only of bigotry but intent, when no such phenomenon has ever been identified. "Discrimination" must be the intentional act of a rational being. Whatever else the chromosomes which cause sickle-cell anemia do, they do not discriminate against blacks.

The 1982 Voting Rights Act remains the most egregious use of "unintentional discrimination" to cloak the dismantling of negative liberty. The legal theory that blacks can be deprived of a vote even if no one deprives them means that "discrimination" has occurred if an accidental fire at a polling place in a black neighborhood forces black voters to walk to a polling place in a white neighborhood. As a quite unavoidable consequence of this theory, the Voting Rights Act counts the proportion of black winners in an election as "relevant" to whether black voters have full use of their franchise.[10] It now becomes possible to overturn an election in which everyone voted for whom he preferred because the number of black winners is not high enough.

9. *Summary*

My principal categorical argument in this paper has been that negative liberty alone can be "distributed" equally among all members of a political community. I have not argued that negative liberty is the preeminent value, but I did maintain that conservative criticisms of negative liberty as too harsh or atomistic are beside the point. I have, also, noted a number of cases in which negative liberty has been curtailed in favor of other values, generally with the aid of some obscurantism.

Philosophy, City College of New York

---

[10] See my statement before the Senate Judiciary Committee, *Congressional Record*, Feb. 2, 1982; also my extended presentation in *Legislative History of the 1982 Voting Rights Act*. Thinking the example of the fire might be contrived, I checked it with a Justice Department Lawyer, who told me "We get cases like that all the time."

PREFERENCES OPPOSED TO THE MARKET: GRASSHOPPERS VS. ANTS ON SECURITY, INEQUALITY, AND JUSTICE*

DAVID BRAYBROOKE

"Vous chantiez? j'en suis fort aise./En bien! dansez maintenant." That's what the Ant said, when she refused the Grasshopper a loan to tide her over the winter. La Fontaine's fable, however, is told from the Ant's point of view. It expresses the scorn of the industrious possessive individualist for relatively improvident people who do not take pains to accumulate capital. Admittedly, the Grasshopper is not a good business risk; and in spite of the animus in the manner of the refusal, it is on basic market principles that the Ant refuses to make the loan.

Would it have been different if the Grasshopper had made an effort to accumulate comparable to the Ant's, but had run into a bit of bad luck – fields flooded at harvest time; a barn struck by lightning? No doubt the Grasshopper's promise to repay next year would then have seemed more reliable. At some rate of interest the Ant might have found the risk of lending worth taking.

I think, however, that a Grasshopper who was not anywhere near as committed to accumulation as the Ant might have something rational to say for herself, beginning (and ending) with the protest that Ants are very hard to live with. The Grasshopper might say – might she not? – that singing and dancing were more important than acquiring property. "No doubt," she might concede, "it is important to make provisions for the winter, even provisions for bigger crops next summer. So not everybody can do nothing but sing all summer long; it's only fair that everybody should in fact do his part to provide. But there should be as much singing and dancing as possible for everybody who wants them. Let's be provident enough to make sure that with everybody doing his part together we save enough to cover everybody's

* Delivered at a conference on Philosophy, Economics and Justice held by the University of Waterloo 20–22 May 1983. Other papers from that conference will appear in the next issue of *Social Philosophy & Policy*. I wish to thank Alastair Sinclair, Lanning Sowden, and Sheldon Wein for helpful comments on a preliminary draft. I am also obliged to Jeffrey Paul, who served as the commentator on the paper at Waterloo. I have made a number of additions responding to his points. Bernard Suits' book, *The Grasshopper: Games, Life, and Utopia*, 1978, has given a Grasshopper grounds for claiming to be the *genius loci* at Waterloo, but my Grasshopper and her kin are more humdrum characters.

needs through the winter. That will mean that each of us will have to aim at saving a little more than what each needs, to allow for disasters that prevent some of us from saving as much. Let's all be provident to this degree; and spend the rest of the time enjoying life."

The Ant will want to be yet more provident, maybe to the extent of leading a rigorously frugal life, maybe with due allowance for modest bourgeois comforts. Should she not be allowed to be? Moreover, even if, as I have been implicitly assuming, there will be plenty of time left over for singing and dancing once reasonable provisions for the winter have been undertaken the Grasshopper hasn't yet said how much she wants to do about economic growth. Will she agree to cut down the singing and dancing a lot to provide for growth? Perhaps; but perhaps not. I shall not try to speak for her on this point.

I shall say this: Whatever provision she is willing, as a moderately provident person, to make for hard times or for growth, she can rationally object to providing for these things through the market. In particular, she can object to allowing the Ant to accumulate as freely as the market and uncircumscribed private property will allow her to. But Grasshoppers have other grounds for objecting to the market, especially to a market in which Ants are present; and so if they have the choice, they may choose not to have a market. If they are to live in the same society with Ants, this inclination deserves at least as much weight, person by person, as the inclination of Ants, which I shall assume is opposed, and favors the market. Even if the Grasshoppers go apart, to form their own joyous society, the Ants will create trouble for them. Finally, the Ants will create trouble for themselves if they do not take some of the same precautions that the Grasshoppers are concerned with.

The Grasshoppers' objections to the market might come up at any time. I shall treat them as coming up at the foundation or refoundation of society on rational terms, under some hypothetical construction congenial to social contract theorists. I do so without endorsing any of the programs adopted in social contract theory. On the other hand, I do so as one who has found them more congenial than theories that begin with sacrosanct *a priori* entitlements, and especially illuminating – in success or failure – on the extent to which rational self-interest can serve as the foundation of ethics. My special target in this paper is the inclination of some contract theorists (notably, David Gauthier) to hold that the market would beyond question be accepted by rational contracting agents as the most suitable means of producing and distributing private goods.[1] Gauthier is inclined to think that given accepted initial factor endowments the market is beyond question in respect to justice

---

[1] David Gauthier, "Justified Inequality?," *Dialogue*, 1982, 21(3), pp. 431–443, at p. 433.

or other moral considerations: no moral issue arises from the operation of the market. Other philosophers (notably, Robert Nozick) supply me with a secondary target in being inclined, with or without any reference to the social contract, to think that transactions in the market are a prototype of justice: provided the goods exchanged were rightly held to begin with, whatever comes about through a fair exchange is just.[2] I think this, too, is highly doubtful; but even if it were true, it would not rule out grounds that rational agents might have for apprehending from the operation of the market, including fair exchanges, dangers to justice and dangers to other good things as well.

The dangers to justice include the danger of imposing market arrangements on people whose preferences at bottom disfavor having a market. How can those preferences be disregarded in favor of contrary preferences without prejudice – without unjustifiably discriminating against Grasshoppers in the provision of things valued? If, as a species of injustice, this looks a bit *recherché*, it is only because the issue is commonly settled without attention, by prejudice. Grasshoppers do really have to be reckoned with; there are in fact many of them among us.

The market that the Grasshoppers would have grounds to reject might be the perfectly competitive market – the ideal market, the market in which a welfare optimum (of sorts) is guaranteed as an equilibrium solution. In an attempt to redress the balance of value-laden terms employed on this subject, I shall call it the fantasy market. It assumes that the technology available is given and unchanging; that every product and every factor of production can be assigned to a sizeable homogeneous class; that no seller or buyer is large enough to affect by his actions alone the prices of products or factors in any class, or even large enough to affect prices by any feasible coalition of sellers or buyers; that all products and all factors are equally available for sale or purchase everywhere in the market; that labor and capital at least are perfectly mobile; and finally (though this assumption has been known to give special trouble), that all agents are perfectly informed (as well as being perfectly rational).

What could Grasshoppers object to in that? They might object that they cannot bring home important real-world objections to it, just because it is a fantasy that, very conveniently for ideological purposes, deliberately sets aside a host of real-world considerations. One might take the fantasy market as offering an instantaneous recipe for the composition and distribution of output. Given an initial distribution of factor endowments accepted as just or accepted as unchangeable, and given the preference maps of all agents, the fantasy market arrives at once at a Pareto-optimal solution, in which the

[2] Robert Nozick, *Anarchy, State, and Utopia* (New York: Basic Books, 1974), p. 151.

Grasshoppers' greater taste for leisure is nicely balanced against the Ants' greater preference for other goods. Don't the Grasshoppers do as well, given their tastes, vis-à-vis the Ants as they could reasonably expect to?

The Grasshoppers might wonder, even so, whether their preferences for goods other than leisure might not be ill-assorted with the Ants', so that after supplying the Ants with frankfurters, rubber bread, and Cold Duck few factor units would be left over to work at high marginal costs on the Grasshoppers' behalf producing milk-fed veal, stone-ground flour, and Pinot Chardonnay. Even with instantaneous optima, one might wish to take some precautions about what sorts of people one is going to have optima.with. However, I shall not press this point here, since I have said nothing about the Ants' tastes, except as regards leisure; and it is the Ants' unremitting industry and inclination to accumulate property that I am specially concerned with.

With the least shift away from an instantaneous solution, real-world objections to the market start up. Suppose that though it is to operate in many respects costlessly, the fantasy market does, nevertheless, take some time to reach the optimum. Then, if the Grasshoppers put some value on having goods produced and supplied in a spirit of brotherly – of brotherly-and-sisterly – love, they might now object to the unlimited scope (apart from force and fraud) given by market arrangements for the pursuit of self-interest. They might accept the market solution, as best answering to the preferences of all concerned, but they would want it arrived at in a different way, as an expression of communal concern and planning (Malinvaud, Milleron).[3] I shall not press this objection either, or follow it up when I turn from the fantasy market, modified in one particular or another, to the market in the real world. Grasshoppers filled with brotherly-and-sisterly love would find narrowly rational, self-interested Ants even harder to get along with than narrowly rational, self-interested Grasshoppers would, but the latter have objections enough, and it is they that I have in mind – Grasshoppers who each of them relish singing and dancing just because of the pleasure that they themselves take in such things.

The next step, still within the realm of fantasy, away from the instantaneous solution toward the real-world market might be to introduce changes in technology, delivered as a series of exogenous shocks. After each shock, the market would operate again to bring about a Pareto-optimal solution, but it would not, except by a miraculous coincidence, be a Pareto-optimal solution as much to everybody's liking as the one arrived at in the previous period. The Grasshoppers in particular might prefer not to have their positions continually unsettled by the shocks, with the attendant risks of losing out as a result. They might prefer to keep the introduction of

[3] J.-C. Milleron, "Theory of Value with Public Goods," *Journal of Economic Theory*, 1972, 5(3), pp. 419–77 (which draws on work by Malinvaud).

technology under communal control and minimize the shocks that it might cause.

If the fantasy market is to be so far modified as to operate in a succession of periods, we might consider introducing savings. The Ants will save; the Grasshoppers, beyond a minimum, will not. Translated into factor endowments (land, capital goods), the Ants' savings will bring them to the beginning of each successive period with ever larger possessions. Thus, at the beginning of any later period the distribution of factor endowments may be skewed away from what was accepted as a just distribution at the beginning of the first. Even so, while competition continues, as the fantasy assumes, the Grasshoppers, if they have the prudence not to multiply, may be steadily better off. They may have skills – maybe their very skills in singing and dancing – that the Ants' accumulation of labor-saving machinery cannot easily supersede. If the Ants – or the Ants' wives – are ready to pay a premium for the public exercise of those skills, the average Grasshopper might even do better than the average Ant, in spite of the latter's steadily growing opportunity to gain income from factors other than the labor that she has to offer. On the other hand, the Grasshoppers' chief marketable skills may be, like the weavers' trade, very susceptible to supersession by the Ants' capital goods.[4] Even if, given general economic expansion with no increase in the labor force, the Grasshoppers' wages rise, the Ants' incomes are likely to rise even more; so the Ants will steadily acquire better and yet better positions for outbidding the Grasshoppers for scarce goods. They will appropriate the ocean beaches; Grasshoppers, "nymphs and shepherds dance no more/By sandy Ladon's lilied banks."

Imprudent in this respect at least, the Grasshoppers may multiply. All that singing and dancing is likely to come to something. In that case, they may individually get no benefit at all from the increased amounts of the other factors, and even become worse off as time passes. As rational, self-interested agents, the Grasshoppers of any one generation may not suffer enough from such consequences to offset in their eyes the pleasures of procreation and family life. Grasshoppers in later generations may, however, find their impoverished condition objectionable, and all the more objectionable because it was not of their own making, or of the making of the Ants contemporary with them.

Grasshoppers of any generation might well become too impatient at this juncture with the fantasy market to continue discussing it. Once the possibility of increasingly unequal accumulations of property had been brought in, they might insist that to get any real sense of the significance of such accumulations the talk of the fantasy market has to be abandoned in

---

[4] In this passage, I am responding to some illuminating comments by Sheldon Wein on the Grasshoppers' competitive position when the Ants acquire capital.

favor of coming to grips with the real market. I shall take this advice. The first thing to be said about the real market is that it coexists with other possibilities of social interaction. Even were the market to remain competitive – that is to say, free of any monopolistic or monopsonistic developments – while the Ants accumulate ever larger amounts of property, those holdings would pose a danger to the Grasshoppers. The Ants will be able to oppress the Grasshoppers, by hiring hit men or by harassment in the courts, and in other ways.

This danger will be compounded by lapses from competition. The Ants will be able not only to outbid the Grasshoppers for goods that become scarcer over the whole market. They will, in individual bargains struck with the Grasshoppers, have more bargaining power – more chance to wait the Grasshoppers out. So that bargaining – a feature of real markets that vanishes in the fantasy market – will run steadily more in the Ants' favor than in the Grasshoppers'. Most terrible of all might be the effect of accumulation in the market for labor. There, in time, in one locality after another, single Ant capitalists or landlords or small coalitions of capitalists and landlords will face relatively large masses of workers – more workers than there are jobs available. In such circumstances, the greater bargaining power of the Ants may enable them to drive the wages of the Grasshoppers at least temporarily below the long-run natural or subsistence rate of wages that would be established were the market fully competitive over all localities taken together.

Sometimes things have worked out this way; sometimes, of course, they have worked out very differently. In favorable circumstances, gross and growing inequalities in property have been consistent with staggering increases all-around in the material standard of living, not only in trinkets, but also in fundamental matters like sanitation, nutrition, and medical care. But the Grasshoppers might be indifferent to some components of this standard of living, opposed to the industrial discipline that had been required to achieve it, and prepared to try other arrangements to capture the material goods that they most valued.

Besides, they might not agree that either the oppression or the risk of oppression which comes hand in hand with unequal property has vanished during the extraordinary, intermittent, worldwide boom of the last two centuries. They might not accept that experience as empirical proof either of the inherent virtues of the market or of its capacity to escape the dangers of the differential accumulation of property. I am not saying that accumulation of property – or, more generally, of control over the means of production – and its concentration in the hands of an elite occur in the market alone; or that processes contrary to accumulation – shirtsleeves to shirtsleeves – do not to some extent offset it. The market, nevertheless, licenses differential accumulation without limit; and the Grasshoppers have reason to refuse that license to any social arrangement.

It is true that during the last two hundred years market societies in the West have been able to tolerate enormous disparities in riches without much direct personal oppression. Millionaires in Canada or the United States cannot openly get away with having people that they object to beaten up on the street, as a displeased nobleman could deal with Voltaire. The inequality of power is exerted instead in adjustments to the tax system and to other governmental policies; and, on occasion, in personal conflicts, in having easier access to the courts and ampler use of them. There are small claims courts; but if their judgments can be appealed, as they can be in Nova Scotia, does not the party with more money still have the advantage?

Moreover, in the contracting position, Grasshoppers like other agents must take a long view. (John Rawls says that the contract is to hold "in perpetuity."[5]) Sooner or later, will not unchecked inequalities of wealth lead to a division between an irresponsible patrician class and an oppressed and demoralized plebs? For two hundred years the rich, secure in their power, and growing ever richer, could easily afford to let the less rich become, cyclically, more comfortable. What happens when the boom stops permanently, or becomes ever harder to resume and ever more fitful? Uruguay, Chile, and Argentina, which until recently were civilized, even progressive countries, may show us what happens. Is it perverse of the Grasshoppers to choose not to run these dangers?

Grasshoppers, in the primordial contracting position, may be assumed to have all the latest deliverances of economic theory, together with the prescriptions for economic policy to be inferred from them. Yet they may have some doubts – may they not? – as to whether it has yet been made clear how a market economy can accommodate technological change without laying whole regions waste, like the obsolete and deindustrialized near-Middle-West of this Continent, including Ontario. They may have some doubts, too, as to whether economists have yet perfected their advice as to how a market economy is to avoid long periods of cyclical unemployment. Moreover, even if sound and comprehensive advice regarding cycles or technological change were forthcoming, Grasshoppers, from their knowledge of political science, might doubt whether the advice is going to be taken.

To choose the market, therefore, may well look to Grasshoppers like a choice attended with severe drawbacks in protracted unemployment and underemployment of resources, human and material. Almost as bad, in the Grasshoppers' view, might be the competitive pressures accompanying

[5] John Rawls, *A Theory of Justice* (Cambridge, Ma: Harvard University Press, 1971), p. 131.

continued employment under technological changes or the forced mobility
that is a condition of continued employment. Moreover, the Grasshoppers
may refuse to make the easy assumption, taken for granted by the economists
and politicians who preside over the periodic shutting-down of Canada and
other countries, that in the long run everybody will benefit more from
technological change, from domestic booms, and from restored international
trade than he may lose from unemployment. Could this be proved in
conformity with the Pareto welfare criterion, applied to people's overall
preferences for one life-plan against another? Merely showing that a greater
dollar-volume of output is generated over whole cycles or whole generations
would not show this, even if the index problems afflicting such comparisons
are disregarded. Moreover, the dollar measures, with or without the index
problems mastered, will not include any serious estimate of the suffering,
humiliation, and demoralization that millions of people experience during
protracted unemployment. A rational Grasshopper might prefer to opt out of
the market far enough to avoid them, whatever abundance of fastfoods and
trinkets she would have to forego thereby.

   For further objections, the Grasshoppers could put forward the long list of
discrepancies between the fantasy market and the real market that Frank
Knight assembled in his classic critique of the ethics of competition.[6] The
list particularizes the effects of various rigidities, barriers, and lapses of
rationality. Some are related, of course, to monopolistic aspects of real
markets; the Grasshoppers would not fail to make the point that with
distinctiveness of products, talents, and locations monopoly is unavoidable in
the real world, so far making the fantasy market irrelevant.

   The Grasshoppers would also press the point that in the real world
externalities are found everywhere; or at any rate they would press this point,
if they were not assured, as some social contract theorists would assure them,
that externalities both negative and positive were going to be taken care of
separately, by other arrangements. They would, notwithstanding, have more
misgivings about this assurance, the more broadly the term "externalities" is
being used. If it is to be used to include all the good and bad things not
automatically provided for in market transactions, including oppression,
technological shocks, and business cycles, a skeptical Grasshopper will
demand details. For Grasshoppers, provisions respecting these things will be
among the most important features of the social contract. If the term
"externalities" is to be used more narrowly, embracing on the negative side
only costs of production not borne by the producers or consumers of a given
product, the Grasshoppers will be quick to point out that taking care of them

---

[6] "The Ethics of Competition," *Quarterly Journal of Economics*, 1923, 37, pp. 579–624;
reprinted in *The Ethics of Competition and Other Essays* (London: Allen & Unwin, 1935).

will go only a short distance toward answering their objections to the real market.

There is at least one more objection that the Grasshoppers might make. They might object to the effects of the market on the characters of the participants. I have, by confining myself to self-interested Grasshoppers, forfeited the chance of putting in their mouths the morally most telling version of this objection. It is, again, that the market encourages action from narrow self-interest alone, and that in the real world the unremitting pursuit of self-interest is likely to spread out from the market to infect personal relations and civic obligations. Thus, on the one hand, the rich press for tax concessions in the name of incentives to investment, and obtain what the less rich perceive as loopholes not available to them. Were they less self-interested, would the less rich not still have some excuse, in the injustice of the tax system, to refuse to cooperate with it? But, thoroughly inculcated in the motives of the market, they are self-interested, too: evading taxes is their way of getting theirs.

Even self-interested Grasshoppers will have a version of the objection about personal character to put forward. The Grasshoppers may fear that their characters, with which they may be quite pleased, will be transformed by taking part with the Ants in a market.[7] Competing with the Ants for success in the market, or just survival, they may become more and more like the Ants, losing among other things their taste for singing and dancing. But the Grasshoppers may consider that taste well-founded; and they may not relish the change of character that would destroy it.

The objections that I have had the Grasshoppers raise are all, it might be said, familiar. I'm not sure they are. They have certainly all been raised before by Marx, Kropotkin, Tawney and others; they even reflect aspects of the practice, or attempts at practice, of real social groups, some of them – the Amish, the Mennonites, the Hutterites, one-farm communes and collectives – continuing today. The objections seem, however, to have dropped out of sight among some of our leading social theorists. Perhaps, they have done so because it is difficult to find a place for them in economic thinking. Economic thinking finds it convenient to focus on mixes of goods, demanded without regard for the mode of producing them and without reflection on the origins and contexts of putting values on them. It also treats every good as interchangeable on the margin with every other. If the Grasshoppers are offered a sufficiently rich mixture of goods with the market, how could they rationally be content with the mixture that they will be left with on rejecting the market?

There is some tendency among enthusiasts for the market, of course, to

---

[7] This is a point that I owe to Sheldon Wein.

try to have the market both ways: perfect, so that all the good things said in the fantasy can be said about it; but also an untrammelled opportunity for self-enrichment. Yet some possessive individualists frankly support the real market rather than the fantasy – laissez-faire, with changing technology, and no limitation either on fair exchange of rightfully acquired goods or on accumulation, short of the Lockean proviso,[8] which is determinate to the point only of operating to prevent the complete engrossment of vital necessities. In the discussion of any original contract, Grasshoppers may properly raise objections about the real market. Is it not the one that in the end they are being invited, more likely than not, to practice?

Furthermore, though it is a point that I shall simply note in passing, it is not logically beyond question that with the market a richer mixture of material goods on any specified list, even a richer mixture of material goods and various specified services, is sure to be obtained. I shall let the question pass, because it is not an essential issue here. Even if doing without the market implies a lower material standard of living, the Grasshoppers may, for the reasons that I have reviewed, prefer to do without it, or to accept it only in a very circumscribed form. Such preferences, whether or not they fall in with the assumptions of economic thinking, deserve as much attention as any others. Economists, in fact, make a good deal of fuss about systematically abstaining from asking for the reasons for preferences; so they could not justify setting aside these, even if they came without reasons. Coming with reasons, they should give pause even to social theorists who are working perhaps with a notion of rationality full enough to call for reasons and who are ready in any case to have agents ascribe utility to goods not exchanged – not exchangeable – in the market.

What impact will the Grasshoppers' objections have upon the process of arriving at a social contract? More particularly, what impact will they have on contractual discussions between Grasshoppers and Ants? I shall assume that if the Grasshoppers were to do the deciding, they could arrange to have a society that would do at least modestly well without a market. Either they are wise enough (with the present resources of social science at their disposal) to avoid letting population grow too rapidly and avoid any other development that might make spending some centuries in a market society the only route out of the kingdom of necessity. Or they would have the resources of present-day society and the same choice of technologies and so be able to refound a society on terms that assure it of a modest standard of living without a market.

The Grasshoppers might, nevertheless, want to have the Ants in the same

[8] Nozick, *op cit.*, p. 177 ff. Nozick leaves the proviso otherwise indeterminate when he sets aside (p. 177) the task of relating a "base line" to "original appropriation" (itself a dubious notion).

society – not in disinterested hopes of humanizing them, but because it would be dangerous to leave the Ants outside. To some extent the Grasshoppers might feel that the increased availability of some trinkets and gadgets was partial compensation for conceding the market some room to operate. Moreover, though they would know of many instances in which nonmarket arrangements had worked very well, they would have to concede that so far, even the largest of them – some monasteries in the Middle Ages, some tribal societies, the Oneida Community – had come nowhere near demonstrating how such a thing as segmental communalism could work on the scale of a modern nation-state. Organizing on such a scale, if such organizing was unavoidable, the Grasshoppers might be ready to show some sober respect for the market as a sensitive device for registering and aggregating preferences even in relatively important matters. They would have to concede, too, as I have already acknowledged, that some of the points that worried them most, in particular the differential accumulation of property and power, occur in nonmarket societies as well as in societies with unchecked markets.

So the Grasshoppers might be willing to bargain about accepting greater or lesser use of the market. The Ants, for their part, putting aside any desire on their part to improve the Grasshoppers' moral character by converting them to the spirit of capitalism, might be ready to bargain with the Grasshoppers because they, too, saw advantages in a larger society, including the possibility of a more extensive market.

One form of compromise might be to let the market operate for some goods and services and not for others. Even a Grasshopper, comparing the prices and offerings of state and provincial liquor commissions with the prices and goods available in Florida, California, Minnesota and other jurisdictions in which business in wine and liquor is left to competitive private enterprise, might prefer the market for these things. Other possibilities would be restaurants, food, clothing, and furniture, though the advantages of catering to individual tastes in these last two connections might be offset by the disadvantages of arbitrary fashion-changes.

Another form of compromise – which might be combined with the first one – would be to adopt various measures to correct for the misadventures of the market: factory legislation; food and drug inspection; workers' compensation; anti-trust action; social security; a drastic and unavoidable tax on inheritances; and, if one could be found, an effective countercyclical policy.

Combined, these forms of compromise seem to come out resembling at least roughly what we have got in late capitalism and the welfare state. One may infer that our present arrangements can be looked upon not merely as incorporating a series of remedies for various failures of the market to meet human needs. They can also be looked upon as the result of a hypothetical social contract between enthusiasts for the market and people who, very different in their basic preferences, find the market something acceptable, if at all, only for limited uses, subordinated to certain stringent conditions. It is common practice in certain quarters to portray the mixed economy and the welfare state as something imposed unjustly upon productive people by unproductive ones – disobligingly denominated "free riders" and "parasites." Due attention to the Grasshoppers' position shows, however, that these things might result from a compromise that did some justice both to champions of the market and to opponents of the market who are yet prepared in their own way to be productive and in particular to put forward their share of social effort.

Perhaps, however, what we have got is at once too much of the market for Grasshoppers and not enough of it for Ants. If they could, would not they be better off parting company, the Grasshoppers to establish some sort of communal economy, with limited use of the market if any use at all, the Ants to a roaring market with no holds short of force and fraud barred? Let us assume that enough other Grasshoppers and enough other Ants turn up to make each society large enough to be viable, at least at the outset.

Alas! the Grasshoppers cannot escape all the difficulties of living with Ants and with the market by setting up on their own. The Grasshoppers may prefer to sacrifice substantial amounts of output in order to have more leisure, more time for singing and dancing; they may prefer to develop technology very slowly, bringing in innovations only on terms that avoid disrupting people's lives. If the Ants meanwhile go all out for output and rapid technological development, they will soon overshadow the Grasshoppers in potential military strength. I am not saying that only a market society would pose such a danger for the Grasshoppers. The Golden Horde was not a market society; nor are the countries whose aggressiveness is most denounced in our press: North Korea; Viet Nam under its present regime; the Soviet Union. We might, however, recall that market societies have been extremely aggressive in opening up markets abroad and forcing trade and development upon countries that did not especially want them. Remember the opium wars waged by Britain against China, in the name of free trade; the warships that carried Perry's demands to Japan; the parcelling out of Africa in the 19th Century; the pacification of the Philippines, resisting co-prosperity with the United States, at the cost of hundreds of thousands of Filipinos dead;[9] the actions of the United States in the last quarter of a

[9] An American general, in the course of *defending* the pacification, estimated 616,000 dead in Luzon alone – one-sixth of the population – by May 1901 (Daniel B. Schirmer, *Republic or Empire*, 1972, p. 231). This estimate has appeared exaggerated to others, including some severe critics of the pacification. Leon Wolff, in *Little Brown Brother*, 1961, claims 250,000 dead all told, including 16,000 counted as killed in action by the United States army, plus 20,000 killed but not counted, plus 200,000 civilians dead of famine and pestilence.

century in Guatemala, Cuba, El Salvador, and Nicaragua. I grant that more than the expansion of markets was and is at issue in many of these cases; my point is that there is enough force in all of them taken together to give the Grasshoppers genuine reasons for fearing aggression from the Ants. They could not but be a bit uneasy living side by side with all that power, anyway.

Must the Grasshoppers then agree to give high priority in their affairs, if not to the market and technology of all sorts, at least to military technology and their defense budget? Can they have what they want in one country? But there is another possibility. Maybe it is not entirely hopeless for Grasshoppers to look to Ants for help, once the Ants – most Ants – realize what is at stake for them. For Ants, too, have something to fear in the cumulative inequalities that the unchecked market will generate, and something to lose from the other aspects of the market to which Grasshoppers object. Most of the Ants must expect to be left eventually far back in the pack; and though they may gain enough to make their comfort secure if they can keep it, small Ants are always liable to be driven out of business by large Ants.

Indeed, the real market jeopardizes in time the very thing that Ants and their theorists most prize – free and fair exchange. Inequalities in wealth may lead to aggrandizements outside the market, as when the rich arrange to have the government modify the terms of trade in their favor, or even transfer more wealth directly to them, or as when, more nakedly, various sorts of direct intimidation are practiced, within or without the law, to seize assets and opportunities. Even if the rich continue to respect the rules of the market, however, the bargains in which they enter with others – with less successful Ants – will reflect their superior bargaining power, and will be specially to their advantage for that reason. The fantasy market, of course, as I have said, has no place for any process of bargaining. The champions of fair exchange and of the market might, however, have expected to have thought more fully about what was required to keep the process fair for all participants. It is true, even with very great differences in bargaining power, the bargain struck may be in the end beneficial to both parties and in a sense voluntary. Such, as Hobbes insisted, is the bargain struck between a bandit and the man whose life he spares.[10]

So the less successful Ants may be interested after all in measures that keep the operation of the market within limits. Indeed, all Ants, asked to make choices in this connection while they are drawing up a social contract, may be interested in such measures. They will know from reading Lester Thurow that the best explanation of success in the market, the sort of success embodied in acquiring within one's lifetime a disproportionately large personal fortune, is a random walk process.[11] Even Ants as confident of

[10] Thomas Hobbes, *Leviathan*, 1651, Chap. 14.
[11] Lester C. Thurow, *Generating Inequality* (New York: Basic Books, 1975), pp. 149–154.

their powers of acquisition as any Ants could be must rationally recognize that things may go wrong for them, so that with James Buchanan and Gordon Tullock they would be interested in having some measures of social insurance against personal disasters.[12]

Will the measures that the Ants are interested in to limit the market be in variety and scope enough like the provisions that the Grasshoppers want to make for themselves apart from the market to encourage both parties to reconsider the project of joining in the foundation or refoundation of one society? I do not have a quick answer to that question; but I think that a social contract theory, recast to allow for preferences opposed to the market as well as preferences enthusiastically favoring one, might, on exploring the question, come upon a basis for compromise in which even were the grounds, considered earlier, favoring a joint society with a mixed economy, not to operate or not to suffice, compelling grounds for both parties could still be found.

The Grasshoppers would have a ground for conceding something to the Ants so as to forestall the Ants from living apart and advancing far beyond them in technology and power. The Ants would have a ground for conceding something to the Grasshoppers in order to have them present, in the same society, as additional support for measures to check the market, and also, possibly, in the institutions that the Grasshoppers set up, as an added source of stability for the economy. Those institutions – consumers' cooperatives, producers' cooperatives safeguarded against monopolistic tendencies, communes, perhaps tiers of segmental communalism – might be less cyclical in initiatives and less subject to cyclical forces from outside.

Of course, they might be these things at the expense of a much less rapid development of technology, as well as of less rapid and less massive capital accumulation. The jointly supported measures for checking the market – anti-trust, reduction of inheritance, redistribution of income – would tend the same way. Both Ants and Grasshoppers, however, might well be willing to pay these costs; and if this is so, there is a basis for far-reaching compromise between them, and thus a basis for thinking that social contract theory can cope with agents as diverse as Grasshoppers and Ants in one contract, though it is going to have to be much more guarded about accepting the market than some theorists have yet allowed, and much more specific in its implications regarding a mix of market and nonmarket arrangements.

Philosophy and Political Science, Dalhousie University

---

[12] James M. Buchanan and Gordon Tullock, *The Calculus of Consent* (Ann Arbor: University of Michigan Press, 1962), pp. 192–193.

ROUSSEAU ON EQUALITY

Maurice Cranston

Rousseau has the reputation of being a radical egalitarian. I shall suggest that a more careful reading of his work shows him to have been hardly more egalitarian than Plato. He was undoubtedly disturbed by existing inequalities, especially as he observed them in France. He had an original and interesting theory about how inequality among men came into being; he also set out what he considered to be the connections between equality and freedom. As a champion of a certain idea of freedom, he wrote in favor of specific sorts of equality; even as Plato, as the champion of a certain idea of justice, wrote in favor of putting every man in his place. The great difference is that Plato believed that men were never equal, whereas Rousseau believed they had once been equal but no longer were.

To the proposition that all men are born equal he could be said to subscribe only in the sense that "all men were originally equal". Rousseau argued that equality prevailed in the state of nature, but he also said it would be wrong to expect, even to desire such equality in civil society. In the final footnote to his *Discourse on the Origins of Inequality* (hereinafter called the *Second Discourse*) he wrote (in 1753): "Distributive justice would still be opposed to that rigorous equality of the state of nature, even if it were practicable in civil society."[1]

Commentators eager to claim Rousseau as an egalitarian, or proto-Marx, ignore this footnote; as for the opinions expressed in the Dedication to the *Second Discourse*, opinions no less at variance with egalitarian ideology, they tend to be dismissed as empty hyperbole, designed to ingratiate the philosopher with the authorities of Geneva at a time when he wanted to recover his rights as a citizen and burgess. But this is a myth. If Rousseau had planned to do this he would have followed protocol, and dedicated the *Second Discourse* to the magistrates of Geneva (as he was advised to do[2], and not stubbornly addressed it to the citizens.

The key sentence in Rousseau's Dedication is this:

---

[1] J. J. Rousseau, *Oeuvres Complètes* (Paris: Bibliothèque de la Pléiade, 1964), III, p. 222 (Hereinafter this work is referred to as *O.C.*; the translations are my own)

[2] See Rousseau's correspondence with Jean Pedriau, in R. A. Leigh, ed., *Correspondence complète de J. J. Rousseau* (Geneva and Oxford: Institut Voltaire, 1965–) III, pp. 55–64.

Having had the good fortune to be born among you, how could I reflect on the equality which nature established among men and the inequality which they have instituted among themselves, without thinking of the profound wisdom with which the one and the other, happily combined in this Republic, contribute in the manner closest to natural law and most favorable to society, to the maintenance of public order and the well-being of individuals.[3]

Rousseau, then, goes on to congratulate the Genevans on being "that people which, among all others, seems to me to possess the greatest advantages of society and to have guarded most successfully against its abuses."[4]

It is clear from these words that Rousseau connects equality with nature, and inequality with culture; and his claim is that a well-ordered society must have the right balance of the two. In one of his poems, *Épitre à Monsieur Parisot*, Rousseau wrote

It would not be good in society
If there were less inequality between the ranks[5]

Admittedly this verse was written in 1742, more than ten years before the *Second Discourse*, but Rousseau never changed his mind greatly. He did not wish to see "less inequality between the ranks," but he had his own ideas as to who should be in the different ranks.

One thing he did change his mind about was the character of the people in the higher ranks in Geneva. What he wrote in *The Social Contract* of 1762 confirms the ideal conception of Geneva that he sets forth in the *Second Discourse* of 1753; his attack on the regime of Geneva in his *Letters written from the Mountains* of 1764, is not an attack on the structures of the Genevan civil society but an indictment of the magistrates for abusing the constitution and their office. Rousseau had been brought up to believe that the republic of Geneva was a model state, a city where the people were sovereign, the law was supreme, and the magistrates governed as the people's trustees. He had also been brought up to know that Geneva was a city divided into several social classes: patricians, clergy, academics, professionals, artisans and more or less plebeian aliens; and of this arrangement Rousseau had no criticisms to offer, but was only careful to insist that his own family was one whose "manners distinguished it from the people."[6] He had indeed been born in an upper-class house belonging to his mother in high Geneva, but unfortu-

---

[3] *O.C.* III, p. 111.
[4] *ibid.*
[5] *O.C.* II, p. 1136.
[6] *O.C.* I, p. 61.

nately reduced in his childhood to life in low Geneva with his widowed father, a mere artisan; and he had run away from Geneva altogether at the age of sixteen rather than endure the humiliations of a *declassé* apprentice in an engraver's workshop.

In the main text of his *Second Discourse*, Rousseau concentrates on the first part of the question posed by the Academy of Dijon: "What are the origins of inequality among men?" rather than the further part "and is it authorized by Natural Law?" He has some arresting ideas on the subject. Readers are apt to be carried away by the sensational first paragraph of the second section (and Rousseau more than once demonstrated his genius as a polemical writer by opening a chapter with a shock): "The first man who, having enclosed a piece of land, thought of saying 'This is mine', and found people simple enough to believe him, was the true founder of civil society."[7] This eloquent utterance has prompted some readers to assume that Rousseau dates inequality between men from the institution of property, which divided men into rich and poor. But this is a mistake. Rousseau rejects the idea that men moved straight from the state of nature into civil society. He depicts an intermediate stage of "nascent society," and that is where he says inequality originates.

Inequality, according to Rousseau, dates from the time when men first started to associate as neighbors. This is a period when the true state of nature – in which each individual lives a wholly solitary life, with no home, no mate, no regular commerce with any other person, ignorant, innocent and idle – terminates; it ends as men start to build huts or furnish caves, for as soon as men begin to live in settled dwellings, they remain with the same female for long enough to acquire an awareness of fatherhood and to found families. As other men construct their dwellings nearby, they are introduced to life as neighbors; and thus, from sheer proximity, society is born. Inequality is born at the same time. For as soon as people see each other regularly, they appraise each other.

"People become accustomed to judging different objects and to making comparisons; unconsciously they acquire ideas of merit and beauty, which in turn produce feelings of preference. . . . Each began to look at the others and to want to be looked at himself; and public esteem came to be prized. He who sang or danced the best; he who was the most handsome, the strongest,

---

[7] *O.C.* III, p. 164. Rousseau goes on to say: "How many crimes, wars, murders; how much misery and horror the human race would have been spared if someone had pulled up the stakes and filled in the ditch and cried out to his fellow men: 'Beware of listening to this imposter. You are lost if you forget that the fruits of the earth belong to everyone and that the earth itself belongs to no one.'" This is naturally a text much used by writers who see Rousseau as a proto-Marx.

the most adroit or the most eloquent became the most highly regarded, and this was the first step towards inequality . . ."[8]

At this point in his argument, Rousseau picks up the thread of his *First Discourse*: culture corrupts – moving further from the state of nature and further into society and inequality, man moves closer to vice. Nascent society was a sort of golden age; the loneliness of the state of nature had ended, and the evils of the civil state were as yet unknown. But corruption developed swiftly; frequent association between the sexes bred love, and love bred jealousy and conflict. Original self-love, *amour de soi*, which is natural and good, turned in *amour-propre*, which is cultivated and injurious.

"As soon as man learned to value one another and the idea of consideration was formed in their minds, everyone claimed a right to it, and it was no longer possible to refuse consideration to anyone with impunity."[9]

Such then is Rousseau's account of the origins of inequality: there are natural differences of looks and talents in individuals; when some characteristics are esteemed more than others, these differences become inequalities; and when the idea of consideration enters men's heads, bringing with it the demand for some esteem and the desire for more, inequality becomes part of the human condition itself.

Repeatedly, Rousseau stresses the fatal role of *amour-propre* in the life of social man; the role is not unlike that of pride in Hobbesian theory which makes men rebel against the equality of their natural condition. For both philosophers, the psychological or moral causes of human conflict are much the same; the main difference is that Hobbes regards the competitiveness of man as a product of nature, whereas Rousseau suggests that it is a product of society. Indeed, Rousseau sees this same *amour-propre* at work impelling men to their greatest achievements as well as their greatest misery.

If this were the place to go into details, I would explain how this universal desire for reputation, for honors, and for preference, in devouring us all, exercises and compares talents and powers, how it excites and multiplies passions, how it makes men competitors, rivals or rather enemies; how it everyday causes frustrations, successes and catastrophes of every kind by making so many contenders run the same race; I would show how the burning desire to have oneself talked about, the yearning for distinction, which nearly always keeps us outside ourselves, is responsible for what is best and worst among men, responsible for our virtues and our vices; for our sciences and our mistakes, for our conquerors and our philosophers; responsible, in short, for a multitude of bad things and a very few good ones.[10]

[8] *ibid.*, p. 169.
[9] *ibid.*, p. 170.
[10] *ibid.*, pp. 188–189.

To sum up, Rousseau traces the origins of inequality among men to their first experience of life in a family and as neighbors in "nascent society," and he attributes its growth to passions which tend to increase rather than diminish as society develops. What then, can exist of equality in advanced or civil society? Clearly it can only be partial or fragmentary, but even so, some sort of "natural" equality must be able to exist side-by-side with the "instituted" inequalities of man's social condition, since Rousseau asserts in the "Dedication to the *Second Discourse*" that they do so co-exist in the fortunate commonwealth of his birth. And although Rousseau does not directly answer the second question posed by the Academy of Dijon – is the inequality between men authorized by natural law? – he does answer a question he sets himself: what forms of equality are necessary to freedom and what forms of inequality are inimical to it?

Natural man, for Rousseau, is free in three senses of the word "freedom." First, he has free will. This is a crucial sense for Rousseau. Hobbes and most of the *Encyclopédistes* were determinists, believing that man was a machine, and if more complicated than any other machine in nature, subject to the same laws of cause and effect. While Rousseau himself invokes the metaphor of the machine in describing living creatures, he insists that the "human machine" differs from the "animal machine" in being autonomous; among beasts, nature alone "operates the machine"; in the case of human beings, the individual contributes to his own operations in the capacity of a free agent: "The animal chooses and rejects by instinct; the man by an act of freedom."[11] This metaphysical freedom, or freedom of the will, is a characteristic of men as such and is possessed by men in all conditions, whether of nature or of society.

The second form of freedom which men enjoyed in the state of nature was necessarily lost on entering society. This is anarchic freedom, and it is absolute since the state of nature, by definition, is a condition where there is no government and no positive law.

The third form of freedom is one which, according to Rousseau, man need not necessarily lose on entering society: this is personal freedom, in the sense of having no master, no employer, no immediate superior. Before the introduction of the division of labor, all men possess this form of freedom. Afterwards some are independent and some are not. Afterwards, some men have this personal freedom and some do not.

In the *Second Discourse*, Rousseau suggests that there is not much left of freedom for most people – apart from their metaphysical freedom – once they have entered civil society. In *The Social Contract* (1762) he confirms this: "Man was born free, but he is everywhere in chains."[12] (Another sensational

[11] *ibid.*, p. 141.
[12] *ibid.*, p. 351.

opening sentence.) But the same book suggests that some people need not be in chains. Where a commonwealth is based on a genuine social contract (as distinct from the fraudulent social contract depicted in the *Second Discourse*), then men can receive in exchange for the anarchic freedom of the state of nature another and better kind of freedom, republican freedom. This fourth sense of freedom is what he is saying (in the "Dedication" to the *Second Discourse*) that the citizens of Geneva enjoy. In the *Social Contract*, Rousseau claims that this republican freedom is a wholly advantageous exchange for the anarchic freedom of the state of nature: one finds himself "transformed from a limited and stupid animal into an intelligent being and a man."[13] Losing "his natural liberty and his unqualified right to lay hands on all that tempts him," he gains "civil liberty and the rightful ownership of what belongs to him."[14] To this is added the moral liberty which makes a man his own master, "for subjection to appetite alone is slavery, while obedience to a law one has prescribed for oneself is liberty."[15]

Republican freedom is, thus composed of civil liberty and moral liberty. The republic, as Rousseau explains, is not only a device for reconciling freedom and law, it is a structure which introduces and depends for its success upon the existence of this completely new and essentially positive form of freedom. The problem of equality is important to him as an aspect of freedom in this sense. If he is a champion of equality, it is simply as a champion of those types of equality which can be seen to be necessary to, or conducive to, republican freedom. Let us consider what these are.

First, Rousseau's republican freedom entails equality of legislative rights; no man or group of men must be able to impose his will or laws on others, and this rules out both monarchical and aristocratic forms of government. Men must be equal as citizens. However, Rousseau makes it clear in the "Dedication" that by demanding an equal vote in legislating he is *not* demanding an equal voice for every citizen in government: "I would have fled from a republic, as necessarily ill governed, where the people . . . foolishly kept in their own hands the administration of civil affairs and the execution of their laws."[16] Rousseau's republic has to have chiefs (*chefs*): "I would have chosen a republic where the individuals, content with sanctioning the laws and making decisions in assemblies on proposals from the chiefs on the most important public business . . . elected year by year the most capable and most upright of their fellow citizens to administer justice and govern the state."[17]

The point that Rousseau dwells on is that superiority of public office shall correspond to superiority of capability and rectitude.

[13] *ibid.*, p. 364.
[14] *ibid.*
[15] *ibid.*, p. 365.
[16] *ibid.*, p. 114.
[17] *ibid.*

In the *Social Contract*, a book I believe to have been inspired by Rousseau's vision of Geneva as a model city-state, an "elective aristocracy" is said to be "the best form of government";[18] which is presumably to be understood as the same thing as the "democratic government, wisely tempered"[19] ascribed to Geneva in the *Second Discourse*. Here again we see that Rousseau does not want to banish inequality, but to have a rationally justifiable inequality. Instead of an aristocracy based on blood (characteristic of feudal regimes, and "the worst form of government"[20]), he looks for an aristocracy based on democratic choice coupled with moral criteria.

Besides this sort of equality of rights, Rousseau's republican freedom requires some measure of equality of condition. In the oration which he envisages addressing to his fellow citizens of Geneva, he says:

> You are neither so rich as to be ennervated by effeminacy and lose in vain luxury the taste for true felicity and solid virtue, nor are you so poor as to need from foreign aid more than your own industry can furnish.[21]

This is one of Rousseau's many attacks on luxury. In France and in Italy he had witnessed (and perhaps even enjoyed for a fleeting moment) the lavish joys that ostentatious wealth could acquire for the privileged subjects of those advanced civilisations, but he had come to believe that it made them the effeminate and corrupt accomplices of despotism. In Geneva, there were substantial inequalities of wealth and prestige between the families who lived in the handsome houses in high Geneva and the workers who crowded into the wooden dwellings beside the lake; but the rich were not conspicuously rich; there were no theatres, ballrooms or carriages; and there were restrictions on the wearing of finery and jewelry. The rich families of Geneva invested their money instead of spending it; and Rousseau, in his *Letter to M. d'Alembert on the Theatre* explained why he attached such importance to the puritan life style of the richest of his fellow-citizens.

The equality in question here, then, is not equality of property or estates, but relative equality in the leading of a simple and austere *train de vie*. And if excessive wealth that manifests itself in luxury and effeminacy is bad, so too is excessive poverty that breeds ignorance, depravity, and dependence. In Geneva the inequality between rich and poor is judged by Rousseau to be in order. Even the working men are educated. They go to state schools, attend divine services and are drilled in the citizens' militia. They are near enough to the rich in their life style and their general culture as to be able to meet

---

[18] *ibid.*, p. 406.
[19] *ibid.*, p. 112.
[20] *ibid.*, p. 406.
[21] *ibid.*, p. 116.

with their superiors in public assemblies and to participate as members of the same sovereign body.

Thus, the equality of condition required by Rousseau for his republican freedom is not so very different from that prescribed by Aristotle for a well-ordered state.[22]

A third form of equality demanded by Rousseau as necessary to republican freedom is equality of civil duties, including universal military service and the payment of equitable taxes. An equal duty on all citizens to bear arms had long been the rule in Geneva. It did not mean that there was social equality between officers and men, only that there was an equal bearing of the burden of defence. In his *Letter to M. d'Alembert*, Rousseau recalls witnessing as a child the officers and men of his local parish militia eating together and "dancing together round a fountain,"[23] but this was a festivity; officers and men were at ordinary times not equals. Different men were appointed to different ranks.

But if the government is to intervene in the ranking of citizens, what are the criteria to be invoked? Rousseau does not want to see the authorities judging merit. In the final footnote to his *Second Discourse*, he writes:

> The ranking of citizens ought therefore to be regulated, not according to their personal merit, which would leave the magistrates with the means of making an almost arbitrary application of the law, but according to the real services they render to the state, which are susceptible of being estimated more exactly.[24]

One form of equality which Rousseau does not suggest is that there should be equality between the sexes. Women were not citizens in Geneva, and he did not suggest that they ought to be. Women should "command" as they did in Sparta; they should "govern our sex," but only in the family:

"It is for you," he said to the women of Geneva, "by your kindly and innocent domination and by your subtle influence, to perpetuate love of the laws within the state and concord among citizens ... to be the chaste guardians of our morals and of all the gentle bonds of peace."[25] Rousseau had once been dependent on an employer with strongly feminist opinions, Mme. Dupin,[26] and he had no patience with such ideas. He argues at length in *Emile* – in Book V, which is entitled 'Sophie, or Woman' – against "the vanity of the disputes as to the superiority or the equality of the sexes."[27] To

---

[22] See: Aristotle, *Politics*, trans. T. A. Sinclair (Harmondsworth and N.Y.: Penguin Books, 1982) p. 319.

[23] J. J. Rousseau, *Lettre à Monsieur d'Alembert*, ed. Fuchs (Lille: Libraire Giard, 1948), p. 181.

[24] *O.C.* III, p. 223.

[25] *ibid.*, p. 120.

[26] See M. Cranston, *Jean-Jacques* (New York: W. W. Norton, 1983), pp. 205–207.

[27] J. J. Rousseau *Emile*, trans. B. Foxley (New York: Dutton, 1974), p. 321.

the feminist proposal that women should be educated as men are educated, Rousseau replies: "The more women are like men, the less influence they will have over men, and the men will be masters indeed."[28] He continues:

All the faculties common to both sexes are not equally shared between them, but taken as a whole they are fairly divided. Woman is worth more as a woman and less as a man: when she makes a good use of her own rights she has the best of it; when she tries to usurp our rights, she is our inferior. To cultivate the masculine virtues in women and to neglect their own is clearly to do them an injury.[29]

The arguments Rousseau advances on the subject of equality seem to me coherent and reasonable, despite his occasional extravagant language. If we accept his concept of freedom, we cannot easily dissent from what he says about equality. But of course we do not have to accept that concept. Benjamin Constant criticized it with arguments that I believe to be still valid.[30] As an inhabitant of the neighboring *pays de Vaud*, Constant was familiar with Geneva and that republican ideal which Rousseau proclaimed. He detected a tendency among Genevans to compensate themselves for their exclusion from the Swiss confederation (the majority of the cantons having refused to admit Geneva because of Calvin's persecution of Catholics), by imagining that their pocket-sized republic was somehow superior and even able to perpetuate in the modern world the values of the city-states of classical antiquity. Constant called Rousseau's notion of freedom "ancient freedom", and contrasted it with "modern freedom." "Ancient freedom" was a form of liberty suited to small face-to-face communities, where it was practicable for every man to participate in person in the legislative business of the state. Geneva was equally tiny,[31] and could, therefore, allow itself to entertain political theories suited to its size. But Geneva was something altogether exceptional in eighteenth-century Europe. The typical states of the modern world, whether they were Empires, Kingdoms, republics, principalities, or confederations, were large; the personal participation of everyone in the political assemblies of the nation was inconceivable. The modern world needed a modern concept of freedom such as was to be found in the philosophers of modernity. What Constant called "modern freedom" was substantially a matter of the individual being allowed to do what he chose to do, so long as he did not transgress the law or injure his neighbor. It is freedom as Locke understood it.

[28] *ibid.*, p. 327.
[29] *ibid.*
[30] See S. H. Dodge, Benjamin Constant's *Philosophy of Liberalism* (Chapel Hill, N.C.: University of North Carolina Press, 1980), pp. 18–51.
[31] In Rousseau's lifetime the population of Geneva was about 25,000, of whom only 1,500 were adult male citizens. See L. Binz *Brève histoire de Genève* (Geneva: Chancellerie d'Etat, 1981).

Constant does not have much to say about equality, and living through the French Revolution he doubtless heard the word *égalité* proclaimed too often to take pleasure in thinking about it. But it is reasonable to ask, if Rousseau discerns certain forms of liberty as necessary to his type of freedom, what forms of equality, if any, are necessary to "modern freedom."

Although I am reluctant to join Sir Isaiah Berlin in speaking of "modern freedom" as "negative," it is, nevertheless, liable to make more modest demands in the matter of equality than is Rousseau's "ancient freedom" or "republican freedom." Equality of civil rights, must, I suggest, be as important to modern freedom as to ancient: since those rights – notably "life, liberty and property" as Locke expressed them are part of the concept of modern freedom.

But what about equality of civil duties? Here modern freedom will expect less: and may even be hostile to the claim. In a city-state like Geneva, universal military service may well be part of the role of the citizen-soldier; but in imperial France or Germany, the *levée en masse* becomes an instrument of a militaristic despotism. It is not illogical that the liberal philosophers of the Anglo-Saxon world should regard conscription as a limitation of people's freedom, whereas Rousseau sees it as an expression of their freedom. What "modern freedom" must entail is an equal obligation to respect the law; beyond that each individual's civil duties will vary with his civil station.

Thirdly, there is the question of equality of condition. I have pointed out that Rousseau did not advocate a radical levelling of society, however often interpreters claim he did. But his concept of republican freedom did require some diminution and some careful veiling of social inequalities. Does modern freedom demand as much? I see no reason why it should be in any way affected by differences of wealth, rank, education, and status. Since civil duties vary there is no call for uniformity.

But since modern freedom imposes an equal obligation to obey the law, some equality – even some basic uniformity – of political, social, and moral culture may well be necessary. "If laws are to be observed," wrote Machiavelli, "there is need of good customs."[32] Good customs mean a more or less equal adherence to a code of right and wrong. Where everyone unconstrained follows the precepts of natural law, the state can afford to leave him alone. In this "modern" sense of freedom, men "cannot be forced to be free," as with Rousseau's form of "ancient freedom" they could be; I do not think "modern freedom" is any the worse for that.

Political Science, London School of Economics and Political Science

---

[32] N. Machiavelli, *Discourses*, trans. L. J. Walker, S. J. (Boston: Routledge, 1975), p. 258.

LIBERTY, EQUALITY, HONOR

William Kristol

As today's battles rage between those who march under the banner of liberty and those who unfurl the flag of equality, even an engaged partisan might be forgiven for occasionally wondering whether the game is, after all, worth the candle. For one thing, neither party simply rejects the other's principle – properly understood. Egalitarians routinely emphasize that their concern for equality is, also, a concern for true liberty; thus Michael Walzer, writing "In Defense of Equality," finds it "worth stressing that equality as I have described it does not stand alone, but is closely related to the idea of liberty."[1] Libertarians tend to be less enthusiastic in their embrace of equality, but almost all endorse some form of equality or other – for example, equality of political rights or equality before the law. It would seem, then, that the differences between egalitarians and libertarians are really over the meaning and scope of equality and liberty, and that putting the issue as one of equality *vs.* liberty may be misleading.

More important, one can wonder whether either the egalitarian or the libertarian combination of the principles of liberty and equality is worthy of support. What society has exalted personal liberty, has taken rights more seriously, than ours? Yet who can easily dismiss Solzhenitsyn's charge that our worship of freedom has resulted in "destructive and irresponsible freedom" being granted "boundless scope," leaving us defenseless against "the corrosion of evil"?[2] The cause of liberty against tyranny surely continues to command our support; but what conclusion ought we to draw from the facts that liberty *in absentia* seems so markedly more attractive than liberty in practice, and that the qualities manifested in the struggle for liberty seem so superior to those that come to the fore once liberty is secured? Is Solzhenitsyn mistaken about "the weakening of human beings in the West"?[3]

If one is entitled to be doubtful about the worth of liberty, how much more so about equality? We tend to speak of equality as a first principle of extraordinary dignity; but is it not in fact, as James Fitzjames Stephen

---

[1] Michael Walzer, *Radical Principles* (New York: Basic Books, 1980), p. 256.
[2] Aleksandr I. Solzhenitsyn, "A World Split Apart," in *East and West* (New York: Harper and Row, 1980), p. 50.
[3] *ibid*, p. 57.

suggested, "a big name for a small thing"?[4] Americans sensibly recognized that they were "substantially equal in all the more important matters" (leaving aside race), and therefore did not set up unfounded distinctions; is this worthy of great praise? Only, according to Stephen, by contrast with the behavior of the French, who first allowed a class of extraordinary privilege to develop, and then "were just in the mood to become rhetorical about it, and to make it the subject not of rational quiet alteration, but of outbursts of pathetic and other nonsense, the effects of which will long be felt in the world." The doctrine of equality has been, by contrast, a "success" in America; but, "it is also a question . . . whether the enormous development of equality in America, the rapid production of an immense multitude of common place, self-satisfied, and essentially slight people is an exploit which the whole world need fall down and worship."[5] As with liberty, then, the cause of equality seems primarily to command our respect by virtue of our distaste for the alternative, a regime of caste or class privilege. But this would leave equality and liberty as merely minimally necessary conditions of a just social order, and conditions whose fulfillment seem in practice to undermine the health of the very social order they justify.

The limited appeal of liberty and equality may account for the fact that these two principles seem to invite a third to complement them. The most prominent candidate for this role has been fraternity. The historical record of this trio would seem, however, only to confirm Stephen's judgment that "when used collectively the words do not typify, however vaguely, any state of society which a reasonable man ought to regard with enthusiasm or self-devotion."[6]

Yet the desire to find something more than merely liberty and/or equality as the legitimating principles of a social order is a persistent one. One sees it even – or especially – in the work of two of our foremost advocates of liberty and equality, Robert Nozick and John Rawls. In order to make libertarianism and its "uniquely justifiable" minimal state inspiring, even thrilling, Nozick turns "to that preeminently inspiring tradition of social thought, utopian theory," and argues that "what can be saved from this tradition is precisely the structure of the minimal state."[7] In fact, Nozick succeeds in trumping the utopians, for he offers us not merely utopia but "meta-utopia," a society of many utopias, "of many different and divergent communities in which people lead different kinds of lives under different institutions."[8] But

---

[4] James Fitzjames Stephen, *Liberty, Equality, Fraternity* (New York: Holt and Williams, 1873), p. 253.

[5] *ibid.*, pp. 253–254.

[6] *ibid.*, p. 3.

[7] Robert Nozick, *Anarchy, State, and Utopia* (New York: Basic Books, 1974), p. xii; see also p. 297.

[8] *ibid.*, p. 312.

Nozick's attempt "to get the best of all possible worlds" by supplementing his libertarianism with utopianism,[9] by making room in utopia for illiberal communities cultivating illiberal virtues, cannot, I believe, succeed. For Nozick's astute observation that the right of "internal opting out" could not be required of all communities, since such a right "would itself change the character of the group from that desired,"[10] also applies to the possibility of external opting out (emigration). For such a right to leave (which is required by the principle of individual liberty) implies, as Nozick more or less acknowledges, a right to be informed of the existence of and the case for alternative communities. But this would decisively limit the extent of communal censorship possible, and thus limit the possibility of the formation of character along certain lines. Nozick states the problem in the case of children: "In some way it must be ensured that they are *informed* of the range of alternatives in the world. But the home community might view it as important that youngsters not be exposed to the knowledge that one hundred miles away is a community of great sexual freedom. And so on."[11] In the end, Nozick's utopianism conflicts with, and must in fact bow to, his libertarianism; but his effort to supplement liberty with a "utopian process" leading to an unknowable future which "will be worth speaking eloquently about"[12] is itself eloquent testimony to the limited appeal of old-fashioned "negative" liberty.

Nozick's utopianism is explicitly a supplement to his libertarianism; one can reject the framework for utopia and stay with the minimal state as (uninspiring) guarantor of liberty. Rawls' utopianism is, by contrast, covert; but (or consequently?) it penetrates far more deeply into the structure of his argument. Rawls' attempts at once to radicalize equality (by ruling out the legitimacy of considering "natural endowments" which are "arbitrary from a moral point of view") and to elevate equality (into an equality of respect and self-respect); he wishes to have moral dignity while repudiating moral desert.[13] His radicalization of the principle of equality is the basis for his

---

[9] *ibid.*, p. 332.

[10] *ibid.*, p. 321.

[11] *ibid.*, p. 330.

[12] *ibid*, p. 332.

[13] John Rawls, *A Theory of Justice* (Cambridge, Ma.: Harvard University Press, 1971), especially pp. 15, 310–312, 440–442. Nozick's comment on this point is telling: "So denigrating a person's autonomy and prime responsibility for his actions is a risky line to take for a theory that otherwise wishes to buttress the dignity and self-respect of autonomous beings; especially a theory that founds so much (including a theory of the good) upon persons' choices. One doubts that the unexalted picture of human beings Rawls' theory presupposes and rests upon can be made to fit together with the view of human dignity it is designed to lead to and embody." (p. 214) See also Harvey C. Mansfield, Jr., *The Spirit of Liberalism* (Cambridge, Ma.: Harvard University Press, 1978), pp. 90–101.

"difference principle," which as he says "transforms the aims of society in fundamental respects."[14] The extent of this transformation is checked by the priority assigned by Rawls to the principle of liberty. But the justification of this priority is weak, depending as it does on the following claim:

> The basis for self-esteem in a just society is not then one's income share but the publicly affirmed distribution of fundamental rights and liberties. And this distribution being equal, everyone has a similar and secure status when they meet to conduct the common affairs of the wider society. No one is inclined to look beyond the constitutional affirmation of equality for further political ways of securing his status.[15]

But if citizens do happen to consider facts like income share – or natural endowments – in allocating status, then, since self-esteem is a primary good and status crucial to self-esteem, it is hard to see why the government would not be entitled to impose illiberal egalitarian measures to ensure equality of status and, thus, of self-esteem; and the priority of liberty over equality would collapse. Rawls' attempt to transcend old-fashioned egalitarianism in the name of equality of esteem thus seems dangerously utopian, whereas Nozick's attempt to transcend old-fashioned libertarianism is merely wishfully utopian.

But is there no account that can be given of equality and/or liberty that is neither utopian nor uninspiring? Could liberty and equality perhaps be understood as honorable?

II

> The principle of honor is of use as a subordinate rule of ethics in all our relations, especially in those which we sustain to our equals: but there is no department of action where it is so much needed as in politics – there is none in which it is so much missed. The decay of it, or its absence from the political department of life, is not only a vast evil of itself, but it deters many young men of refined tastes from seeking to do public service for their country. . . .[16]

Theodore D. Woolsey, "The Relations of Honor to Political Life" (1875)

---

[14] Rawls, *A Theory of Justice*, p. 107
[15] *ibid.*, p. 544.
[16] *An Address delivered before the Phi Beta Kappa of Harvard College*, July 1, 1875 (New Haven: Judd and White, 1875), p. 3.

Honor occupies ... an unambiguously outdated status in the *Weltanschauung* of modernity.[17]

Peter L. Berger, Brigitte Berger, and Hansfreid Kellner,
"On the Obsolescence of the Concept of Honor"

The prospect of linking together the modern doctrines of equality and liberty and the notion of honor may seem a doubtful one. Clearly there is a considerable tension between a politics oriented towards equality and liberty and what one might call the prerequisites of honor: as Tocqueville points out, "it is the dissimilarities and inequalities among men which give rise to the notion of honor," and "honor is only effective in full view of the public," a view that recedes in favor of the private sphere in a society dedicated to securing individual liberty.[18] On the other hand, the doctrine of equality will not cause all dissimilarities to disappear, nor will the doctrine of individual liberty entirely do away with the public sphere; so Tocqueville can speak of "the contemporary American conception of honor."[19] For "honor plays a part in democratic ages as well as in those of aristocracy, but it is easy to show that it presents a different physiognomy."[20] The prescriptions of honor will be less odd and less well defined, as well as fewer in a democracy, and therefore less easy to discern; "the law of honor exists, but it is often left without interpreters."[21]

Tocqueville's enterprise might be said to be to teach his readers how to interpret, and thus to guide, democracy in an honorable way. Today we see the limits of his success. We do still speak of honor in our public life ("Peace with Honor"), but the concept now means without excessive disgrace or embarassment. In our private lives the phrase, honoring one's debts, is not yet entirely archaic. But our theorists of equality and liberty speak not at all of honor. For Rawls honor becomes the primary good of self-respect, and self-respect is itself democratized almost beyond recognition: "as citizens we are to ... avoid any assessment of the relative value of one another's way of life. ... This democracy in judging each other's aim is the foundation of self-respect in a well-ordered society."[22] Nozick correctly identifies Rawls' difficulty: "When everyone, or almost everyone, has some

---

[17] Peter L. Berger, Brigitte Berger, and Hansfried Kellner, *The Homeless Mind* (New York: Random House, 1973), p. 83.

[18] Alexis de Tocqueville, *Democracy in America* trans. George Lawrence (Garden City, N.Y.: Doubleday, 1969), II,iii.18 ("Concerning Honor in the United States and Democratic Societies"), pp. 626–627. I have occasionally corrected the translation.

[19] *ibid.*, p. 624.

[20] *ibid.*, p. 623.

[21] *ibid.*, p. 623–624.

[22] Rawls, *A Theory of Justice*, p. 442.

thing or attribute, it does not function as a basis for self-esteem. Self-esteem is based on *differentiating characteristics*; that's why it's *self*-esteem."[23] Nozick, thus, judges it unlikely that self-esteem can be equalized; but he, too, is sufficiently egalitarian to be interested in avoiding widespread differences in self-esteem, and the best way to achieve this would be "to have no common weighting of dimensions," no "commonly agreed upon dimension on which will be based people's self-esteem,"[24] no public sphere which would support a common conception of honor.

If honor seems to lack interpreters today, the reason can surely be traced back to its repudiation in the thought of those modern political philosophers who laid the groundwork for our belief in equality and liberty. Hobbes' egalitarianism led him to debunk honor, reducing it to "the opinion of power" and asserting that it does not "alter the case of honor, whether an action . . . be just or unjust."[25] Locke's liberalism seems to leave room for a discussion of honor only in the context of explaining the Biblical injunction to honor thy father and mother, an injunction Locke explains away for the purpose of distinguishing patriarchal from political power, and subordinating the first to the second.[26] Hobbes' debunking of honor follows from the fact that his doctrine of human equality is based on the passion of fear and on the fact of our fearful condition: "In the movement from the principle of honour to the principle of fear, Hobbes' political philosophy comes into being."[27] As for Locke, his inattention to honor follows from the primacy of the necessity of human appropriation, given the virtual worthlessness of the materials provided by nature or God. The notion of honor seems to involve an assertion of human pride, and the claim that there exists some sort of natural or divine support for such an assertion, which in turn calls for human deference; at the bottom of the modern philosophic doctrines of equality and liberty are a denial, even a negation, of both human pride and human deference.

Yet Tocqueville found that there did exist an American conception of honor; and the American Founders, who established a regime based on the principles of equality and liberty, did not entirely shun the term, or the notion, of honor. Is there – or can there be – an "American" understanding of liberty and equality that makes it possible to think – and not simply in a wishful or edifying way – of equality and liberty in conjunction with a certain (democratic and liberal) notion of honor?

[23] Nozick, *Anarchy, State, and Utopia*, p. 243.

[24] *ibid*. pp. 244–246.

[25] Thomas Hobbes, *Leviathan*, ed. C. B. Macpherson (London: Penguin, 1968), p. 156.

[26] John Locke, *Two Treatises of Government*, ed. Peter Laslett (New York: NAL, 1968), pp. 345–361, especially section 70.

[27] Leo Strauss, *The Political Philosophy of Hobbes: Its Basis and Genesis*, trans. Elsa M. Sinclair (Chicago: University of Chicago Press, 1952), p. 128.

III

The first question that offers itself is, whether the general form and aspect of the government be strictly republican. It is evident that no other form would be reconcilable with the genius of the people of America; with the fundamental principles of the Revolution; or with that honorable determination which animates every votary of freedom, to rest all our political experiments on the capacity of mankind for self-government.[28]

Federalist #39

The determination to rest all our political experiments on the capacity of mankind for self-government may require a strictly republican form of government. But why is that determination honorable?

For a deed to be honorable it must be difficult to do and very much worth doing. Mankind has the capacity for self-government; but that capacity is not easy to realize; establishing and maintaining self-government is difficult. In addition, self-government at its best can be good government; the question the people of America will decide will be "whether societies of men are really capable or not of establishing *good government* from reflection and choice, or whether they are forever destined to depend for their political constitutions on accident and force."[29] The task of self-government is honorable both because it is difficult to do at all and because it can produce good government when done well.

If the capacity of mankind for self-government is problematic, the right of self-government seems not to be. The right follows quite directly from the truth that we Americans "hold" to be self-evident, "that all men are created equal."[30] This truth is the first cause of the separation from Great Britain because it is the basis of the general right of revolution; and as the Declaration of Independence is both the declaration of the causes of our revolution and the declaration of the fundamental principles of the new nation to be established after the revolution, this truth is the first cause of the American republic. Human equality is a universal fact that we hold or assert to be true; our particular nation claims to take its bearings by a universal and abstract truth, one whose meaning was defined with tolerable clarity by

[28] "Publius" (Alexander Hamilton, James Madison, and John Jay), *The Federalist* (New York: Modern Library, n.d.), #39, p. 243.

[29] *Federalist* #1, p. 3. Emphasis added.

[30] For the following interpretation of the Declaration and its principles, I am indebted to Harry V. Jaffa, *Crisis of the House Divided: An Interpretation of the Lincoln-Douglas Debates* (Seattle: University of Washington Press, 1959), and especially to Mansfield, *The Spirit of Liberalism*, ch. 5.

Jefferson nearly fifty years later: "The general spread of the light of science has already laid open to every view the palpable truth, that the mass of mankind has not been born with saddles on their backs, nor a favored few booted and spurred, ready to ride them legitimately, by the grace of God."[31] But the assertion of this truth is not by itself, perhaps, particularly honorable – especially if Jefferson is correct that this is not a truth terribly difficult to discern. The truth of human equality becomes honorable only when it is understood as imposing upon us the task of self-government.

Men are equal in possessing certain unalienable rights; the end of government is to secure these rights, while deriving its just powers from the consent of the governed. This second consequence of equality – that government derives its powers from the consent of the governed – accounts for the right of revolution; but the other consequence of equality – that government exists to secure our rights – limits the proper occasion of revolution to "whenever any form of government becomes destructive of these ends." We are only justified in exercising our right to revolution when it is "necessary" to revolt, and the Declaration takes this limit on a willful right to revolt so seriously that it devotes a good deal of space to specifying particular facts which prove that this necessity exists. Only because of these facts, which demonstrate the tyrannical intentions of the present King of Great Britain, is revolution not merely a right but also a "duty": "when a long train of abuses and usurpations, pursuing invariably the same object evinces a design to reduce them under absolute despotism, it is their right, it is their duty, to throw off such government, and to provide new guards for their future security." By the same token, the revolution can only be said to be fully justified if it does result in "their future security," that is, if it does lead to the establishment of a government which does secure rights and which does derive its powers from the consent of the governed. The Declaration's account of the right of revolution, then, implies both the determination to assert the capacity of mankind for self-government, and the responsibility of vindicating that capacity.

The Declaration also suggests one key aspect of that responsibility. For the two consequences of the principle of equality, consent and rights, do not automatically coincide: it is possible for government by consent to abridge individual rights, and it is possible for government to secure individual rights by abridging the requirement of consent. The internal reconciliation, so to speak, of the requirements of just government – of rights and consent – may be as difficult a task as reconciling the characteristics and requirements of republican government with the characteristics that any government that is to survive must possess, such as energy and stability. It is the difficulty of

---

[31] Thomas Jefferson, letter to Roger C. Weightman, June 24, 1826, in *Selected Writings*, ed. Harvey C. Mansfield, Jr. (Arlington Heights, Illinois: AHM, 1979), p. 13.

achieving this twin task, along with the presumed worth of a government that preserves rights and depends on the consent of the governed, that makes self-government honorable.

Arranging republican government so that it can meet these challenges, external and internal, is of course the goal of the Constitution, as explicated in *The Federalist*. There we learn that the necessities of foreign policy require Union, and one with an energetic government, but that these necessities can be accommodated to government by consent and with the preservation of rights. This requires a considerable amount of education by Publius of his readers as to the harsh realities of politics, and especially of foreign policy – and a debunking of the notion that "this portion of the globe" is likely to be exempt from "the common calamities that have befallen other parts of it."[32] On the basis of this education Publius can persuade his readers to countenance, indeed to endorse, institutional arrangements which lean against the tendency or "genius" of "republican liberty."[33] Similarly, the genius of republican liberty has certain characteristics that, left unchecked, might endanger rights or, eventually, the perpetuation of government by consent of the governed; here, too, Publius has to persuade his readers to endorse arrangements such as life tenure for judges, arrangements that do not come easy to the republican temper.

Publius' method of persuasion in these cases is precisely to appeal to our honorable determination to govern ourselves. For example, Union is not to be accepted as an unfortunate necessity: "According to the degree of pleasure and pride we feel in being republicans, ought to be our zeal in cherishing the spirit and supporting the character of Federalists."[34] Our pride in being republicans ought to make us do what is necessary to make sure that republicanism is successful.

In *Federalist* #39 Publius comments on the inaccuracy with which the term republic has been used in political disquisitions, and offers his own definition: a republic derives all its power directly or indirectly from the people, and is administered by persons holding their offices for a limited term or during pleasure or good behavior. "It is *essential* to such a government that it be derived from the great body of society, not from an inconsiderable proportion, or a favored class of it; otherwise a handful of tyrannical nobles, exercising their oppression by a delegation of their powers, might aspire to the rank of republicans, and claim for their government the honorable title of republic."[35] Publius appeals to republican pride to support what is, after all, the non-controversial aspect of his definition. But he, then,

---

[32] *Federalist* #36, p. 223.
[33] *Federalist* #37, pp. 227–228.
[34] *Federalist* #10, p. 62.
[35] *Federalist* #39, pp. 243–244.

shows the consequences of that pride, or the consequences we must admit if we are to take pride in being a republican: we must allow indirect appointment by the people, and the possibility of tenure during good behavior; "otherwise every government in the United States, as well as every other popular government that has been or can be well organized or well executed, would be degraded from the republican character."[36] That is, we must accept life-tenured judges, something we republicans are reluctant to do, because otherwise republican government would not be good government, and the title of republic would not be an honorable one.

For maintaining a well-organized and well-executed popular government – one that can survive, and that can preserve its principles of consent and securing rights – America would deserve to be honored. It would stand apart from the rest of mankind, thus fulfilling Tocqueville's condition for having a notion of honor.[37] But it would stand apart as a representative of mankind, thus embodying a peculiarly democratic conception of honor. *Federalist* #11 nicely captures the difference between this ground of national honor and what might be called aristocratic national honor.

> ... Europe ... has ... extended her dominion over them all. Africa, Asia, and America, have successively felt her domination. The superiority she has long maintained has tempted her to plume herself as the Mistress of the World, and to consider the rest of mankind as created for her benefit. ... Facts have too long supported these arrogant pretensions of the Europeans. It belongs to us to vindicate the honor of the human race, and to teach that assuming brother moderation.[38]

America seeks honor not by ruling over others but by vindicating the claim of the capacity of mankind for self-government; America distinguishes herself as the particular representative of the human race who vindicates the honor of the human race.

America's role as representative of the human race reminds us of the role of the representatives who wrote the Declaration of Independence. It is the representatives who call their fellow citizens' attention to the British King's design of tyranny; it is the representatives who declare independence on behalf of their fellow citizens; and it is the representatives who, for the support of their Declaration, "mutually pledge to each other" their lives, their fortunes, and their "sacred honor." The representatives claim honor not as rulers over their fellow citizens but as representatives of them, acting on their behalf. When fifty years later the dying Jefferson had to turn down

[36] *ibid.*
[37] Tocqueville, *Democracy in America*, II,iii,18, p. 626.
[38] *Federalist* #11, p. 69.

an invitation to participate in a celebration of the anniversary of the Declaration, he wrote,

> I should, indeed, with peculiar delight, have met and exchanged there congratulations personally with the small band, the remnant of that host of worthies, who joined with us on that day, in the bold and doubtful election we were to make for our country, between submission of the sword; and to have enjoyed with them the consolatory fact, that our fellow citizens, after half a century of experience and prosperity, continue to approve the choice we made.[39]

This bold statement makes clear that the choice was that of the representatives, acting on behalf of their fellow citizens.

It would have been foolish for the representatives to have allowed the truth of equality to blind them to the fact that a few had to step forward to spur their fellow citizens to put an end to their patient suffering, and "to right themselves by abolishing the forms to which they are accustomed." Equality does not preclude, indeed it allows, a few representatives to achieve honor by leading the people, just as it allows the American people to achieve honor by acting in advance of and in the interest of the rest of mankind. And the task of self-government is difficult enough so that even if the Declaration were to fulfill Jefferson's hopes, and become to the world "the signal of arousing men to burst the chains under which monkish ignorance and superstition had persuaded them to bind themselves, and to assume the blessings and security of self-government,"[40] there would still be honor for any nation that successfully preserved self-government. And representatives like Jefferson would still be needed, despite the "general spread of the light of science,"[41] to help the people establish and preserve it.

IV

> In the United States professions are more or less unpleasant, more or less lucrative, but they are never high or low. Every honest profession is honorable.
>
> Tocqueville, *Democracy in America*, II, ii, 18

The preservation of self-government is no mean task; but is it truly honorable? One could imagine a well-constructed system of government by consent that was energetic and stable, and secured rights; is this the full meaning of "good government by reflection and choice"? Does it not matter

[39] Jefferson, letter to Weightman, in *Selected Writings*, p. 12.
[40] *ibid.*, pp. 12–13.
[41] *ibid.*

how the rights that are secured are exercised? If the right to pursue happiness is used entirely for low or banal pursuits, or if happiness in any meaningful sense is never secured, if life in a liberal democracy is merely the joyless quest for joy, then how honorable is the preservation of the structure that makes this quest possible?

One should begin by noting that here, too, as in the case of consent, there exists a kind of internal minimal standard by which one can judge a better and worse exercise of rights. If the pursuit of happiness leads to utter irresponsibility or enervation, the security of rights, and the preservation of self-government, will be endangered. So the very principles of liberty and equality, properly understood, allow for some discrimination among the private pursuits of citizens in a liberal democracy, and suggest the directions in which legislators might, usually indirectly, seek to push their fellow citizens. That such a discrimination among private pursuits makes possible, and indeed implies, a liberal democratic notion of honor, is explained by Tocqueville in volume two of *Democracy in America*.

The dominant fact of our age is equality of conditions. This fact gives rise to "a mother thought or to a principal passion"[42] that drags all other sentiments and ideas along in its course, Tocqueville explains in Part Two of Volume Two why the passion of equality is stronger than our taste for liberty – because human beings are short-sighted and ignorant of their true interests – and how it threatens liberty and self-government by fostering individualism.[43] He then shows how this threat can be countered:[44] it seems that the principal passion of equality can above all be checked by the mother thought that binds Tocqueville's book together,[45] which is, here, identified as the "science of association."[46] The taste for liberty must be supplemented by or educated by this science, which sees the possible connections among individuals and groups, and which makes possible an "art of association," an art of putting together individuals and groups – and ideas, sentiments, laws, and mores – for the sake of preserving liberty and self-government, and, indeed, civilization.[47] Central to the art of association in America is the peculiarly American doctrine of self-interest well-understood, first however elaborated as a doctrine by Tocqueville. This doctrine encourages and justifies public-spiritedness on the grounds of private interest and need, and "if it does not lead the will directly to virtue, it approaches virtue insensibly through habits."[48] Thus, "at first it is of necessity that men attend to the

---

[42] Tocqueville, *Democracy in America*, II,ii,1, p. 504.
[43] *ibid.*, II,ii,1–3, pp. 503–509.
[44] *ibid.*, II,ii,4–9, pp. 509–528.
[45] *ibid.*, Introduction, p. 20.
[46] *ibid.*, II,ii,5, pp. 513–517.
[47] *ibid.*
[48] *ibid.*, II,ii,8, pp. 527.

public interest, afterward by choice. What had been calculation becomes instinct. By dint of working for the good of his fellow citizens, he in the end acquires a habit and taste for serving them."[49] The public-spiritedness necessary for the preservation of liberty arises on a base of interest, even of necessity.

This is very much the theme of Tocqueville's discussion of honor in Chapters Eighteen of Parts Two and Three of Volume Two of *Democracy in America*. Tocqueville explains that since everyone in a democracy works or has worked or has parents who worked for a living, we assume that "to work is the necessary, natural, and honest condition of all men." Work is thought to be honorable in a democracy, even work for pay, whereas in aristocracies work for pay is, at least in public, despised. And "as soon as these two assumptions are made, that work is an honorable necessity of human nature and that it is always clearly done, at least in part, for pay, the immense difference separating different professions in aristocratic societies disappears." Every honest profession becomes honorable.[50] This doctrine seems to complement the teaching of self-interest well-understood: the pursuit of happiness, even when primarily understood, as it is in our times, as the attempt to flee or overcome natural necessity, need not degrade human beings to the status of mere reactors to the spur of necessity. If we accept the claims of necessity openly and honestly, we can understand our manner of the pursuit of happiness as somehow chosen by us – and therefore, to an extent, honorable. For the successful pursuit of happiness as we understand it does impose certain requirements on us – above all, honesty, and other bourgeois virtues: the "needs" of a commercial trading nation lead us to honor hard work, the quiet virtues which favor trade, a kind of courage in economic matters, and the chastity which supports the domestic harmony so important to business success.[51] Thus, on the basis of need or interest an "American conception of honor"[52] is constructed, one that supplements the doctrine of self-interest well-understood in shaping the exercise of rights so that their exercise is consistent with the preservation of self-government.

But Tocqueville also points to the insufficiency of this conception of honor which virtually reduces honor to honesty and a few other bourgeois virtues. For while this conception gives us a sort of minimal standard for judging the exercise of rights, it does not really speak in a satisfactory way to the question of whether our exercise of our rights is truly admirable – or even whether it is truly satisfying. According to the Declaration, the people should organize a government in a form "as to them shall seem most likely to

---

[49] *ibid.*, II,ii,4, pp. 512–513.
[50] *ibid.*, II ii,18, pp. 550–551.
[51] *ibid.*, II,ii,18, pp. 550–551, and II,iii,18, pp. 616–627.
[52] *ibid.*, II,iii,18, p. 621.

effect their safety and happiness." The doctrine of self-interest well-understood and of honorable work might be said to effect our safety; but what of happiness? According to Tocqueville, the Americans, despite pursuing their self-interest well-understood, are not happy.[53] We are preoccupied with the satisfaction of material needs, with the things of this world; we seek an infinitude of goods which the inevitability of death thwarts, and we seek a perfect equality that can never be attained.[54] Thus we are restless and sad. For we fail to realize that the soul, too, has its needs and interests; our doctrine of self-interest well-understood still does not do justice to the complexity of the self. We thus find ourselves engaged in an ultimately pathetic quest for bodily happiness, a quest interspersed with moments of fierce and strange spirituality.[55]

Thus, Tocqueville's discussion of Americans' love of material well-being[56] modifies his apparent endorsement of the doctrine of self-interest well-understood. For this doctrine may not succeed in preventing us from losing sight of "those more precious goods which constitute the greatness and glory of the human species". Self-interest well-understood seems not to preclude the possibility of human degradation: "while man takes delight in this proper and legitimate quest for prosperity, there is a danger that in the end he may lose the use of his sublimest faculties and that, bent on improving everything around him, he may at length degrade himself. That, and nothing else, is the peril."[57] Beneath the dangerous passion of equality, which is checked by self-interest well-understood, is the love of this-wordly well-being, which Tocqueville tells us is the dominant national taste: "The main current of human passions running in that direction sweeps everything along with it."[58] Materialism is a deeper threat than equality, or is the deeper version of the threat of equality; and self-interest well-understood seems an insufficient response.

Or can self-interest well-understood be made to point beyond itself, thereby raising the souls of democratic citizens rather than merely extending our this-worldly horizons? Tocqueville suggests that this is the case. By setting distant goals for human endeavor in this world, by accustoming democratic citizens to protracted effort for the sake of a long-term project, the moralist and legislator accomplishes his "most important business." The extension of self-interest over time may lead ultimately, one might say, to its extension upwards:

[53] *ibid.*, II,ii,13, p. 538.
[54] *ibid.*, pp. 537–538.
[55] *ibid*, II,ii,12, pp. 534–535.
[56] *ibid.*, II,ii,10–17, pp. 530–549.
[57] *ibid.*, II,ii,12, p. 534; II,ii,15, p. 543.
[58] *ibid.*, II,ii,10, pp. 530–532.

I have therefore no doubt that, in accustoming the citizens to think of the future in this world, they will gradually be led without noticing it themselves toward religious beliefs.

Thus the same means that, up to a certain point, enable men to manage without religion are perhaps after all the only means we still possess for bringing mankind back, by a long and roundabout path, to a state of faith.[59]

The doctrine of self-interest well-understood can thus be elevated to a concern with the soul as well as the body.

That such an elevation is possible is in fact suggested by the very fact of our attachment to the doctrine of self-interest well-understood. This attachment, as Tocqueville points out, cannot after all be explained by self-interest. Indeed, the doctrine does not even account for some of the disinterested, spontaneous acts "natural to man" that Americans do, let alone accounting for itself. "But the Americans are hardly prepared to admit that they do give way to emotions of this sort. They prefer to honor their philosophy rather than themselves."[60] If Americans thought through our desire to honor our philosophy, our desire to live according to a principle – even a principle which celebrates self-interest – we would see the limits of our understanding of self-interest, and of our understanding of what is honorable.

V

And for the support of this Declaration, with a firm reliance on the protection of Divine Providence, we mutually pledge to each other our lives, our fortunes, and our sacred honor.

Declaration of Independence

Is there any support in the Declaration for an understanding of honor that reaches above the level of the successful preservation of self-government and the pursuit of self-interest well-understood? Perhaps. For at the end of the Declaration the representatives pledge their honor as individuals to each other as individuals – not, say, to their countrymen. The representatives' honor, in other words, seems not to be derived from their status as representatives. What is the ground of this individual honor? We note that it is referred to as "sacred honor"; and we note that in the penultimate

---

[59] *ibid.*, II,ii,17, p. 459.
[60] *ibid.*, II,ii,8, p. 526.

paragraph of the Declaration the representatives, stepping forward as individuals for the first time, appeal to "the Supreme Judge of the world for the rectitude" of their intentions. At the beginning of the Declaration the representatives had explained that "a decent respect to the opinions of mankind" required the American people (speaking through their representatives) to declare the causes which impelled them to separation. The people seem to take their bearings by mankind; and in *The Federalist* the American people acquire honor by vindicating the capacity of mankind for self-government. The representatives, on the other hand, appeal on their own behalf to the Supreme Judge of the world; their honor seems to rest not on the capacity of mankind, but on their truthfulness as judged by God. The pledge to one another of the representatives' sacred honor cannot, it seems, be understood merely in light of what is necessitated or justified by even an honorable devotion to liberty and equality. We might say that in speaking only in terms of liberty and equality, the signers of the Declaration prefer to honor their philosophy rather than themselves. In so honoring their philosophy, they teach us that human honor depends upon and derives from a standard superior to, though not inconsistent with, human safety and happiness.

Kennedy School of Government, Harvard University

SOME THOUGHTS ON LIBERTY, EQUALITY, AND TOCQUEVILLE'S *DEMOCRACY IN AMERICA*

Werner J. Dannhauser

I. INTRODUCTION

1. *In praise of Tocqueville.* The young United States was lucky – and deserving of its luck – to find as profound an interpreter of its principles as Alexis de Tocqueville (1805–1859). So deeply, so philosophically, did he comprehend this country in *Democracy in America*[1] that today's reflections on liberty and equality in America either copy Tocqueville or fall short of understanding. The following reflections will be guilty of both plagiarism and superficiality but they do intend to capture something of Tocqueville's spirit. He gave this nation its due. He brought to his endeavors some advantages we no longer enjoy. For example, he had first-hand experience of democracy's great alternative and predecessor, aristocracy; he knew both sides because he was both sides.

Of course, some advantages accrue to those of us who have come after him, even apart from having *Democracy in America* to study. The United States may not be old but it is older now; we can take later developments into account. Thus, we no longer lack poets or poetry; we probably suffer as much from crime as from vice; and juries do not function all that well. But no dwarfish ability to climb the shoulders of a giant nor special dispensation from history can compensate us for the lack of Tocqueville's genius: the breadth of vision that recalls Montesquieu and even Aristotle, an intimacy, reminiscent of Rousseau, with modernity's demons, a sad coming to terms with human contingency that puts one in mind of Thucydides. All honor to Alexis de Tocqueville.

2. *Ruminations on Procedure.* At times I will attempt to divine "the view from Tocqueville's head" but I will not be trying to solve any of the problems that continue to vex Tocqueville scholarship.[2] Thus, I will not have much to

---

[1] Alexis de Tocqueville, *Democracy in America*, trans. by George Lawrence (Garden City, New York: Anchor Books, 1969). Quotations from Tocqueville are all from this edition. Page references are given in the text.

[2] A good introduction to these problems can be found in Marvin Zetterbaum, *Tocqueville and The Problem of Democracy* (Stanford: Stanford University Press, 1967). The book and its author have taught me more about Tocqueville than I can readily acknowledge by specific citations.

say about the problem of Tocqueville's historical determinism or lack of it, about the extent of his allegiance to modern as opposed to ancient thought, or kindred difficulties.

In seeking something like a Tocquevillian approach I mean, among other things, that it is not necessary, not desirable, and probably not possible to begin a meaningful discussion of liberty and equality with a rigid definition of terms. The discussion of political matters may move toward a precise terminology but it cannot begin from that point. All of us bring more or less adequate notions – called opinions – of liberty and equality to any genuinely political discussion of liberty and equality. Were we to ask a man "Are you free?" and he were to answer "I'm free at 4 this afternoon" we would realize at once that we were talking not to a sensible citizen but to a fool, a professor of philosophy, or a foolish professor of philosophy.

In line with the above I will make no attempt systematically to distinguish among liberty, freedom, and even independence, three overlapping terms. I am content to imitate the talk of political beings as they worry about what to do or avoid doing.

Such a procedure can claim to be in harmony with that of Tocqueville's, who "tried to see not differently but further than any party." (p. 20)

II. SOME THOUGHTS ABOUT LIBERTY

3. *Personal.* A naturalized citizen, I came to these shores in 1939. My arrival resembled that of millions of other refugees accepted by the United States: from the deck of a ship I sighted the Statue of Liberty and was deeply moved.

No Statue of Equality greets the immigrant. Why not? Liberty strikes us as more lustrous an object of desire than equality. American history bears witness to a preference for liberty over equality. We have a Liberty Bell, not an Equality Bell. Many understand equality as the leading issue of our Civil War, but we think of having fought that war to "free the slaves," not to make them equal. In their songs, Americans frequently extol liberty, rarely equality, and that includes American slaves: "O before I'll be a slave, I'll be buried in my grave and go home to my Lord and be free."

The praise of liberty – and relative neglect of equality – goes beyond these shores and continues today. The German Communists in the Spanish Civil War sang not of equality (*Gleichheit*) but of freedom (*Freiheit*). We know of "freedom fighters"; would we not be surprised by "equality fighters"? This evidence should not be dismissed because it emphasizes rhetoric; political rhetoric provides us with one of our best clues to political reality.

One can openly oppose equality as a principle but the opponents of liberty usually deny their opposition. They identify themselves as advocates of "true freedom." The praise of liberty can doubtless be exposed as hypocritical on many occasions, but we know from La Rochefoucauld that hypocrisy is the tribute that vice pays to virtue.

Tocqueville surely adds to the luster of liberty with *Democracy in America*, but we must not suppose that he merely forces open doors with his praise. Luster can be lost. Perhaps he feared that men might not always, and no longer, be willing to fight for freedom and if need be die for it? Perhaps he sensed that the liberty that men were praising in the nineteenth century was as much gilded as golden? Perhaps he knew that in our time liberty need only be loved more but understood better?

5. *Gods, Men, Beasts.* Trying to understand liberty somewhat better, we soon notice that it does not always possess the kind of luster that first attracted our attention. In fact we associate it with beasts as well as men; when we speak of the former as free, or at least as "born free," we do not simply abuse language.

If even animals can live in freedom, it is only to be expected that uncivilized human beings can enjoy many of the blessings of liberty. We have no particular trouble understanding Tocqueville when he talks about the wild freedom of savages or discusses with some sympathy the liberty that once informed the lives of American Indians. (see especially pages 318–320, 330–333)

Sometimes, to be sure, liberty is even more lofty than has been suggested. The gods are free in a way precluded to man, if only because they are free of the constraints of death. And when we pray to God we assume that His power, freedom and will are co-extensive.

Tocqueville's main concern, however (and hence our own), remains with human freedom and more specifically with political liberty, a liberty unknown to beasts, not completely accessible to uncivilized human beings, and not necessary to the gods. Tocqueville tends to limit his discussion of liberty in a way similar to John Stuart Mill, who begins *On Liberty* by excluding freedom of the will from consideration and discusses primarily "the nature and limits of the power which can be legitimately exercised by society over the individual."[3]

6. *Tocqueville and the Range of Liberty.* Tocqueville's partiality to liberty makes itself manifest in a number of ways, especially by the fact that he dwells much more extensively on the abuses of equality than on the abuses of liberty. His occasional use of the term "true liberty" (see for example pp. xiv, 33, 46) points to the existence of false liberty but he does not make all that much of it.

Indeed, we may surmise that even the lowest kinds of liberty are good.

[3] John Stuart Mill, *On Liberty* (London: Penguin Books, 1974), p. 59.

The proud lion roaming in the jungle is to be preferred to the caged animal if only because he is somehow more of a lion. Liberty is in most cases a precondition and in some cases a cause for things becoming what they truly are or are meant to be; liberty is part of nature's way.

The range of liberty as something we can observe in gods as well as beasts helps us to evaluate the various manifestations of human liberty. It helps to ask whether a particular liberty pertains to those aspects of us that manifest our kinship with beasts or those we are tempted to call "divine." We need liberty to take care of our souls as well as our bodies.

7. *State and Civil Society.* Politics used to refer to everything done by the *polis* and the *polis* did almost everything human beings can do. Today we distinguish both in theory and practice between the social and political.

The distinction causes us no difficulty in our everyday lives; we are brought up to observe and embody it. We know, for example, what it means to keep politics out of a conversation or a decision. What we sometimes overlook is that the political sphere has assigned limits because of political decisions, many of them enshrined in the United States Constitution. We should also remember that the idea of a limited politics must itself be limited, if only by common sense. When somebody says that "the country is in danger" or "the country is going to the dogs" it will not do to ask him whether he means the state or the society.[4]

Notwithstanding the limits of the limits of the distinction, it is useful enough for Tocqueville to use it. In fact he organizes his book around it. (see p. 417) Nevertheless, he emphasizes that he has written "a single book" (ibid.), and he sometimes attributes repetition to the organization of his work.

8. *Liberty Against the State.* The spheres may overlap here and there, now and then, but they are clear enough for most practical purposes. A threat to liberty appears whenever a transgression of limits occurs, whenever a "strong and dominating authority" steps over the line. The most obvious threat to liberty comes from the state. Liberty is most manifestly liberty against a tyrannical government, as those subject to one know, and those who have never lived under one find it difficult to understand. (see pp. 250–253)

For present purposes, we need not distinguish between tyranny and despotism, and certainly not between authoritarianism and totalitarianism, though Tocqueville might help us to develop – or rediscover – a sensible political vocabulary. For now it suffices to speak of oppression.

There are degrees of oppression. The state may have too many formal rights even though it does not always use them, or it may exercise power without any entitlement. Without doubt slavery constitutes the greatest

---

[4] This formulation, as do others in this essay, comes from my teacher, Leo Strauss.

abomination, the greatest negation of liberty. (see pp. 136, 345–346, 380)

9. *Liberty Against the Democratic State.* The state that threatens liberty and does its best to extinguish it need not be the executive committee of an entrenched minority.[5] It can represent the majority, boast of its popular support. Both Tocqueville and Mill have made us sensitive to the tyranny of the majority. (see especially pp. 246–261) Democracies tend to become careless about that vigilance which is known to be the price of liberty. "Nowhere has the law left grander scope to arbitrary power than in democratic republics, because they feel they have nothing to fear from it" (p. 206). A democratic state can suffocate many liberties, including the freedom to think unorthodox thoughts, in various insidious ways (see, for example, pp. 254–256).

10. *Liberty Against Society.* The majority that rules in democracies does not need to work its way through laws and other explicitly political measures. Society lets people know that certain things are just not done, though one may be allowed to do them by the law. Disapproval can be as threatening as a jail sentence. One not only obeys; one conforms. Tocqueville has taught us all we need to know about the degradations associated with conformity.

Indeed, many Americans think too much about the dangers of conformity and not enough about its merit. We all know people who think they are free when they dress differently – worse – than other people, whose idea of liberty is to defy the manners enshrined by tradition, who fear for the Free West when even the most sensible restraints on behavior are imposed. They loathe conformity so much it no longer matters to them what it is *to* which one conforms.

11. *Two Cheers for Negative Liberty.* We have talked about liberty *against* the state and *against* society. Liberty can be understood as something negative, as the "mere" absence of external constraints. Because of that, "freedom from" can be compared invidiously with "freedom for." The distinction has been made most eloquently by Nietzsche,[6] but excessive love of political freedom or fondness for democracy are not among his noteworthy characteristics.

The case against negative liberty commands respect. Let us, however, not sell short the merit and beauty of liberty as meaning above all that we are left alone.

On the collective level, after all, that is what we call independence, self-

---

[5] Karl Marx and Friedrich Engels, "The Communist Manifesto," in *Marx and Engels: Basic Writings on Politics and Philosophy*, ed. Lewis Feuer (Garden City, New York: Anchor Books, 1959). p. 29.

[6] Friedrich Nietzsche "Thus Spoke Zarathustra," in *The Portable Nietzsche*, ed. and trans. by Walter Kaufmann (New York: Viking Press, 1956), pp. 174–176. I am also indebted to Isaiah Berlin, *Four Essays in Liberty* (London: Oxford University Press, 1969) pp. 118–172.

determination, sovereignty. An aura of respectability and even nobility attaches to these terms. We feel that nations and other collectivities ought usually to be free to decide their own destinies. In most cases they ought even be allowed to make their own mistakes.

If we hold it better, most of the time, for collectivities to be free should we not give the benefit of the doubt to individuals whenever possible? That would mean that each of us commits himself to minding his own business – and it has long been known that minding one's own business has something to do with justice.[7]

Leaving others alone need not entail indifference; it can betoken respect. It involves the realization that the goodness that issues from grappling with one's own demons is more enduring, more reliable than any correct behavior we impose. By cherishing freedom we cherish human inwardness. In the best case, we cultivate it.

But even if it produces no great and shining deeds, we cherish the absence of constraint, or else, alas, we take it for granted. We walk by the policeman without lowering our voice; we change jobs without notifying the proper authorities; we take a trip without obtaining a permit. These freedoms begin to matter more once they are lost. Nor will it do to call them little freedoms. A relative absence of fear of the police has much to do with the very atmosphere enveloping our lives, and women's "right to choose their husbands freely" (p. 597) constitutes a vital part of their lives. The freedom *from* external constraints does not assure the use of freedom *for* the living of the good life, but it is worth preserving, protecting, enhancing.

12. *Protecting Liberty.* Since it is worth doing, how does one do it? We associate the furtherance of liberty with the furtherance of democracy but Tocqueville teaches us to reflect about the unreflective link we establish between democracy and liberty. He does so both by praising the liberty to be found in aristocracies (see, for one of many examples, p. 473) and by stressing democratic dangers to liberty.

Yet, though we cannot simply equate democracy and liberty (see p. 683), democracy and liberty do go hand in hand these days; Tocqueville speaks of the "democratic liberty and enlightenment of our age." (p. 363) The only plausible liberty today is liberty *for all*, so that the protection of liberty today becomes indistinguishable from the protection of liberal democracy.

13. *Religion and Liberty.* Having reinvented the wheel, we can continue to think about the preservation and furtherance of liberty. In this respect one finds it difficult to keep religion out of the picture; reading *Democracy in America*, one finds it impossible.

---

[7] Plato, *The Republic*, 443a–444e.

Let us begin again with "negative" liberty. In the United States, government does not tell us when to worship, how to worship, whether to worship. That remains a private matter by virtue of the public laws depending on the First Amendment. Government leaves us alone when it comes to religion and we have legal recourse to force others to leave us alone as well.

The religion Americans practice freely teaches them much about freedom; in Tocqueville's words, it helps to teach "Americans the art of being free." (p. 290) It does so by teaching, among other things, that man is worthy of being free because God created him, that his inwardness should be cherished because the sparks it houses are divine. Tocqueville quotes none other than Cotton Mather when he writes of "true liberty" (see xiv, 33, 46), suggesting that true freedom, or at least the truest freedom is freedom under God. The divine hallows our liberty even as it limits it.

Tocqueville goes so far as to suggest that religion provides the only firm foundation for liberty. "For my part, I doubt whether man can support complete religious independence and entire political liberty at the same time. I am led to think that if he has no faith he must obey, and if he is free, he must believe." (p. 444)

Immediately after this passage, Tocqueville refers to "the great usefulness of religion." He does not refer to its truth. We need not inquire into the strength of Tocqueville's own piety, but we must ask whether the mounting attacks on the truth of religion have not impaired its usefulness. Later in the nineteenth century, Nietzsche, who admired Tocqueville, was to proclaim the death of God.[8] Was Tocqueville unwilling or unable to face that event? Did he deny its occurrence? Did he think that the institutions we call "organized religion" could survive the death of God and continue to function in the service of liberty?

Those are good questions, which is to say that they will not be answered here. Instead three lame conclusions will be offered. First, religion, or something like it, is needed to transfigure negative liberty into something higher. Second, negative liberty is a good even without such transfiguration. Finally, Tocqueville offers other suggestions for the preservation and furtherance of liberty.

14. *Earthly Concerns.* Liberty needs more nurture than the love of God and obedience to His words. It requires cultivation by mundane deeds in the arena of daily life. For example, Tocqueville stresses not only the utility of faith but the usefulness of participation in local government, "that fertile germ of free institutions." (p. 33)

---

[8] Nietzsche, *op. cit.*, p. 124.

He even goes so far as to refer to local liberties as the modern art that will correct the modern natural tendency toward centralization, with its concomitant affinity to oppression. (p. 674)

The exalted freedom to become what we are, to become the best that we are, can be threatened by neglect of what we call the nitty-gritty side of liberty. One must practice liberty (see pp. 132, 191, 194, 243), participate in the management of the community's affairs. One needs both "a taste for freedom and the skill to be free." (p. 287)

It is partly because a people must be habituated to the life of liberty that Tocqueville so frequently praises local, provincial freedoms. (see also pp. 96–7, 396, 511, 662, 676) To some extent the praise constitutes an element of his insistence that liberty needs not only dedication but institutions, a formal framework in which to thrive.

Thus, for a country to keep its liberty it must tend to the independence of its courts, the integrity of a limited political jurisdiction, vigorous though not necessarily highly principled parties. It must see to it that the existence of all kinds of associations is protected by law. Administration needs to be kept decently decentralized; magistrates must be limited as to their powers both by law and prevailing mores. Liberty needs lawyers; their proliferation is either a necessary evil or the same kind of good as bitter medicine; it requires, besides a government dedicated to liberty, "secondary bodies temporarily composed of private citizen." (p. 696)

We have neglected to discuss freedom of the press; the excuse for this omission must be that almost nobody neglects it when discussing liberty. Suffice it to say, then, that according to Tocqueville "freedom of the press is infinitely more precious in a democracy than in any other nation." (p. 697).

15. *Economic Concerns.* Liberty, we have seen, flourishes only in certain settings. Does liberty require a *capitalist* setting? Is capitalism simply in the economic sphere, as its passionate defenders sometimes insist?[9]

Tocqueville never refers to "capitalism," a term popularized by the enemies of the phenomenon they were describing, but he does proclaim the virtue of private property. By having things we can call our own, we learn to respect the rights of others to their own, to their liberty (see especially p. 239). Moreover, he argues for the desirability of middle-class rule. (p. 209) On these two grounds alone – others can readily be found – Tocqueville *ought* to be understood as a capitalist by anti-capitalists.

Looking at the matter from a different side, one can say that the "negative liberty" previously mentioned entails a commercial society with free enterprise. Men want to be free *from* the more severe constraints of material wants.

[9] In this context, one can still learn a good deal from Friedrich A. Hayek, *The Road To Serfdom* (Chicago: University of Chicago Press, 1944).

They also want to be free *to* enrich themselves, to risk money, to change jobs, and to bestow wealth on their children.

The alleged or real baseness of economic pursuits hardly constitutes the distinguishing characteristic between materialistic capitalism and materialistic socialism so it need not concern us in this context. One should, however, mention that the hustle and bustle associated with the commercial life energizes society and, hence, the practice of liberty. Also: the commercial life may be the immoral equivalent to war.

16. *The Abuses of Liberty*. Tocqueville includes a chapter in *Democracy in America* entitled "How an Aristocracy May Be Created by Industry" (pp. 555–558). The chapter serves as the center of gravity for left-wing interpretations of Tocqueville.[10] Such interpretations include the understanding that capitalism – "the system" – is the greatest threat to liberal democracy. Not even this chapter, to say nothing of the work as a whole, sustains such an interpretation.

It is, however, true that the abuses of liberty come to sight with particular ferocity in the economic domain. To encourage commerce means to encourage acquisitiveness. The energizing of society is inseparable from the unleashing of greed.

One might try to argue that, strictly speaking, liberty cannot be abused because the abuse of liberty amounts to license and no longer deserves to be called liberty. Tocqueville, indeed, suggests that liberty is a mean between servility and license (see, for example, p. 94), but if we choose to try to speak strictly we must simply come to the conclusion that the use of liberty forever produces the abuse of liberty.

Examples come readily to mind. Liberty needs a free press, and no free press anywhere at any time confines itself to the cultivation of virtuous deeds and men. Similarly, there can be no liberty without freedom of association, but nobody should assume that church choirs and library committees will constitute the majority of associations.

Liberty may become injurious to liberty; "habits form in freedom that may one day become fatal to that freedom." (p. 254) Tocqueville displays enthusiasm for the fine effects of freedom of association but he doubts "whether there has ever been at any time a nation in which it was wise not to put any limits to the freedom of association." (p. 524)

Libertarian interpretations of Tocqueville tend to become as "thin" as Marxist interpretations. Tocqueville does not show any particular reluctance to curb freedom at certain times.

Lines will always be hard to draw in politics. But one does well to

[10] See for example, Harold J. Laski, "Alexis de Tocqueville and Democracy," in *The Social and Political Ideas of Some Representative Thinkers of the Victorian Age*, ed. by F. J. Hearnshaw (London: Harrap, 1935), pp. 164–186.

challenge those who oppose sensible restraints by proclaiming "I'm for it, but where do you draw the line?" They are usually not for it.

17. *Personal.* I passed the Statue of *Liberty* but upon landing my parents and I had to deal with the Department of *Justice.* Liberty may lead to justice; it may even resemble justice, but it is not the same as justice.

III. SOME THOUGHTS ABOUT EQUALITY

18. *Equality as Democracy.* Equality resembles democracy more than liberty resembles democracy; at times Tocqueville uses the terms "equality" and "democracy" almost synonymously. (see, for examples, pp. 417–418, 695–696) We all find it easier to think of aristocratic liberty than of aristocratic equality. Wherever equality thrives, one must think of democracy, even when the praise of equality emanates from quarters hostile to our liberal democracy.

Would Tocqueville call the Soviet Union and other communist countries democratic? One suspects he would, being quite convinced that democracy and oppression can go hand in hand. What is more, the countries in question call themselves democratic.

In occupied Berlin, the Western sectors call themselves "free"; the Soviet sector refers to itself as "democratic."

19. *Looking for Equality.* Let us return to these shores and refine our terminology a bit. When we look for liberty we find liberties "of" something: freedom of speech, worship, etc. The same goes for equality. Tocqueville follows common sense when he discusses, among other topics, equality of enlightenment, of death, of races, of children, of women, of wealth, of education.

To follow Tocqueville means to concentrate not on the above kinds of equality but on what he calls equality of conditions, meaning social conditions, "the creative element from which each particular fact derived"; the "nodal point" of Tocqueville's observations. (p. 9)[11]

20. *Equality as Self-Evident.* We are children of a two-hundred year old democratic regime, so we tend to take equality of social condition for granted. Our Declaration of Independence refers to the self-evident truth "that all men are created equal." We no longer ask for evidence at all.

Nothing seems more obvious to us than that aristocratic privileges ought not to exist in these United States. In our Constitution, the 8th paragraph of the 9th section of the first article states that "No title of nobility shall be granted by the United States." That must be among the least contested parts of our Constitution.

[11] See Marvin Zetterbaum, "Alexis de Tocqueville," in *History of Political Philosophy*, ed. Strauss and Cropsey (Chicago: Rand McNally, 1972), pp. 715–718.

21. *Historical Roots.* Today we refer to equality of conditions as equality of opportunity. It is not, however, today's discovery; in fact it antedates our regime. The Anglo-American immigrants brought "equality of conditions with them to the New World." (p. 305)

Indeed, Tocqueville writes of "a thousand years of equality" (p. 363) before the reintroduction of slavery, and, as we shall shortly see, the principle of equality even has roots in a more ancient past.

Age bestows a luster all of its own. We cannot help but identify the old with the good and the true.

22. *Historical Enshrinement.* Abraham Lincoln voiced the nation's commitment to equality in the most eloquent possible way. In today's prosaic times, it behooves us to recall something of the poetry of equality.

On August 22, 1864, President Lincoln addressed the 166th Ohio Regiment. He concluded as follows:

> I happen temporarily to occupy this big White House. I am a living witness that any one of your children may look to come here as my father's child has. It is in order that each of you may have through this free government which we have enjoyed, an open field and a fair chance for your industry, enterprise and intelligence; that you may all have equal privileges in the race of life, with all its desirable human aspirations. It is for this the struggle should be maintained, that we may not lose our birthright – not only for one, but for two or three years. The nation is worth fighting for, to secure such an inestimable jewel.[12]

No evidence exists that Lincoln even heard of *Democracy in America*.

23. *Commentary.* Lincoln did not tell the soldiers they could aspire to the Presidency; he referred to their children. He counseled patience and moderate expectations.

Lincoln referred to equal privileges in the race of life. He did not promise anybody a victory or even a tie in the race of life.

24. *Objection Overruled.* Cynics dismiss the thoughts and sentiments expressed by Lincoln as poppycock. Theoretically, they maintain, each of us may look to have our child elected President, but practically there are well-nigh insuperable obstacles. The cynic will most likely cite economic inequality.

Yet within the lifetime of most of us, the son of a poor man has become President – Richard M. Nixon – and the son of a rich man has become President – John F. Kennedy.

25. *Common Sense.* Let us think of a hospital nursery. A dozen newly-born

[12] Abraham Lincoln, *Selected Speeches, Messages, and Letters*, ed. T. Harry Williams (New York: Holt, Rinehart and Winston, 1962), pp. 271–272.

infants are lined up for viewing. What can we tell about them? Very little. We would know little even if we knew much about their parents. Beethoven's parents showed absolutely no promise of rearing a great musician. That black child may grow up to be a Frederick Douglass, that white child a Charles Manson. We know next to nothing. That is the common sense of granting equal privileges in the race of life.[13]

26. *Religion and Equality.* The principle of equality draws strength from a source even more venerable than Abraham Lincoln, and far more ancient, the Bible.

The very first chapter of Genesis affirms an essential equality of men – and women – by virtue of their creation: "And God created man in His own image, in the image of God created He him; male and female created He them." (I:27)

We might, then, say that our love of liberty is rational because it has roots in the part of our tradition stemming from Athens, but that our love of equality is sacred because it has roots in that part of our tradition stemming from Jerusalem. Tocqueville remarks: "Jesus Christ had to come down to earth to make all members of the human race understand that they were naturally similar and equal." (p. 439)

Christianity may have allied itself with inegalitarian aristocracy throughout much of its history, but that alliance went against its grain. On its deepest level, Christianity teaches that men are equal not only because of their common ancestry as creatures of God, but also because all men can attain to the highest life, the life of faith as opposed to the life of reason. Very few men can become philosophers but all men, though sinners, can be candidates for sainthood.

The idea of the infinite preciousness of each and every human life also stems from Jerusalem rather than from Athens.

The connection between equality and Christianity has been understood not only by friends of liberal democracy like Tocqueville but by its vehement enemies. Again, it must suffice to refer to Nietzsche.[14]

27. *More Earthly Concerns.* Once more, we must acknowledge Tocqueville's power to observe mundane realities as well as exalted realities. The origins of equality can be found not only in the Bible but in the laws of inheritance, "those laws whose principal object is to control the fate of property after its owner's death." (p. 51)

It follows that the friends of equality who wish to further it must be concerned with what we have called the nitty-gritty realities. Tax policy can

---

[13] I owe this example to a conversation with the late Herbert J. Storing.

[14] Nietzsche, *op. cit.*, pp. 211–214.

be as significant as divine worship in this respect,[15] and proclamations of equality of rights may not be as important as realizing the relationship between newspapers and equality (see, for example, p. 520).

28. *Present Dangers.* Having given equality something of its due, we must turn to its negative aspects. The following list of dangers is meant to be representative, not exhaustive; it is culled from *Democracy in America*, which presents the reader with a veritable catalogue of calamities connected with the principle of equality.

It causes envy and restlessness of heart. (pp. 310–311)

It engenders "restless and insatiable vanity." (p. 613) One must be equal to the Joneses and that means becoming morbidly sensitive to the esteem that can be bestowed or withheld by the Joneses.

It encourages a restless ambition rendered a bit unsavory by the pettiness of its objects.

It has a deleterious effect on language.

It devalues honor. (See pp. 626–36)

It supplements more rational controls by the rules of public opinion: "Whenever conditions are equal, public opinion brings immense weight to bear on every individual. It surrounds, directs, and oppresses him." (p. 643)

Finally, and perhaps worst of all, the love of equality proves to be insatiable. As it conquers obstacles, the remaining barriers become more repugnant to it. (See, for example, pp. 537–538). Tocqueville states:

> When conditions are unequal, no inequality, however great, offends the eye. But amid general uniformity, the slightest dissimilarity seems shocking, and the completer the uniformity, the more unbearable it seems. It is therefore natural that love of equality should grow constantly with equality itself: everything done to satisfy it makes it grow. (p. 673)

29. *Future Dangers.* As equality marches on, it becomes more problematic and, usually, more pernicious. The greatest dangers will probably come in the future, as inherited checks on equality grow feeble, the luster of liberty dims, and the love of equality over-reaches itself.

When the desire for equality over-reaches itself, it changes from equality of social condition or equality of opportunity to what we can call egalitarianism. Tocqueville does not make that distinction, but one can argue for its consistency with his intention and thought.

It will remain an open question whether equality of social condition must inevitably lead to egalitarianism.

---

[15] In this connection see Tocqueville's *The Old Regime and the French Revolution* (Garden City, New York: Anchor Books, 1955).

30. *Sameness*. Usually, when somebody claims equality with somebody else he does not claim identity. We can desire an equal right to vote without intending a situation where everybody votes the same way.

We should realize that the distinction between equality and sameness is more clear in English than in languages like French and German.

In any event, as equality becomes egalitarianism it begins to find differences as such an affront. To be truly equal comes to mean to be indistinguishable.

A germ of common sense inheres in the increasing insistence on sameness. To understand human differences means to evaluate them in terms of "better" and "worse". If my being different forever entails superiority or inferiority, it threatens equality.

Hence egalitarianism must labor ceaselessly to minimize individual differences, to create similarities on the way to identity. It tries to make all men alike even if such a molding of men weakens them.

Tocqueville writes: "In our day everything threatens to become so much alike that the particular features of each individual may soon be entirely lost in the common physiognomy." (p. 701)

One of the signs of increasing sameness is the near extinction of the kinds of eccentrics we find depicted in novels of former times. It ought to go without saying that ambulatory schizophrenics, of whom there is no shortage in the United States, are not eccentrics.

31. *Nature*. The dangers of egalitarianism go far beyond the reduction of eccentrics to an endangered species.

The fight against social inequalities can frequently enlist our sense of fairness. For example, all of us have noticed that the correlation between wealth and virtue is, to put it mildly, inexact.

However, as we remove social barriers to inequality we soon discover *natural* barriers. In fact, the removal or arbitrary barriers may accentuate natural ones: "Natural inequality being very great, fortunes become unequal as soon as every man exerts all his faculties to get rich." (p. 457)

What happens when egalitarianism comes up against inequalities that are not the result of man-made institutions? Sometimes these inequalities can be convincingly declared irrelevant. Nature has made some people short and others tall – so what? But nature has also made some people beautiful and others ugly, some intelligent and others stupid. It is not always fitting to shrug and say "So what?"

Various strategems suggest themselves. One can declare nature to be more flexible than is commonly realized and work to change her. But after a while, how can we tell the difference between changing nature and wounding or even destroying her?

One can close one's eyes, do one's best to deny all reports received of the hierarchical nature of nature. One fools oneself – and others.

Finally, one can declare war on nature.[16] Nature can be castigated as unfair, unjust. But such war cannot be waged with impunity. It produces resentment. It costs us the sense of gratitude that enriches those who accept the world as it is and declare it wonderful, full of wonders.

32. *Feminism.* In recent years radical feminism has been the most characteristic form of egalitarianism. It wavers between two extremes. Sometimes it denies any meaningful differences between men and women, thus denying the natural differences that have never escaped the notice of men and women. Sometimes it denies the importance of many things that join men and women, once more denying the evidence of nature. At all times it denies the possibility that the nature of nature may be hierarchical.

Men and women differ enough, and complement each other in so many ways, that one may well claim ignorance of the possible superiority or inferiority of men. Radical feminists denounce such professions of ignorance. Evaluation as such becomes suspect. Radical egalitarianism leads to relativism, which is the first stage of nihilism.

33. *Personal.* I used to think that even if one knew that inequality reigns in our world one should not talk about it because it is humiliating to be reminded of one's inferiority.

But every time I read a great book – such as *Democracy in America* – I am reminded of my intellectual inferiority to greater minds. And I know now that the realization of such inferiority need not cripple.

34. *A Way of Seeing.* Pushed beyond the idea of equal opportunity, to repeat, the love of equality becomes egalitarianism. The latter must be understood as a world-view, a way of comprehending all things. We can only sketch the contours of this cast of mind.

The egalitarian thinks in horizontal rather than vertical terms. He accentuates similarities and distrusts differences.

He thinks both dogmatically and skeptically; egalitarianism fosters and spreads Cartesianism (see especially p. 417).

He believes in perfectibility and universal enlightenment. (Every man can *too* be a philosopher).

His mind has a practical bent; when it turns from practice to theory his mind glazes over with abstractions.

He generalizes too recklessly; he hunts for general causes everywhere, especially in understanding history. (pp. 494–495)

35. *A Way of Life.* Ideas have consequences, to coin a phrase. Egalitarian

[16] The most seminal thinker on the "conquest of nature" remains Francis Bacon.

ideas influence the whole democratic way of life, even as they may be influenced by it.

Nations in which egalitarian ideas thrive are characterized by a passion for material well-being, by a decent pettiness or a petty decency, by a high estimation of the life of work and gain, by the devaluation of honor, by a prevalence of the prosaic over the poetic.

The mores of a democracy reveal the passion for equality. Equality frowns on looking up as well as looking down, and what results may be a seeming absence of manners rather than bad manners.

36. *The Wave of the Future.* Nothing at present seems able to stem the march of equality. Politically, genuinely inegalitarian measures become ever more unthinkable. Thus, it may be true that one ought never to trust anybody under thirty, but what support could one get for *raising* the voting age? Thus, too, one could make a case for giving the wiser or more virtuous a greater share of ruling, but what support could one get for a slogan of "one man – two votes?"

37. *Equality High and Low.* Having cast some doubt on equality (or egalitarianism) we should try to restore the balance. Equality may force the higher to flatter the lower, but it also confers a manly self-assurance on many decent, ordinary men. It may cause social and political upheaval, but it can also manifest a gentle mien (see, for example, p. 432). It fosters not only resentment but benevolence.

Tocqueville states the case beautifully:

> There is indeed a manly and legitimate passion for equality which rouses in all men a desire to be strong and respected. This passion tends to elevate the little man to the rank of the great. But the human heart also nourishes a debased taste for equality, which leads the weak to want to drag the strong down to their level and which induces men to prefer equality in servitude to inequality in freedom. (p. 57)

38. *Equality and Justice.* The abuses of equality may well be more dangerous than the abuses of liberty, but Tocqueville does not turn his back on equality. He knows the costs of equality but he also knows that societies that have equality as a principle are "more just than others" (p. 704) and are, therefore, not without greatness and beauty. Equality is not justice but it resembles justice.

IV. SOME THOUGHTS ON THE RELATIONS BETWEEN LIBERTY AND EQUALITY

39. *Liberty, Religion, Equality.* In the hurly-burly of daily political life in the United States the demands of liberty frequently conflict with those of

equality. The struggle for civil rights provides a standard example. When we try to guarantee everybody equal access to overnight accommodations we may pass legislation that interferes with a small proprietor's real liberty to restrict the kind of people to whom he wants to rent a room.

In adjudicating such problems it may help to realize that both liberty and equality can justly refer to their descent from Christian ideas (see pp. 287–8, 295–6, 442–449).

40. *Earthly Roots.* Liberty and equality, joined together, also have a respectable secular pedigree.

John Locke describes the state of nature as a state of "perfect freedom" as well as of equality. Civil society secures both equality and liberty.[17]

In the United States, one can point to a student of John Locke, Thomas Jefferson, as a distinguished teacher of both liberty and equality.

We today can include Alexis de Tocqueville as among those who tried to teach us how we can be both equal and free.

41. *Personal.* Liberty and equality intermingled in the neighborhood talk I learned when coming to these shores.

I remember two expressions especially, part of the daily speech of my friends and me. We often said, "It's a free country, ain't it?" We usually said it when we were discovered doing something we were not supposed to do.

And we often said, "I'm just as good as you." We almost always said that to our superiors.

42. *Interlockings.* To ask about priorities when it comes to liberty and equality resembles asking about chicken and eggs. One finds it difficult to tell which is desired for the sake of which. Men can yearn for liberty in order to spread equality and they can yearn for equality in order to spread liberty.

Because we are both free, we must respect each other as equals. Because we are equals, you must not rule me without my consent.

The Declaration of Independence assigns a kind of priority to equality by making it the first self-evident truth. So, occasionally, does Tocqueville (see, for example, pp. 66–7. He writes: "Equality, which makes men independent of one another, naturally gives them the habit and taste to follow nobody's will but their own in their private affairs. This complete independence . . . soon suggests the notion and the love of political liberty." (p. 667)

At the same time, equality presupposes the presence of certain liberties. Democracies often replace aristocracies. The latter may have enjoyed considerable liberty. Such liberties go far to moderate the love of equality, so that a country may be judged lucky if it enjoys liberty before equality.

43. *Similarities.* Plagiarizing from Tocqueville with even greater abandon

[17] John Locke, *The Second Treatise of Government* (Indianapolis: Bobbs–Merrill, 1977), pp. 4–5.

than usual, we can compile an incomplete laundry list of the things liberty and equality have in common.

Both liberty and equality depend on the principle of self-interest correctly understood. (p. 82, pp. 525–8)

Both thrive most easily in small political entities. Extended republics present problems for both liberty and equality.[18]

Both contribute to the vitality of the nation.

Americans love both; they are both elements of our patriotism.

Both give birth to "manly habits." (p. 578)

Both are venerable; our fathers bestowed on us a love of both equality and liberty (see p. 279).

Both benefit greatly from a free press. (see especially p. 517)

Both are needed to fight against tyranny. History grants only limited options. Honorable men today have little choice but to assent to liberal democracy. They may have a choice between a complacent consent to its survival and a noble concern with its ennoblement.

44. *Differences.* Liberty and equality can be compatible – the United States is living proof of that – but compatibility does not imply identity.

The differences, to be sure, may not be the ones that first come to mind. For example, we tend to think of equality as social and liberty as individual. It is surely easier to think of a solitary individual as free than as equal. Yet by dissolving hierarchical bonds on society equality may isolate individuals, while liberty may socialize them by encouraging freedom of association.

Liberty and equality differ not only in paradoxical but in perfectly obvious ways. Liberty may increase inequality, especially in the economic sphere (see especially p. 457).

45. *The Democratic Preference for Equality.* Liberty and equality may be sisters but democratic nations face the danger of liberty's becoming the permanent "weak sister."

Tocqueville teaches us all about that situation, in a chapter entitled "Why Democratic Nations Show a More Ardent and Enduring Love for Equality Than Liberty." (pp. 503–506) The chapter is perfect, which means that one cannot really summarize it. It should be read, studied. It is especially impressive because Tocqueville's articulation of the conflict is prefaced by his imagining a harmony, "an extreme point at which freedom and equality would meet and blend," a situation in which "men will be prefectly free because they are entirely equal, and they will be perfectly equal because they are entirely free. Democratic peoples are tending toward that ideal." (p. 503)

46. *A Scenario.* Let us imagine a situation in which love of equality

[18] The authors of *The Federalist Papers* (New York: Anchor Books, 1961) still felt compelled to argue the case for large republics. See, for example, pp. 73–74, 100–101.

overcomes liberty. Extreme egalitarians do well to cloak themselves in a rhetoric of moderation. They may say: "We want no more than equality of opportunity, but it must be genuine." They may use the image of the "race of life" as Lincoln did. Nobody can deny that wealth provides a headstart in the race of life, poverty a handicap. Let us then do away with all possibilities of leaving money to one's children. Every child will start the race of life equally rich, equally poor.

We can assent but we should understand that it is not exactly ignoble for parents to wish to provide for their children, to work hard at the lower things so that their children may enjoy the higher things.

An equal economic start will soon prove to be a first and futile step. Some will try harder, and that may be through no virtue of their own. Some come from a good family that prepares people for the race of life, some from a bad family. To come from a good family is a headstart; to come from a bad one is a handicap. Ergo: let us abolish the nuclear family. (Let us take seriously certain parts of Plato's *Republic* that may not be meant to be taken seriously.)

That would not do the trick. Certain runners have better physical endowments than others. Certain runners have better minds than others. Good bodies and minds are a headstart; bad bodies and minds are a handicap. We must have a eugenics program. So be it.

And we are still talking about equality of opportunity.

Two obvious questions come to mind. First, when along the line did liberty disappear? Second, who would want to live in a place that chased equality of opportunity this way?

V. CONCLUSION

47. *In the Spirit of Tocqueville.* The author of *Democracy in America* ends one of the early chapters of his book with a sentence that begins with a haunting phrase: "Once the American republics begin to degenerate . . ." (p. 111)

Philosophers understand that no work of man abides. Some day there will be no United States. It sobers us to think that we may perish of the conflict between liberty and equality or of our lack of dedication to either or both. And it pains those of us who are not philosophers to contemplate human contingency.

Tocqueville, however, is no teacher of despair. By seeing our regime as a whole he allows us to see its strengths and beauties. Our imperfections do not negate our achievements; we have made liberty and equality work, and work together, tolerably well.

We are not perfect, but a political philosopher like Aristotle, who teaches us to judge by the highest standards, also teaches us the nobility of saying: Sparta has fallen to our lot; let us adorn it. The same spirit informs Tocqueville's work.

The United State has fallen to our lot; let us adorn it.

Government, *Cornell University*

TOWARDS A THEORY OF TAXATION*

J. R. Lucas

"Towards a Theory of Taxation" is a proper theme for an Englishman to take when giving a paper in America. After all it was from the absence of such a theory that the United States derived its existence. The Colonists felt strongly that there should be no taxation without representation, and George III was unable to explain to them convincingly why they should contribute to the cost of their defense. Since that time, understanding has not advanced much. In Britain we still maintain the fiction that taxes are a voluntary gift to the Crown, and taxing statutes are given the Royal Assent with the special formula, *"La Reine remercie ses bons sujets, accepte leur benevolence, et ainsi le veult,"* instead of the simple *"La Reine le veult,"* and in the United States taxes have regularly been levied on residents of the District of Columbia who until recently had no representation in Congress, and by the State of New York on those who worked but did not reside in the State, and so did not have a vote. Taxes are regularly levied, in America as elsewhere, on those who have no say on whether they should be levied or how they should be spent. I am taxed by the Federal Government on my American earnings and by state governments on my American spending, but I should be hard put to it to make out that it was unjust. Florida is wondering whether to follow California in taxing multinational corporations on their world-wide earnings. There is some debate on whether such a move is expedient: but nobody to my knowledge has suggested that, in order to make it just, multinational corporations, or their overseas shareholders, should be given representation in the state legislature. Indeed, were anyone to make such a suggestion, he would be laughed out of court, so dead is the contention that representation is a necessary condition of taxes being justly levied. And yet I do not want to bury the Colonists' argument utterly. They had a point. Although the main issues in an adequate theory of taxation are those of justice, there is also room for a quasi-Lockean approach in which we try to make sense of taxes as a sort of bargain in which the taxpayer surrenders his individual quid in return for a share of a collective quo.

* My thanks are due to Loren E. Lomasky, R. M. Hare, and John Gray for comments and criticisms which I have incorporated into this final version.

If we are to develop a theory of taxation and address ourselves to the Colonists' grievance, we need to purge ourselves of contemporary complacency and take an unfashionable stance. For it is generally accepted among modern thinkers that high taxes are a Good Thing. It is partly a streak of masochism, which requires psychiatry to cure it rather than argument. But it is also due to mistaken views of political morality which are open to rational debate. It is widely taken for granted that it is Wrong to be Rich. It may, indeed, be true that it is wrong to be rich, but it needs to be argued for, not taken for granted, and if it is argued for, the arguments will have an important bearing on how the principle is to be applied in practice. It is quite plausible to maintain that to seek riches has a bad effect on the character. It is arguable that even to possess them imposes an unacceptable cost in wordly worry and concern. Jesus said it was hard for the rich to enter the Kingdom, and advised the young man to give away all he had. It is a matter of dispute whether his advice was directed to just that particular young man or was a general precept addressed to everyone. Many Christians have heard and heeded a call to poverty, although many others have believed that they should live in the world and make the most of its resources, for others as well as themselves. but whatever their decision, the question is one of personal morality, not public morality. It may be right for me to be a slum priest, forgoing money, family and freedom for the sake of the Gospel: but that is a decision that only I can take. It is no good if you decide that I should be poor, celibate and under rigid discipline, or if I wish that vocation on you. There is no merit in the choice unless it is made wholeheartedly by the person concerned, and it is unlikely to work – the unwilling mind will continue to dwell on the goodies it has unwillingly renounced, and its underlying bent will manifest itself in all sorts of covert ways. Just as it is better to marry than burn, so it is better to be rich than be always thinking about money, or always being angry at others being rich. Even if we are generally persuaded, as medieval men were generally persuaded, that the vocation to poverty was a better one than that to involvement in the world, we should still not make it a basis of our public morality which we reckon to be incumbent on all men irrespective of their personal inclinations. We may all commend the example of St. Francis, but still should not conclude that the Queen should play the part of Robin Hood.

It is often thought that the State should redistribute from rich to poor not because it is Wrong to be Rich, but because Equality is a Good Thing. I have argued against egalitarianism at length elsewhere and shall not weary you with repetition. In the context of taxation, however, there is one variant of the egalitarian argument which is superficially attractive. It seems natural to regard the relief of poverty as a possible aim of public policy – one does not have to be an egalitarian to regard poverty as a bad thing, and only extreme advocates of *laisser faire* would say that it should be no concern of the State. But then we seem to have a licence for Robin Hood. Whenever there is a choice we should always devote public funds to the fashionable minority group of the moment rather than reduce the higher rate tax demands on the Duke of Westminster. It is this contention that I want to controvert, and in particular the second half. As regards the first half, it has been increasingly recognized that there are limits to what can be achieved by public expenditure in the way of relieving poverty. No matter how much we spend, the poor will always be with us. But although this is a reason for doubting the efficacy of egalitarian policies, there are always going to be some expenditures which look like they might do some good for some poor people; and unless there is some counter argument for not taxing the rich to the limit, the plea of poverty will win the day.

Some thinkers seek to block the Robin Hood argument by claiming that taxation ought not to be redistributive. This claim is ambiguous. In one sense, taxation cannot help but be redistributive. The tax collector takes money from me, and distributes it to soldiers, sailors, and civil servants. Even if there were no welfare payments as such, much of my money would go on expenditures which benefited others much more than myself: airports and the M25 for the rich, the health service for the ill, public education for the uneducated. We cannot lay down that taxation should not be redistributive in this sense. But even if it is permissible for taxation to have redistributive effects, some people would still argue that it should not be *intended* to redistribute resources. It is, they argue, contrary to the nature of the State that it should extract from an unwilling individual taxes for any other purpose than the protection of his rights against criminals at home or aggressors from abroad. Such a theory of the State is difficult to refute because it is difficult to formulate coherently. I do not think that any such theory of a Minimum State can be sustained. I have argued the point elsewhere, but only cursorily.[1] For our present purpose, I do not claim that no such theory could be put forward, but only that other theories of the State are put forward and acted on, and that for these, too, a theory of contributive justice is needed. Most people do not believe in the Minimum State. They want to engage in collective action, *e.g.*, in sending a man to the moon, and see no reason why they should not act collectively through the mechanism of the nation-state. And if they may engage in collective action generally, then they can choose as a permissible goal of collective action the relief of poverty, which will be redistributive not only in effect but – at least in one obvious sense – in intention too. Of course, there may still be reasons for being chary of adopting redistributive policies because they are inherently divisive and

[1] J. R. Lucas, *The Principles of Politics* (Oxford 1966) (pbk. ed. 1985), Section 67, pp. 287–295.

often give rise to abuse. But keeping pork barrels out of politics is a counsel of prudence rather than the imperative of political morality. Many redistributive policies at present practiced are unwise, and some are plain wrong. But I cannot see that there is, or even could be, a cogent argument, either of justice or of expediency, for holding that the relief of poverty or the amelioration of misfortune is not a proper object of public concern or public expenditure; I can, however, see arguments, both of justice and of expediency, for saying that the tax burden should be fairly borne by the whole community and not put disproportionately upon the shoulders of the rich.

Aristotle considers the allocation of benefits and burdens together under the title of distributive justice. But the cases are not all similar. When benefits are being distributed, I am not likely to shirk my share, and if I do, no great problem arises: if I do not want my piece of cake, there are plenty of others who will take it up for me. With burdens, however, each person is naturally reluctant to bear them, and so is tempted to shirk and may actually do so. Fare-dodging, free-riding, tax-evasion, and generally not pulling one's weight, are endemic problems when in pursuit of a collective goal we have to call on individuals to make unwelcome sacrifices as their contribution towards it. These problems ought to be considered quite separately from those of distributive justice, and I propose the name "contributive justice" instead.

Essentially the problem is that it is in each person's interest, selfishly considered, not to contribute, but if we all fail to contribute, the collective goal will not be achieved, and we shall all be worse off. Although it seems to be a sensible policy for me not to pay my taxes, or not to buy a ticket, relying on everybody else to pay his bit all the same, if it is sensible for me, it is sensible for anybody else, and if it is sensible for anybody else it is sensible for everybody else, and if it is sensible for me and everybody else it is sensible for us all, and yet if we all did it, the results would be disastrous. And so I oppose my seeming self-interest, which I can see to be short-sighted, by an enlightened self-interest, which is longer term and can embrace others as well as myself. But it makes sense for me to contribute only on the condition that everybody else does. If I act on enlightened principles and they act according to their short-sighted, seeming self-interest, then it is I who am being a fool, not they. I need assurance that if I do my part, they will do theirs. Only if I can rely on them is it individually rational for me to do what it is collectively rational for us to do.

Protagoras was the first to formulate the problem, and Plato saw in it the rationale of the many agreements and tacit understandings which underlie law and conventional morality. Hobbes reckoned covenants without swords to be but empty words, and so sought a sovereign armed with coercive power. In recent years a paradigm example, called the Prisoners' Dilemma, has been much studied with the aid of the Theory of Games. At one level of reasoning Hobbes has been vindicated. Coercion is needed, because some people are moved only by short-term self-interest, and others fear that this is so. Coercion, in the form of tax inspectors and penalties for tax evasion, is essential, because otherwise some will not pay their share, and others, knowing or believing this, will then be reluctant to pay theirs either, for fear of being mugs. But the argument does not go as far as Hobbes thought. The reason is, at the crudest level, that not even Leviathan has enough eyes to see everything that is going on. Nobody knows how much revenue is lost through fiddling and non-declaration, but there is plenty of reason to suppose that it is quite a large sum. Threats by themselves cannot be totally effective because they can only be invoked on the basis of adequate information, and the State is not possessed of perfect information, and can obtain the information it needs only with the co-operation of its subjects. That co-operation will be forthcoming only on the basis of loyalty and trust. Although I shall do what I am told by the Gestapo or the K.G.B., I shall not tell them more than I can help or expose myself to their attentions in the way that I am prepared to co-operate with the reasonable demands of a civil society which does not threaten me and with which I can quite largely identify.

Hence, although the State needs to have some coercive power at its disposal in order to bring sanctions to bear on those who will not otherwise keep their covenants, it cannot rely on the sword alone, but must secure a general measure of agreement to its general aims. Although I want to be assured that those who break the law will be punished, so that I am not being a mug when I myself forbear to break it, my own reason for keeping the law is not primarily that I shall be punished if I break it, but that I see the rationality of my, and everyone else's, keeping it, and am reasonably assured of others' actually doing so.

The fiscal application is clear. Taxes must be not simply what I can make others pay on pain of punishment, but what I can see good reason to pay as a matter of enlightened self-interest and reasonable identification with my fellow members of the State, and in reasonable confidence of their paying too. If these conditions are satisfied, then I will be fairly well disposed to pay my share. And if I can see that it is satisfied for everybody else, I can suppose that they are likewise fairly likely to pay. The temptation not to pay, although present, is well resisted by my recognition of the rationality of the demand and the knowledge that others too will be able to recognize the rationality of what is demanded of them. I am not going to feel myself a mug if most of the others are paying too, and the tax-evaders are a small minority, and in danger of being found out and not only penalized but severely stigmatized as well. Fare-dodging does not seem clever because we all can see why fares should be paid, and know that most other people pay their fares, and do not want to copy Professor Joad.

The case has become very different with taxation, especially income tax. I can still remember the time when it was thought to be a moral duty to pay one's taxes, and tax evasion was a serious social crime. Nobody thinks that now. A generation of high and avowedly punitive taxation has eroded the moral basis of fiscal policy, and has developed in Great Britain an Italian attitude towards the Inland Revenue. The rot set in from the top. Rich men felt – were encouraged to feel by some Chancellors – that they were being unfairly taxed, and ceased to feel any moral obligation to contribute to the Exchequer the very large amounts demanded of them. They became less scrupulous about declaring unconsidered trifles, and understandably eager to rearrange their affairs so as to minimize the tax man's exactions. For forty years successive Finance Acts have sought to block up one loophole after another, but have by and large been defeated by the fact that people who run things have to have discretion, and cannot be stopped, except by moral considerations, from using their discretion to their own advantage. The employer finds a job for his wife, sends the works van to collect his son from school, and gets the milk-maid to lend a hand in the rose-garden. The Inland Revenue seeks to forbid it, but finds that it is forbidding the employer to take on anyone, or is requiring the doctor and his receptionist to live in sin in order that she may be paid for answering the telephone. And the example spreads. If the director or the Cabinet Minister has a company car, why not the executive or Assistant Principal? Top people are inherently influential, and if they try to avoid paying taxes, those lower down follow suit. Even if top people do not, they are thought to. For it is known that the rates are very high, and judging others by myself I reckon that if I were paying 60% on my marginal income, I would see to it that any extra money that came my way came in some untaxable form. And if I believe that Lord Vestey and all the others at the top have sewn up their affairs pretty neatly, I shall soon persuade myself not only that I should be a mug to pay my 30%, but that I have a positive duty to fiddle.

The account I have given is depressingly familiar. But what is to be done? We cannot go back to the pre-Daltonian Garden of Eden. Public morality, although easily eroded, is difficult to restore. Nevertheless, there are measures open to the Government. The crudest, although not the most fundamental, is that tax avoidance is a tedious, inconvenient business. Money is usually much more useful than a perk. I would rather have cash than a company car. In fact, I would settle for quite a lot less cash than the cost of a company car, simply because it was less hassle and enabled me to choose between a new car and a holiday in Dalmatia. Although not all perks would be commutable for cash – some serve a functional purpose – many are. And although once established, a perk is likely to continue, the marginal disutility of paying people by perk instead of in cash could be assessed, and could provide useful pointers to the economically efficient marginal rate of taxation. Better a 35% rate which was generally paid than a 65% which was largely avoided.

More important, however, would be a shift in the context of discussion of fiscal policy. At present it is carried on almost entirely in terms of what can be got out of other taxpayers, instead of what can fairly be asked of each. We need to put at the forefront of the debate "Is it fair to ask this poor man to pay 30% at the margin?" "Is it fair to ask this man to pay 25% of his total income in tax?" "What is the most that it is fair to demand?" These are crude questions, but for that very reason widely intelligible. If people are able to understand what is being asked of them and of others they can appreciate the issues of contributive justice involved and, *per contra*, the questions need to be crude, so that they shall be widely intelligible, and that people can understand not only their own burden but what is being asked of others, and can reckon it fairly tolerable and so likely to be borne. Contributive justice is crucially concerned not only with people's perceptions of their own situation but their perceptions of other people's situation and their perception of other people's perceptions of their own situation. It has to be crude in order to secure *second*-order intelligibility, and thus provide the general assurance, essential if we are to escape from the Prisoners' Dilemma, that other people too will contribute their share.

For this reason the rationale of all sorts of taxation, and especially of progressive taxation, needs to be articulated and discussed. Although often a *per capita* contribution seems appropriate, as in a club subscription or public transport fare, we can argue that a proportionate contribution is a more appropriate premium to pay for the protection of one's property and life style from anarchy and external enemies. The argument for progressive taxation is less obvious. Perhaps a pools winner is getting proportionately more from the State than a wage earner, and perhaps he is willing to shoulder a proportionately heavier burden, but the argument needs to be made out. "If you were to win the pools would you think it fair to have to pay 40% of your income in tax?" – if people are asked that question they are likely to have a much clearer idea of the issues at stake than if they think of it merely as what others are going to have to pay. And if they can answer that question hypothetically in the affirmative, they will know why pools winners should, and will have some reason to suppose they would, pay their contribution to the Exchequer. A climate of opinion would begin to grow up of mutual understanding and shared expectations about what different people in different circumstances were to pay, and this would greatly militate against avoidance.

Three underlying issues arise in the debate on fiscal fairness: the justice of selective disincentives; the individual's benefit from the collective good; and the real burden of the sacrifice imposed. The selective imposition of some burdens is justified not simply on grounds of contributive justice, but in order to further some other public policy. We tax alcohol, tobacco, and gasoline, partly in order to discourage people from drinking, smoking, and driving; drinkers, smokers, and drivers put both themselves and others to inconvenience and risk. This is not the only reason for taxing these commodities, but it does give some sort of justification, not itself intrinsic to contributive justice, for picking on some people rather than others on whom to levy taxes. It is because it has been generally reckoned wrong to be rich that the top rate of tax in Britain was set at 98%. But if it is not inherently wrong to be rich, then this extrinsic argument for high income tax fails.

The second justification for imposing heavier burdens on some rather than on others is by reference to the benefits received in return. Some collective goods, although in principle available to all, are in practice enjoyed only by a minority. Only a small proportion of citizens avail themselves of consular services. Many poor people never go abroad at all. Only a minority of people go to university or have children who go to university. Public libraries and municipal museums are open to all, but not patronized by all. If all public expenditure were financed by a poll tax, it would be unfair on the poor, who would be paying for facilities for the rich which the poor either had no opportunity of using or no wish to use.

Collective goods of this type can be individualized by subscriptions: in Britain the National Health Service has always been financed in part by a *per capita* levy, Mr. Heath tried to introduce museum charges, and there is a growing reluctance on the part of the taxpayer generally to pay for university education for the few. But it is not a clear-cut issue. Many collective goods are difficult to price and cumbersome to provide through market mechanisms. We cannot rule out their being provided by some sort of collective action, even though sometimes the appropriate collective may not be the nation-state. In quite a few cases the collective good will be provided by a public authority, and funded from taxation, but it is not obvious that everyone should pay the same tax. What differentiating principles are apropriate?

The underlying concept, here, is that of the Good Bargain. Each taxpayer is paying a certain amount of taxes and enjoying various collective goods. Nobody is enjoying all the collective goods provided, but those that he is enjoying would cost a great deal more to obtain if they were not provided collectively. My pennies spent on the municipal baths give me no return, but the fire service would cost me much more if I had to pay for it privately. Of course, there is a measure of indeterminacy about the total cost of everyone paying privately for such collective goods. Sometimes only by having actual market alternatives can we agree on a basis of comparison. Often, however, a taxpayer will be broadly content if he perceives himself as receiving some valued services which seem reasonably commensurate with the outlay demanded.

It follows that a rather large margin of efficiency of public over private provision is required before we can justify the compulsory provision of a public service at the expense of the taxpayer. Each taxpayer is going to see a number of the public expenditures he has to help finance as doing no good to him. The remainder have got to carry the cost of the unwanted ones. The elderly couple derives little joy from free schooling but finds the public library a great boon, as, also, clean streets and the availability of the district nurse. They will not grudge half their rates going on education so long as the services they actually use seem a good value for the rates they have to pay, that is so long as those services could not obviously be provided by the market at a cheaper price. This often will be the case, but not always or necessarily: it provides a constraint both on the general political question of what services the public authority should provide and the particular fiscal question of how much the individual can be asked to contribute.

Those with large houses in plush neighborhoods, or with large incomes, or large cars, can reasonably be asked to contribute more because typically they benefit more. Different people will avail themselves of different goods, but each will avail himself of some, and there will not be any general category of exploited taxpayers who have to pay a lot and do not receive a fair return. Although each would like to opt out of some items of public provision, which do not benefit him personally, he would suffer more by others opting out of the provisions which do benefit him. Granted reasonable efficiency of collective action, he gains on the swings what he loses on the roundabouts, and the package as a whole is one that it is in his enlightened self-interest to accept.

The difficulty with this sort of argument is the packaging. If the State is allowed to determine the package on offer, it can make any level of taxation appear to be fair: if the individual, the package can be unpacked until we have a set of separate subscriptions for communal goods, with individuals opting out whenever it is in their individual interest to do so. There is a certain analogy here with the problem of political obedience that Locke inherited from Hobbes. Hobbes offered a big package. The subject had to obey the sovereign regardless, because the sovereign gave him security. In the same way, if there is just a single tax package, and part of the benefit it confers is security, internal and external, then it can carry a pretty pricey tag. If, however, we can set up a more detailed dialogue between the individual and the community, we can make political obedience conditional rather than absolute, and relate benefits to burdens in detail rather than have them all inextricably lumped together. Although one would pay almost anything to be secure, that benefit is one which everyone enjoys and everyone values, and therefore the burden of providing for defence and the maintenance of law and order should be laid on everyone. In time of war the rich may be called on to sacrifice most of their wealth to pay for defense: but if they are being called on to sacrifice most of their wealth, then an equally burdensome sacrifice should be called for from the poor. The fact that the benefit of security justifies a pricey tag cannot be used to justify loading the burden of taxation on the shoulders of one class of taxpayers rather than another, because we all benefit from security, and contributive justice requires that we all contribute.

The basic benefits of civil society are relatively easy to identify and price, and we can make a stab at apportioning the burden of providing for them. The more optional communal benefits are more difficult to package. We need to distinguish two questions: whether they should be in a package at all, and whether the cost of providing them is being fairly apportioned. The former question is predominantly a political one. Representation was seen as a means of securing that collective policies were in line with the Colonists' wishes. Of course, representation is neither a necessary nor a sufficient condition of that. Many governments have conferred benefits on their populations which were recognized as such although there had been no formal representation of the people's wishes, and in any form of representative government a lot of people get outvoted and saddled with policies they do not want. Nevertheless, representation does help. If there is a system of representation, although we cannot tell each individual taxpayer that he wants the benefits he is being asked to pay for, we can tell him that he is a member of a group which by and large wants them. So the question of whether the benefit should be provided is answered, moderately well. The only question left is whether the burden is being fairly shared. Here, it seems to me, we can make use of a presumption of equality. If the community calls on me to bear an equal share of the cost of carrying out a collective decision, even though it is one I may have opposed, I have no complaint. If the share is heavier than that asked of others, contributive justice requires that we consider all those also being asked to contribute the same amount, and ask whether they as a class are benefiting as much as they are having to pay. If they are, they are getting a good Lockean bargain, and are not being too badly done by. If super-tax payers as a whole are getting a lot of opera, foreign consular services, and national parks, which it would cost them more to provide for themselves by private subscription, then they are not being milked by the tax man. But if they are being asked to pay more without there being any justification in terms of benefits enjoyed or available for enjoyment, then their complaint that they are being unfairly "taxploited" stands.

The duties levied on alcohol, tobacco, and gasoline can be partly justified by the fair bargain argument. Consumers of these commodities are disproportionately heavy consumers of health services, which in most countries are at least partly funded out of general taxation. Drinkers and drivers also occupy a disproportionate amount of the time of the police and the judiciary. Large sums of money are spent on roads. The road lobby in Britain frequently makes out that all the money raised by road taxes should be spent on roads. The argument is fallacious, because it ignores the other costs imposed on the community by road users. But the fact that it is put forward at all, shows that there is felt to be something in the fair bargain argument.

Besides benefits directly linked to contributions, we can take into consideration, also, partial and contingent correlations in deciding what packages of benefits and burdens may be fairly imputed and apportioned. A propensity to consume dutiable commodities picks out a class of taxpayers who benefit from the provision of certain other minority interests: almost all those who benefit from country parks consume petrol, almost all opera goers drink wine. This, again, is only a partial justification, and depends on the fact that contributive justice is only rough justice, and that classes of contributors need only roughly correspond with classes of beneficiaries.

With regard to direct taxes, the fair bargain argument justifies proportionate taxation, as opposed to a simple poll tax. It might yield a partial justification of progressive taxation, although the main justification, in so far as it is justifiable, must rely on the third underlying principle of fiscal fairness, which is that the burdens should be equal not in monetary but in real terms: The widow's mites cost her much more than the rich man's largesse. And so we conclude that taxes should be not only proportionate but progressive. But there is a limit to this principle. If we take £1M from a man with £1.25M it is not clear that this is costing him less than the 30% levied on the ordinary taxpayer. As a first approximation we can vary the good bargain argument to become the hard bargain argument. The hard bargain argument considers the provision of collective goods where there is no possibility of their being supplied by the market, and then considers how hard a bargain would have to be before someone felt he could not afford to accept it. The classical example is defense, but that has the disadvantage of being so strong as to be unselective – although the rich man will certainly give his all to preserve his life, so will the poor man; so that although we could tax the very rich very heavily for Trident, we could equally tax everybody else, and it would be unfair to demand enormous sacrifices of the one and not the other. Other public goods are less extreme. In times past, public benefactors who were rich would produce public goods at their own expense, and we can see this as giving an approximate indication of what they could afford. We can intelligibly ask, "How much would those with £10,000 per year be willing to pay for a public good if they alone were having to foot the bill." "How much would those with £15,000 per year? "How much would those with £20,000?" "How much would those with £30,000, etc.?" This would give a measure, although only a rough one, of equality of sacrifice. Of course, it would not be the same for each individual, or for each sort of public good. As always in political economy, we cannot be asking everyone his opinion, or have everyone making actual choices. We have to impute values, and say on behalf of people what decisions it would be reasonable for them to take in hypothetical circumstances. I do not pretend that there would be uniform agreement on the answers. But there would be an advantage in adopting an approach which was informed by a concern for fiscal fairness, and which asked rather more precise questions than those usually canvassed when taxation is under discussion.

It would help when we were discussing tax brackets if we considered hypothetical communities in which everyone had the same income, £10,000, £20,000, £30,000, etc., and asked how much each member of such a community would be willing to pay, on condition that every other member of that community did the same, in order to secure a particular public good. This would tell us for each public good how affordable it was at different levels of wealth, from which we could tell what level of taxation for the purpose of securing that good, imposed an equal burden of perceived sacrifice for people of different wealth. There would be a further, but surmountable, difficulty in grossing up the different scales for different public goods into one overall scale. Anglo-American constitutional practice is averse to assigning particular imposts to particular purposes, but there is nothing wrong in principle in doing this as a theoretical exercise, so that if, for example, poor Americans set great store on the United States sending a space probe to Pluto, and a low store on third world aid, and American millionaires did not care much about NASA but were keen on famine relief, then the NASA budget should be funded by a few cents a dollar on everyone's income tax, and foreign aid on the marginal rates paid by millionaires. Such a theoretical exercise is possible, and would, I think, be helpful in securing justice between different classes of taxpayers.

Contributive justice is always rough justice. It cannot take into account all the peculiarities of the individual case, but must categorize members of the community in broad general terms. So long as the contributions are not too onerous, it does not matter – I do not quibble over my National Trust subscription. It is only when we have very high taxation that we have to deal with all sorts of special cases, and make special and complex provision for them. But complexity destroys intelligibility. I don't know what other people are having to pay, have no idea if it is fair, but have a shrewd suspicion that a clever accountant could avoid it. Hence, conversely, if we are to have a system that can be seen to be fair and will command general support, it must be simple, broadly-based, and not too onerous. What exactly that means in practical terms, I leave for future discussion. For myself, I have often been attracted by F. A. Hayek's suggestion that the top rate of marginal tax should not be more than the ration of public expenditure to Gross Domestic Product. But that I leave to discussion. The one point I want to urge is that we should formulate afresh the principles of our taxation policy, and debate them in terms of justice. For too long the taxpayer has been talked of as though he were a milch cow, without any regard to his own rights and legitimate interests. We have had a high taxation rhetoric, with ever increasing complexity and avoidance. But in reality the yields have been much less than the rhetoric suggests. A new rhetoric, of justice rather than dairy management, would release many energies at present devoted to fiddling for more productive purposes; and might actually increase the yield.

Philosophy, Merton College, Oxford.